The
Antique Furniture
Trail

Rosewood card table c1835, in typical William IV style

Sheraton-style elbow chair c1795,
in satinwood with floral decoration

The Antique Furniture Trail

V. J. Taylor

DAVID & CHARLES
Newton Abbot   London

(above)
An early 18th century, Louis XV kingwood, tulipwood, marquetry and ormolu-mounted *table à ecrire* of slight kidney-shaped outline. The top has a central tooled leather cartouche panel between sprays of flowers within double scroll bordered panels quarter veneered, framed by a brass edge. The cabriole legs with pierced rococo scroll ornament, terminate in scroll feet

This book is dedicated to my good friend and mentor Charles H. Hayward, who was Editor of *Woodworker* magazine for many years, and a fount of knowledge on all things appertaining to furniture and woodwork.

And also to my wife, Enid, to thank her for her prowess with the word processor.

British Library Cataloguing in Publication Data

Taylor, V. J. (Victor John), 1920–
    The antique furniture trail.
    1. Antique furniture – Collectors' guides
    I. Title
    749.2

ISBN 0-7153-9127-5

Typeset by Typesetters (Birmingham) Ltd,
Smethwick, West Midlands
and printed in Portugal
by Resopal
for David & Charles Publishers plc
Brunel House   Newton Abbot   Devon

ACKNOWLEDGEMENTS
Colour illustrations on pages 6, 10, 12, 15, 17, 21, 26–7, 28 (upper), 30, 34, 38, 41 (both), 44–5, 46, 53 (both), 55, 57, 163, 166, 168, 171, 173, 179, 180, 181, 182, 185, 187 reproduced by courtesy of Christie's.
    Colour illustrations on pages 1, 2, 4, 9, 12, 28 (lower), 29, 31, 32, 33, 39, 43, 47, 48, 49, 50, 164, 177, 178, 187 reproduced by courtesy of Phillips Fine Art Auctioneers

Contents

Introduction

The title, **The Antique Furniture Trail**, seems appropriate for this book which is intended to help those who have had what seems to be a valuable piece of antique furniture in the house for years; or who have inherited some old furniture; or who like to attend sales in the hope of finding a treasure.

Identifying and dating a piece of antique furniture (and other kinds of antiques for that matter) is very much like solving a 'who-done-it'; and we must look for a clue here, a clue there, and probably follow one or two false leads until arriving at a solution.

The Customs and Excise has decreed that an antique must be an artefact at least one hundred years old. In books like this it is difficult to know at what period to start, so, using their criterion, the cut-off time is on or about 1900. Unlike most books on the subject, the designs are examined retrogressively, and this method of working backwards seems logical on two counts. First, far more antique furniture is likely to be available dating from the nineteenth century than from, say, the seventeenth; second, it fits in very neatly with the deductive method.

Some readers may be irritated by the way in which many dates are qualified as 'about' or 'circa'. To do otherwise would be difficult if not impossible as, unlike their French counterparts, few British craftsmen marked their furniture. Consequently, very little is known about their lives and work, and such information as we have has been gleaned by patient research among bills, receipts, letters, diaries, wills and contemporary magazines. Such data is bound to be incomplete. If every maker had been as business-like as the firm of Gillows of Lancaster, whose workshop records have been preserved, the situation would be transformed.

British furniture only has been included and it is mainly in the 'vernacular' style – that is, furniture as used by ordinary people, designed to last and give many years of service. Of course this was the largest class of furniture made, and its history is as fascinating, if not more so, than that of the grandiose and opulent pieces that were status symbols of the wealthy. Indeed, it has been difficult to decide what to include and what to leave out from the vast range of designs available; we hope enough have been given for the book to fulfil its purpose. A bibliography has been included for those who wish to carry their researches further.

Although many readers will not wish to sell their antiques, the price guide which has been provided will at least give them an idea of the values for insurance purposes; similarly, it will ensure that future generations who inherit the heirlooms will realise their worth. And those who attend sales in search of a bargain may find that the price guide will save them from missing one, or from paying more than they need!

Welcome to the antique Furniture Trail!

Beautiful breakfront bookcase c1790 in satinwood, cross-banded with rosewood. The drawer section has a bowed front, the fronts of the drawers and doors being decorated with marquetry

Buying and Selling Antique Furniture

For the beginner, auctions can be rather daunting – shrouded in mystery and intrigue. A raised eyebrow or an itchy nose and perhaps the auctioneer will think I am bidding? The plain fact is that the auctioneer is a professional who knows the difference between an itch and a bid. Often he can be heard in 'the room' (saleroom) asking if someone is bidding or not; and if there is a protest of 'I was bidding' after the hammer has fallen, he invariably replies 'Please bid more clearly, sir!' So, please don't be put off from attending an auction, it can be great fun and tremendously exciting.

The Golden Rule when buying is quite simple: buy what you like and not what you think is a good investment because that is when you burn your fingers, it is much better to buy what will give you pleasure and enjoyment over the years.

However, a word of caution: the auctioneer is there to sell and he earns his income from commission on all sales. You must mark your catalogue with your top bid and do not go beyond that figure. Self-discipline is very important if you want to avoid that infectious disease – 'Auction Fever'. Consider taking a friend with you who can be your restraining influence or, perhaps, leave a bid 'on the books', that is to say, you ask the saleroom to bid on your behalf with a commissioned bid. This way you are not going to be tempted beyond your maximum bid. Always bid decisively by raising your hand or indeed your catalogue, and if your bid is successful, the hammer is brought down in your favour, which means yours was the highest bid, exceeding any reserve that might have been placed.

After the sale you will have to pay for your purchase and collect your goods. If you intend paying by cheque, make prior arrangements with the auctioneer, to avoid any unnecessary delays. As for collecting, that can be immediately after the sale or the following day, but if you find the purchases are too bulky then the auctioneer can advise which local carrier to use.

Selling or buying through auction can involve both parties in paying commission to the auctioneer. He always charges the vendor a commission which can range from 10 per cent to 15 per cent, and is usually based on value. For example, 10 per cent would be charged on items selling for more than £100 while 15 per cent is the fee for everything below that figure. The purchaser is liable for what is known as a buyer's premium, which in general is 10 per cent, though it can be as low as 5 per cent. This created a lot of excitement when it was first introduced in 1975, with noises of boycotts by the trade and cries of collusion because both Sotheby's and Christie's made almost simultaneous announcements of their intentions to impose a 10 per cent buyer's premium. It is now established practice, however, and you should make provision for this premium when fixing your final bid. Not all auction houses charge a premium, but always check your catalogue or ask a member of the saleroom staff.

Buying antique furniture through auctions can be great fun but remember these are goods that have come together from various sources (unless of course it is an *in situ* contents sale) and should be viewed with care. In general, the two days preceding the sale are set aside for viewing and you should take the opportunity to examine thoroughly any items that take your fancy. Don't be afraid of asking questions; the specialists are all too keen to help any prospective buyer. You are, however, buying the goods as seen with all the problems that result, such as cleaning and restoration.

If that is not for you, then consider visiting a dealer, preferably a member of either BADA (British Antique Dealers Association) or LAPADA (London and Provincial Dealers Association). There are, of course, one or two other areas, such as the Cotswolds, where the local reputable dealers have got together and formed the Cotswolds Antique Dealers Association, though some of those would already be members of the two national associations. Dealers who are members of these groups are bound by their own stringent rules, and provide some safeguard for the purchaser. Here you will find pieces in pristine, showroom condition – restored, cleaned and polished ready to tempt potential buyers! Always make sure your purchase is backed up with a detailed receipt that gives your piece the full necessary documentation in case it later turns out not to be as claimed. This form of buying should be pleasurable and trouble-free, taking you to all parts of the country in your quest for a desired treasure.

Finally, whom should you get to appraise your own furniture? If you are considering selling, then approach one of the firms of auctioneers in your area who would arrange for a representative to call and give you free verbal advice about saleroom values and their charges, including perhaps, transport (carriage) and photography (should the item merit illustration in the catalogue). Settlement can range from ten days to one month after the auction, less of course all the charges, but including VAT at the current rate. The alternative would be to call in a reputable dealer (possibly a member of BADA or LAPADA) to make an offer for the piece. This has the advantage of immediate settlement.

Whatever you do, once your enthusiasm is fired you will enjoy seeking out that special piece of furniture for your home, and along the way you will meet some wonderful characters who can become good friends. Their infectious love of furniture and its history is catching, so beware! Have fun, and happy hunting!

Bill Simpson is former regional director of Sotheby's, now freelance writer and independent valuer.

Mahogany sofa table c1820, crossbanded with rosewood, in the Regency style

CHAPTER 1

Is it a fake?

This chapter explains what you should look for on your antique furniture, both from the point of view of dating and identifying it, and also to determine whether or not it is a fake. Obviously the first requirement is to define a fake, and the generally accepted definition is that it is a piece intended to deceive a would-be purchaser into believing it is the genuine article. This apparently simple statement actually contains several pitfalls – when, for instance, does a piece of furniture which has been extensively restored become a fake? And is the reproduction of an antique a fake?

As noted, the criterion is whether the intention is to deceive. The United Kingdom Institute for Conservation states: 'It is unethical to modify or conceal the true nature of an object through restoration. The presence and extent of restoration must be detectable, though it need not be conspicuous. All restoration must be fully documented.' This, then, sets the limits within which restoration is acceptable.

Turning to repairs, it is generally considered that genuine repairs are acceptable even if they are of poor workmanship; the basis for this is that it is unreasonable to expect that a piece of furniture should survive several centuries of use without some repairs being necessary. Of course, a genuine piece that has been repaired will not command the same price as its unblemished counterpart, but its authenticity should not be impaired.

Adaptations where a piece has been cut down to fit into a recess or otherwise altered to suit particular conditions are in similar case to repairs. My brother-in-law (who is a master craftsman) once had to lower the height of a *tridarn* (see Chapter 15) to get it into the kitchen of a Somerset cottage – although this has probably reduced the monetary value it has not affected the authenticity.

Tallboy in mahogany c1765, the upper section being surmounted by a dentilled cornice, and having canted-and-fluted corners. The veneers on the drawer fronts are particularly fine and are perfectly matched. Note the scrolled feet

The reproduction furniture trade is a thing apart, and the writer must confess to working in it during the 1930s. However, although the articles produced were copies of classical or traditional designs, they could easily be identified as such. Thus, we turned out reproductions of eighteenth-century wine and tea tables, stools, fire screens, and the like, but they were all French polished and this style of finish did not arrive in England until the 1820s; and no attempt was made to disguise the Guest, Keen, and Nettlefold's screws!

There is some comfort in the fact that the days of the professional faker are over. Their heyday was the period between 1900 and 1930, but now the costs of labour and material are so high that the game is no longer worth the candle. The fakers copied spectacular and ostentatious designs that could fetch high prices, and not the kind of everyday vernacular furniture dealt with here. Herbert Cecinsky's book *The Gentle Art of Faking Furniture* is well worth reading as he relates some amusing anecdotes and, of course, he also deals with the more esoteric aspects of faking that are beyond the scope of this book. Unfortunately his book has been out of print for many years, but some public libraries still stock it.

It is essential to guard against the practice called 'marriage' in the antique trade, although in many instances it could equally well be described as 'divorce', or even 'cannibalism'. It consists of taking two separate pieces of furniture and marrying them to produce a single design which will sell for a higher price. This kind of treatment can yield such diverse pieces as bureau-bookcases, chests on chests, cabinets on stands, and Welsh dressers, all made from two originally separate pieces.

On the other hand such designs, when original and genuine, can be dismantled into their component parts and with some judicious additions and magical cabinet making each can be made into two pieces, and this could logically be described as a divorce!

Cannibalism can be most ingenious. One of the best examples of the genre is the small side table that has been made from legs which were formerly

Rosewood card table c1810, with baize-lined top, and brass mounts and decoration

balusters from an old staircase, and fitted with a small drawer that probably started life in a chest of drawers or a small table. Another practice is to obtain some old panelling and fix this to the back of a long stool or bench to make a settle; the Victorians were particularly fond of using panelling in this way. So much so that a London cabinet maker wrote to his sister in 1839 'We have made much of it [panelled furniture] lately, it sells for more than new such is beginning to be the taste of some that can afford it'. Tripod tables are a favourite target, too, and many a plain and

simple table has been carved with acanthus leaves on the knees and fitted with an imitation piecrust top to take it into a higher price-bracket.

Such creations often give themselves away by not looking right. The general proportions may look wrong, or a top may look too large for the pillar supporting it, or the veneering does not match. It is difficult to explain how you can acquire the instinctive feeling that something is wrong, other than to say it comes from long acquaintance with pieces that are authentic. The obvious advice is that you should take every opportunity to study genuinely antique examples in the many museums and stately homes where they are displayed.

There are, however, many other clues that can help to establish whether or not a piece is genuine, and here are some of them.

First of all, stand back and look from a distance before getting involved with the details. Does all of the piece have a consistent colour and patination, as it should? If it is mounted on a stand, or legs, or on a pillar, do these supports look of the right proportions or are they too delicate or too clumsy? What you are looking for here is evidence that a marriage has taken place.

Are the woods the correct type for the period? And are they consistent throughout the piece? As an example, take the hypothetical instance where a dealer has four chairs which are similar but not matching; as individual pieces they will fetch much less than if they were a set. A clever chair maker is engaged to transform them into a matching set, which means that he has to incorporate new parts made from his secondhand timber stocks. He would be foolish to make the most prominent features such as the front legs and the back splats from wood inconsistent with the design or the period, but the secondary parts such as the side and back seat rails and the underframing could well be made in other woods.

Does the pattern of any veneer carry through? For instance, the pattern of the veneer on the drawer fronts of a chest of drawers should be continuous over all of them. If not, could it be that one of the original drawers was missing or damaged and that a drawer from a similar chest has been altered to fit?

Are there any screw or nail holes which seem inexplicable? Or for that matter, any holes which have been filled? Look for them particularly on drawer fronts. Sometimes drawers from another piece have to be cannibalised and cut to fit; this usually means that the holes for the handle fixings are in the wrong places and have to be disguised.

If the piece has drawers, is their construction the same throughout, and are the dovetails made by the same craftsman in every case? If so, it is likely that all the drawers are original. Dovetail joints made by hand are almost as individual as handwriting, so check the conformity of the sizes of the pins and tails and the angle of slope. There should be the minor imperfections that creep into anything made or done by hand; perfect uniformity, particularly if the sizes of the pins and the tails are equal, indicates that the dovetails were cut by machine. Look, too, for the scratched line where the craftsman ran his marking gauge across the end of the drawer side to mark the depth of the dovetails; this is almost always present on handmade dovetails but never on those made by machine.

Timber always shrinks across the grain and not with it. Therefore, on a genuinely antique circular top of the kind used on tripod tables, the top will not be perfectly round but will be fractionally smaller when measured across the grain, If this is not so, the top could well be a replacement.

Tables of the sixteenth and seventeenth centuries often had clamped tops (see fig 1). The boards comprising the top were tenoned into clamps, which were fixed across the ends. The purpose of the clamps was to minimise shrinkage in the boards and to provide neat ends to the table top. Over the centuries the boards will have shrunk across the width, leaving the clamps standing proud at the corners: if this is not the case, the clamps (or the boards) are probably replacements.

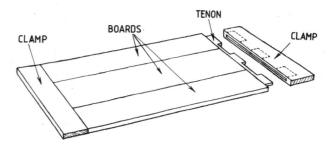

Fig 1 Clamping table top

Sometimes drawers have to be shortened in depth to fit into a carcase which was not made to accept them. Invariably this was done by sawing the drawer sides to the new, shorter length; the dovetail pins were sawn off the drawer back which was then nailed and glued between the drawer sides – a state of affairs never found in genuine antiques.

There are many methods of simulating age. One was to apply a coat of thin glue and then sprinkle on some dust to the appropriate parts of, say, a cabinet. These places could be around the bottom of the inside, under the top, or at the back of the shelves – the moral is to make sure that the dust is dust, and not an antiquing ploy!

Wear and tear marks: one must use common sense when assessing these. Fakers often tend to overdo things in their enthusiasm and a good example to consider is the wear on the bottom rails of an antique oak refectory-style table. The rails were fixed at a convenient height so that diners could put their feet on them away from the rushes which were strewn on the floor; naturally this caused a lot of wear on the top edges and some fakers seized on this feature. Sometimes they overdid things by wasting away the wood in places where a person's feet would never reach; similarly, the wear on the edges of the top of such a table would normally be restricted to the positions in front of the diners, but the faker would apply the distressing indiscriminately. Incidentally, the favourite tool for this job was a wire brush!

There are, of course, areas that are bound to become worn over the years. Wear on drawer sides and runners is an obvious example; flap and gate-leg tables will have marks on the underside of the top where the gate-leg or supporting fly bracket has scraped it during opening and closing of the table. The feet on the legs of some old oak tables have frequently almost disintegrated because they have absorbed moisture from damp or wet floors; if they have escaped this particular fate the faker with his wire brush will soon bring it about. In contrast, dining chairs that have stood on carpeted floors will have the bottoms of the legs almost burnished from being constantly moved about on the carpet pile; of course, this does not apply to legs fitted with castors.

Other small pieces such as stools and small tables that were constantly moved about will also show this burnished effect on their feet. Also, the finish on them should show wear and rubbing on the parts where the hands would fall naturally to pick them up; the same applies to the areas around door and drawer knobs and handles on all kinds of furniture. So this is where your detective instincts plus some common sense come into play.

It sometimes happens that an antique dealer decides that a plain piece of furniture such as a table or chair with uncarved cabriole legs would command a higher price if the knees were carved with shells or acanthus leaves. This kind of 'improvement' is quite easy to spot, as you can see from fig 2A and B. The drawing at A shows how the carving stands proud of the surface on a genuine carved leg because an extra thickness of wood was allowed for it when the leg was sawn out; at B a plain leg has been carved with a similar pattern but the carving has had to be cut out from the existing depth of the wood.

We come now to a word – patina – that stimulates some antique experts to heights of lyricism. It is the term that describes the surface finish which is the result of many years' dusting and polishing; it is a satin-like finish with a deep lustre and is certainly attractive to see and touch. And, as any restorer (or faker, for that matter) will tell you, it is impossible to imitate successfully. The only way to gain useful experience of its qualities is to visit museums, stately

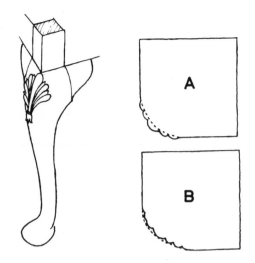

Fig 2 a: Carving on leg stands proud; b: Carving is cut out from existing wood

homes, or reputable antique dealers where it can be examined closely. A good tip is to look closely at antique furniture in churches whenever you can; almost invariably it has never been handled roughly and the patina is all it should be. Incidentally, brasswork, ormolu, and gilding can each acquire a patina, which is a very good reason for never attempting to clean any of them yourself as it is easily ruined.

During the 1920s and 30s particularly, there was a demand for what was called a 'rubbed antique finish'. This was achieved by applying a dark-coloured stain and then immediately wiping it away again from the main areas. The aim was to imitate the effect seen on some old furniture (usually oak) where the edges, outside corners, and centres of panels remained light in colour when compared with other parts where dust and polish tended to accumulate and become darker. The contrived finish fooled nobody and was simply a sales gimmick to make the furniture look different.

Distressing is the process by which fakers imitate the wear and tear that any piece of furniture is subjected to during use. The favoured tool for this job was called a chipper, and consisted of an old plane iron (cutting blade) fixed at right angles to a wooden handle; it was used in the manner of an adze to chip away simulated wear marks. Other expedients included dropping a brick wrapped in cloth from a height of a foot or two to produce bruises, and beating strategic parts of the furniture with a light chain or a steel-link burnisher to produce the many small indentations and scratches which are always found on old pieces.

To mention woodworm holes is to conjure up

visions of furniture being blasted by shotgun pellets to simulate the flight holes of these pests; visions which, incidentally, are purely imaginary. Fake woodworm holes can be made much more easily and just as convincingly with the point of a marking awl. It may seem unnecessary to point out that the evidence of woodworm can only be detected by the presence of the flight holes on the surface and not by being able to see the small chambers they make. We know of one repairer whose enthusiasm outran his knowledge when he included a repair piece with the tunnels running longitudinally and exposed to view – something which never happens in nature. In any case, the presence of woodworm holes does not necessarily indicate age as the pests will infest most woods if the conditions are right. Remember, however, that the true Cuban and Honduras mahoganies, cedar, rosewood, and oak heartwood, are seldom attacked.

Table and chair legs are parts always liable to damage, and repairing them is probably one of the

Walnut credence table c1670, with folding semicircular top, and fitted with a single drawer

largest sources of the modern restorer's work. Tapered legs of the kind used on Pembroke tables are quite delicate; check to see if they have been repaired by examining the grain along the length. It should, of course, run continuously but if a new piece has been spliced in as a repair, the line of the grain will be broken. Remember, too, that such legs are tapered on the inner sides only; if you come across one that is tapered on both sides it is likely to be a replacement. Employ the same method on turned legs, too; a split or broken leg could have a decorative ring or bulb turned on it to disguise the defect.

This summary by no means exhausts the repertoire of the faker but it does contain most of the clues that do not need technical expertise; if you would like to study the subject further, the books included in the Bibliography will help you.

CHAPTER 2

Joints and drawer construction

As already stated, trying to prove the age and authenticity of a piece of antique furniture is rather like solving a 'who-done-it' by looking for clues. The problem is that many of them are hidden in the construction and unless the piece can be taken apart (as in the case of restoration) they remain invisible. There are, however, usually enough that can be seen and examined without damaging the piece.

Medium and good class Victorian furniture is generally regarded as incorporating some of the finest cabinet making and veneering of any period. This was due to the technical improvements of the mid-nineteenth century when more progressive firms installed machine saws and planers; such accessories as glues and sandpapers had also been improved. The result was that their furniture was produced with tight, hairline joints, and every nook and cranny well smoothed off.

These features are very evident when a Victorian reproduction of, say, an Elizabethan chair is compared with its prototype. On genuinely old furniture of the sixteenth and early seventeenth centuries the joints were draw-bored and pegged (see fig 3). This involved offsetting the hole bored through the tenon from the hole through the mortise so that, when the peg was inserted and driven home, a wedging effect was produced which pulled the joint tight. Even so, the joint line is almost always clearly visible from a short distance because the makers had only Dutch rushes (the scouring rush) or rough-scaled fish skin for smoothing off. Anyone who has cut a mortise and

tenon joint by hand will know how difficult it is to smooth off the end grain perfectly square even with modern abrasives, let alone the primitive materials our ancestors had at their disposal.

Similar remarks apply to carved decoration. Until the Victorian era, carved wood was left with a finish straight from the tool and rarely smoothed afterwards, because of the difficulty of doing so. This gave a crisp, sharp, and vigorous appearance, which is lacking from Victorian work where usually the edges were rounded off. There was another difference, too, where a piece of carving included a relatively large flat area. Formerly such areas were difficult to abrade with either rushes or fish skin and they were often filled with random punchmarked patterns rarely found on Victorian pieces.

The makers of Victorian reproductions happily mixed decorative motifs from several periods on one piece – no wonder their designs were sometimes referred to as being in the 'Eclectic' style! Not only did they mix decorations but they also added their own curlicues and arabesques in the name of 'improvement'.

PEGGED JOINTS

These were used to lock the tenons in the mortises because until the eighteenth century glues were unreliable in consistency and unpredictable in behaviour. In any case, animal-based glues, which were the only ones available, are easily soluble in water and

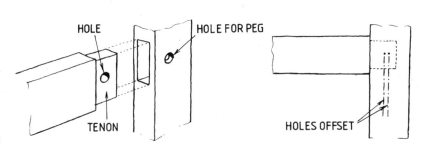

Fig 3 Draw-boring

Mahogany dressing commode c1760, with carved, canted corners. The top drawer is divided into partitions and has a blind fretwork front

in the damp, unheated homes of the sixteenth and seventeenth centuries their behaviour was unpredictable.

On old examples you will find that the pegs invariably stand proud of the surrounding surface by 1mm (⅟₃₂in) or so; this is because the wood around them has shrunk over the years – as the pegs were made with the grain running lengthwise they were not subject to shrinkage. The pegs were usually made from the same timber as the piece itself although on some country-made furniture willow pegs were used, presumably because they were already rounded by nature.

This peg projection is by no means an infallible indication of age since reproduction furniture manufacturers recognised its value as a mark of authenticity and included it in their designs. What is often not

realised is that genuinely old pegs are round on the outside only, and were left roughly shaped on the inside as they came from the drawknife used to shape them.

DRAWER CONSTRUCTION

This can be a useful guide, bearing in mind that four principal factors are involved, namely: the arrangement of the component parts of the drawer front; the type of dovetails used; the direction of the grain of the drawer bottom; and the way the drawer bottom is fixed in.

By the end of the eighteenth century the method of constructing drawers had been more or less standardised for the next century at least, as shown in fig 4. Here, the sides were lap dovetailed into a solid drawer front; the grain of the drawer bottom ran parallel to the front, and the bottom itself was fitted dry (without glue) into drawer beadings. The reason for not gluing the bottom was so that if it shrank or swelled, the wood could move freely in the grooves. In some drawers the bottom extended beyond the drawer back for 6mm or so (¼in) so that if it did indeed shrink, the surplus could be pushed up to fill the gap.

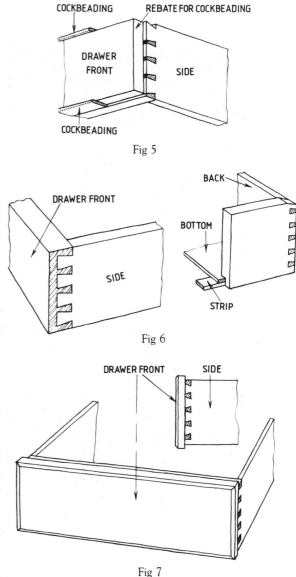

Fig 5

Fig 6

Fig 7

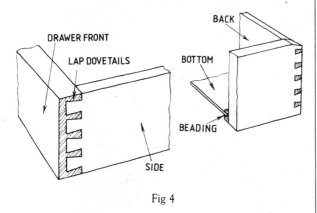

Fig 4

It should be explained that a piece of timber shrinks *across* the grain; any shrinkage in its length is so small as to be negligible. Dovetail joints were invented for this reason as they effectively spread any tendency to shrink or swell across the whole width of the drawer side, and thus prevented a large split from developing in any localised spot. Lap dovetailing, by the way, refers to a dovetailed joint in which the sockets do not penetrate right through the thickness of the wood – when they do, the joint is called a through dovetail.

During the 1770s the fashion was for cockbeaded drawer fronts as shown in fig 5, where the cockbead, with its grain running lengthwise, was rebated into the bottom and sides of the drawer front but occupied the full thickness at the top. The grain of the bottom ran parallel to the front, and the bottom was inserted as in fig 4.

Earlier in the eighteenth century, around 1740, there was another way of fixing drawer bottoms, as shown in fig 6, where the grain still ran parallel to the front and the bottom was contained in rebates in the drawer sides. Thin strips were nailed on and they not only held the bottom in place but also acted as drawer bearers.

Before about 1730, most drawer bottoms had the grain running from front to back, although it is not invariably the case. A development in drawer fronts was introduced about that time; mahogany was just becoming fashionable and drawer fronts were being made from it in the solid. As you can see from fig 7, the front was rebated all round at the back so that when the drawer was fitted into the carcase, the front overlapped and acted both to keep dust out and to prevent the drawer from being pushed in too far.

Actually, the idea originated around 1710 to 1720 at the end of the Walnut period. The details are shown in fig 8, and the method allowed the cabinet maker to practise a little economy by using pine instead of the more expensive walnut. It was common to use pine for drawer fronts from about 1680 to 1720;

the remainder of the drawer material was oak, except in some furniture made by country joiners when any suitable local wood such as ash, cherry or chestnut was employed.

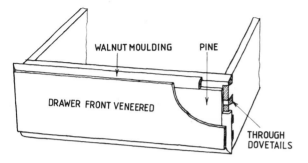

Fig 8

Fig 9 shows three variations of the drawer front that date from about 1690 to 1710, when walnut veneered fronts were considered essential. Note how the fronts were all made of pine covered with veneer; the remainder of the drawer stuff was oak (as already mentioned); the grain of the drawer bottoms ran from front to back.

Before the Restoration in 1660 there were two completely different ways of fixing drawer fronts. Fig 10 shows a drawer of about 1660; the front was jointed to the sides with one large, coarse dovetail, and runners on the carcase fitted into grooves channelled out of the sides. The whole thing was in oak and because the sides had to be thick enough for the channelling, the drawer was heavy and clumsy. Figs 10B and C show other methods used about 1640 – note how nails were employed to strengthen the joint.

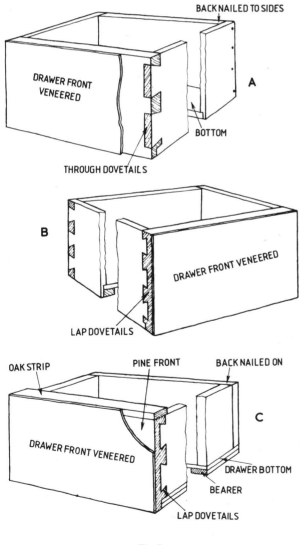

Fig 9

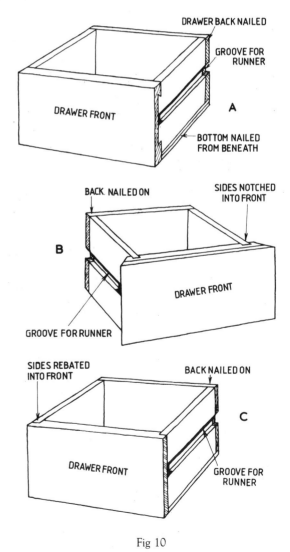

Fig 10

NAILS AND SCREWS

Nail making was a very ancient craft and was a meagre source of income for the very poorest classes until machine production took over from handwork. Our modern wire nails with flat heads are completely different from those used in the years until the middle of the nineteenth century; the old-style examples roughly resembled the modern deckhead nail.

Screws were first used in the late seventeenth century and the earliest ones were in brass, with hand-filed threads that were irregularly spaced and horizontal in profile. The first lathe-made screws with diminishing spiral threads appeared about 1750, followed by the modern style of screw from the middle of the nineteenth century. The early cabinet makers obviously did not have much faith in the holding powers of screws as each one invariably had a brass pin inserted alongside it.

FIXING TABLE TOPS

Edwardian and late Victorian table tops were fixed to the frame by buttoning, or pocket screwing, both of which are shown in fig 11 at (A) and (B) respectively. A third method, (C), called cleating, was utilised on tops made up from several boards – the elongated screwholes accommodated any tendency of the timber to shrink or swell.

Once screws had become reliable, pocket screwing was also used on table tops from the early years of the eighteenth century. The pockets were made using gouges and were therefore rounded; during the Victorian period they were frequently made with chisel cuts and were consequently triangular.

Until about 1700, table tops were fastened by means of oak pins driven down from the top into the frame rails beneath, and the only screws used were for fastening any hinges.

FURNITURE BACKS

In most good quality Edwardian and Victorian furniture the backs of such pieces as wardrobes, bookcases, and the like were as carefully executed as the parts that showed. But on furniture made during the eighteenth century and earlier the backs were

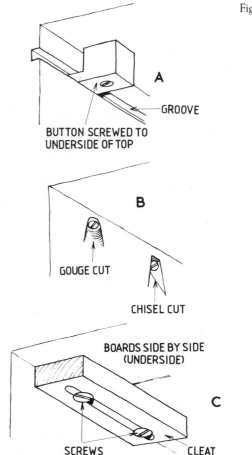

Fig 11

A — GROOVE
BUTTON SCREWED TO UNDERSIDE OF TOP

B
GOUGE CUT
CHISEL CUT

BOARDS SIDE BY SIDE (UNDERSIDE)
C
SCREWS
CLEAT

often surprisingly crude. In such cases, the back comprised several boards of pine or oak nailed to the edges of the carcase; sometimes, but by no means always, the edges of the boards were rebated to fit over one another. The inside of the back, which could be seen, was planed smooth and, in bookcases and display cases, a cloth or velvet lining was glued to it.

Do not condemn what might at first sight appear to be shoddy workmanship in a part which would not be seen. The labour involved in preparing thin boards was immense. First the boards had to be hand-sawn from a thicker piece of timber and then hours were spent in laborious planing. It's little wonder that the makers had no intention of spending too much time and labour on parts rarely seen.

Walnut gateleg table c1700, with a polygonal top. The legs and stretchers are bobbin turned

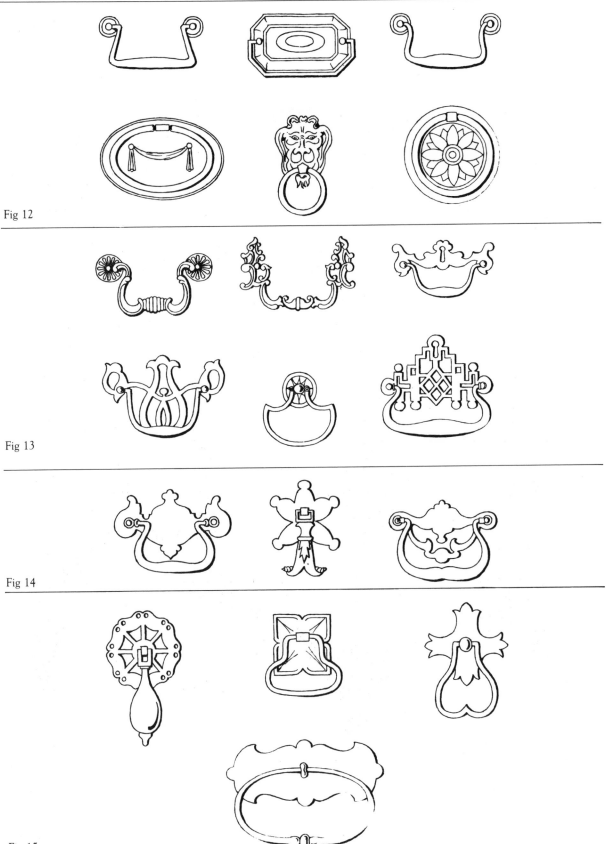

Fig 12

Fig 13

Fig 14

Fig 15

HANDLES

These can be helpful in determining the age of a piece although you must always check that they are not later replacements. The Victorians, in particular, were fond of replacing original handles with others more to their taste – often wooden knobs! Strangely, the wooden knob seems to have been the only handle design originated by the Victorians, and it appeared most frequently on chests of drawers; other furniture was adorned (or otherwise) with handles from every period regardless of propriety.

Fig 12 shows a representative selection of handles and backplates from the Regency and Sheraton periods, 1790 to 1830; fig 13 the same from the Chippendale period, 1750 to 1775; fig 14 the Walnut period, 1660 to 1730; and fig 15 from Tudor and Jacobean times, 1558 to 1645.

Methods employed for fixing handles can also be useful as clues. Thus, about 1770, circular nuts with slots cut in them, were introduced. Previously, from about 1730 onwards, square nuts were used; about 1710 bail-type handles were fixed by the pommel method. The pommel was a ball of metal, usually brass, from which protruded a metal rod with a screw thread at the end; this rod was inserted through the drawer front and a nut screwed on at the back. Each end of the bail of the handle was inserted into a hole in its pommel, so that each handle had two pommels. Before 1710, handles were fastened by snapes – a snape is a forked strip such as you find on a modern paper fastener. The snape was fixed to the handle, the fork inserted through a hole in the drawer front and then bent back on itself on the inside.

CASTORS

These, like handles, can help to date a piece if they are original. Fig 16 shows some typical examples, as follows: (A) a Regency style box castor with a foliar design on the toe; (B) a lion's paw box castor of the Regency period, 1790 to 1830; (C) a round or square tapered socket castor, 1780 onwards; (D) square box castor with bevelled edges, about 1780; (E) bull-nosed box castor, about 1780; (F) square socket castor, about 1760 to 1775; (G) early castor about 1740 to 1750 – it had a brass body and the wheel consisted of leather discs. Even earlier examples at the beginning of the eighteenth century were fitted with hardwood rollers or balls made of boxwood or laburnum.

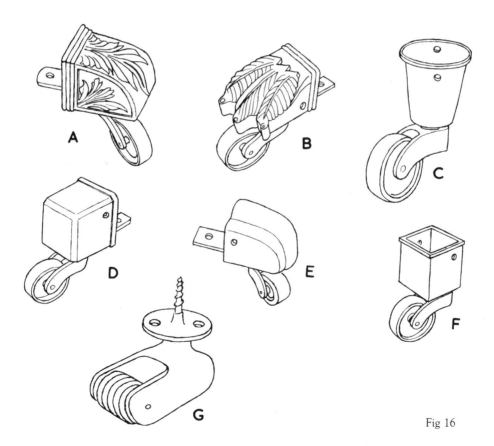

Fig 16

MOULDINGS

These can also point to the date of a piece but as favoured mouldings tended to be used over long periods, they cannot be regarded as precise indications.

A moulding is a patterned profile fashioned on the edge of a piece of wood, either by hand planing with a moulding plane, or by a scratch, or (after about 1850) by a machine called a spindle moulder. Mouldings can be employed in three ways: (A) as a stuck, or struck, moulding when it is worked on the edge of a solid piece of wood; (B) as a planted moulding when

it is a strip of wood with the profile worked on it, and fixed to the main frame; and (C) a bolection moulding which is rebated at the back and fixed on the edge of a frame – many window mouldings are bolection mouldings. All three are shown in fig 17.

Five basic shapes, derived from the classical orders of architecture, can be combined to make up almost any moulding profile. They are shown in fig 18, and are: (A) the ovolo; (B) the scotia; (C) the cavetto; (D) the cyma recta (also called an ogee); and (E) the cyma reversa (called a reverse ogee). Fig 19 shows some of the most frequently used mouldings of the various periods.

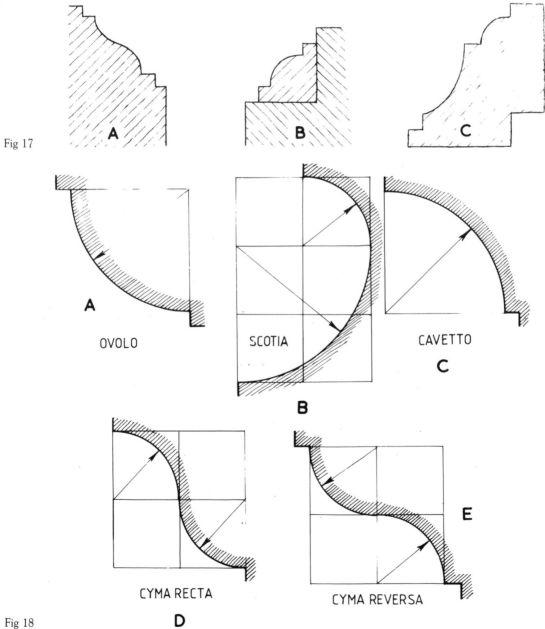

Fig 17

Fig 18

24

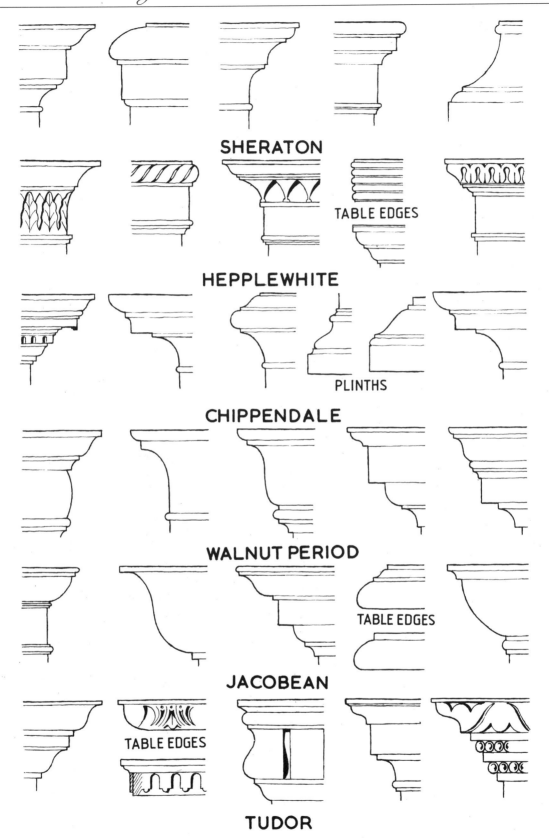

SHERATON

HEPPLEWHITE

TABLE EDGES

CHIPPENDALE

PLINTHS

WALNUT PERIOD

JACOBEAN

TABLE EDGES

TABLE EDGES

TUDOR

Fig 19

WOODS

To give advice on the best ways to identify particular woods would need a book on its own. Several good ones are available, but they all assume that the reader is interested in timber which has been recently felled and converted (that is, sawn into planks, etc) for the purposes of woodwork. This is not very helpful, as many woods change their colour with age, although the characteristics of the grain remain the same.

Here are the principal characteristics of some commonly used woods:

AMBOYNA (from the Philippines and Borneo) is light brown and gold in colour with an irregular, tightly burred figure. The colour tends to fade with age.

ASH, EUROPEAN: creamy white to light brown in colour with a long straight grain; the tree also yields burr veneers with tightly packed knots. It fades to a golden colour.

BEECH, EUROPEAN: light straw in colour when first cut, but this darkens to a medium brown over the years. Although straightgrained the grain pattern is featureless; it was (and is) widely used for chairs and upholstered furniture frames as the grain is tight enough to take tacks without splitting.

ELM, BRITISH: light brown with a twisting, irregular, and strongly marked grain. Generally it retains its colour but may tend to darken a little. It was the timber most used for Windsor chair seats as it was virtually the only tree that gave planks wide enough.

KINGWOOD (from Brazil): also called prince, princes' wood, violet wood, or violetta. The timber is a deep violet-brown colour which fades to a pale pink with a brown tint over the years.

OAK, AMERICAN WHITE and AMERICAN RED: the former is sometimes called chestnut oak, and the latter Spanish or swamp oak. Both are straight-grained but the surfaces tend to be fibrous. The red variety is a medium to dark brown colour as opposed to the white, which is a fawn colour – both fade with age.

OAK, BRITISH: this is sufficiently known not to need a description of the colour, but the grain pattern can vary enormously, depending on the way the log is converted. It tends to darken with age, although if an old piece is cut through, the exposed surface has the same colour as freshly converted wood.

Home-grown oak was the predominant wood up to about 1660, and almost all of it was converted by being riven, which exposes what is called the quarter-figure. This is a figure where the medullary rays, which conduct food and moisture to the sap wood, appear as silvery flecks known variously as clashes, felts, flashes, or silver grain.

There was a very practical reason for this method of conversion. At that time there were only two ways of converting a log into boards suitable for use in furniture: one was by pit-sawing and the other was by riving. True, a few saws worked by water or hand power were in use in Europe but they were very rare in Britain.

Most villages and large estates had saw-pits and in large towns the pits were permanently manned by sawyers, each pit having a top-man and a pit-man. The villages and estates had to wait until an itinerant team of sawyers visited them and this was not always convenient and was, in any case, expensive. The village carpenter or joiner preferred to use riven oak that he could prepare himself. He knew that riven timber is always stronger than sawn. Any reader who

has chopped up small logs for firewood will know the principle involved – if an axe is driven into the end grain of the log, it will split roughly into two halves. Each half can then be split lengthwise into quarters, and so on; what the now-perspiring reader is doing is a primitive form of riving.

Traditional riving or cleaving employed a similar but more sophisticated method. First, a wedge was driven into the end grain of the log with a large mallet called a beetle and as the timber began to split, more wedges were driven in to make the split run the whole length. The process was repeated until the log was converted into billets, which could be dressed with an adze. What proportion of riven oak as opposed to sawn oak was employed in any particular piece of furniture depended on when the sawyers paid their last visit and on what stock of sawn stuff, if any, was on hand.

OAK, JAPANESE: the first imports did not begin until 1905 and the timber is therefore not in the scope of this book.

MAHOGANY (from the West Indies and Central America): as you can see from the historical chart, the first commercial imports of the various mahoganies began about 1725, and were known under several names such as Jamaica wood, baywood, and Spanish, Porto Rico, San Domingo, and Honduras mahoganies.

For the purpose of this book the varieties can be reduced to two – Cuban and Honduras. Of the two the Cuban is superior, having a deep red colour, a beautiful grain, and a surface which polishes superbly; over the years it matures to a dark honey colour.

MAHOGANY, HONDURAN: is lighter in colour, being a rich mellow brown; the texture is not so glossy as in the Cuban variety and it makes a perfect groundwork for veneering. It fades to a pale cream colour.

One characteristic of both mahoganies distinguishes them from the African varieties, which began

An early oak dresser, early 17th century, with geometrically panelled drawer and door fronts

(*top left*) Oak side cabinet with a marble top and shallow pull-out trays along the top; it was probably used as a kind of enclosed dresser. The pilasters with split-turned balusters, plus the geometrical style of the mouldings, indicate a date about the time of the Restoration, c1660

(*left*) American extending dining table c1836, in a style reminiscent of the late 18th century – witness the foliated swags on the frieze rail and the carved acanthus leaves on the bulb of the leg

(*above*) Mahogany writing and reading table c1790. The leather-lined top which rises on central supports can be adjusted to a suitable angle by means of a ratchet

to be imported from the middle of the nineteenth century. It is the presence of straw-coloured narrow lines spaced at approximately 25mm (1in) intervals across the grain which indicate where the tree switched from making spring wood to autumn wood. Additionally, in the case of Cuban mahogany, the grain contains minute specks of what appears to be a white filler but actually is a purely natural feature.

ROSEWOOD: two varieties of this wood concern us; one comes from Brazil and was at one time called Rio rosewood; the other, from India, was called Bombay blackwood or Indian rosewood. Both are dark purple-brown and often have bands of black and dark brown stripes; the colour of neither timber seems to fade with age.

SATINWOOD: another species with two varieties of interest. First, the West Indian satinwood, which was probably the first to be imported: it is a rich yellow colour with a straight close grain which sometimes shows a mottled effect. Second, the East Indian wood which is more open-grained than the dense West Indian; the yellow colour is also paler and tends to become cloudy when polished. The colours of both varieties fade over the years.

WALNUT, EUROPEAN: the wood from young trees is light brown in colour and the grain is indeterminate; the older the tree the better the figure, the deeper the colour, and the darker the striped figure. When fully seasoned it is very stable and is unlikely to shrink, warp, or split; with age it lightens to a honey colour. Unfortunately, woodworm are very partial to it and you must not be surprised to find their flight holes.

Walnut burr veneers are well known; what is often not realised is that much of the highly decorative burr veneer used in the 1870s and 80s was actually Circassian (or Caucasian) walnut from around the Black Sea, and no self-respecting Victorian piano was to be found without it.

WALNUT, AMERICAN BLACK: imported from the eastern states of the USA, this wood does not resemble European walnut as it has very little figure or grain pattern; it is a uniform rich purple-brown colour with black streaks. With age the colour fades to a light purple-brown. Like its European counterparts, it is a stable timber.

WALNUT, AMERICAN RED: sometimes called Virginian: this can resemble mahogany, particularly if it has been polished with this in mind; the grain is, however, finer and the figure undistinguished. It ages to a warm brown.

Two-section chest c1690, in walnut except for the oak-panelled sides. Fitted with three long drawers and one extra deep. William and Mary style and (*left*) Satinwood secretaire-cabinet c1790. The crossbandings are in rosewood, and the sliding secretaire section is partitioned and leather lined

SATIN WALNUT: (from the USA) is not a walnut at all, but the American red gum. Strictly speaking, the name should be applied only to the heartwood, which is a soft medium brown with occasional black stripes; the brown fades to a straw colour.

YEW, EUROPEAN: varies in colour from biscuit to pale red and has a beautifully lustrous surface. The figure frequently breaks into bands of pink and tan colours, and the wild configuration of the grain in yew burrs is quite unique. The colours do not fade with age but become mellower.

Verbal descriptions of timbers are bound to be poor substitutes for the real thing; it is difficult for anyone not in the trade to see actual wood specimens, although they are sometimes displayed at woodworking centres. It is again a matter of examining antique furniture in museums, etc.

The Art Veneers Co Ltd, Industrial Estate, Mildenhall, Suffolk IP28 7AY, supplies veneer samples of most woods; however, you must appreciate that the samples are of recently converted woods and you must make allowances for ageing.

CHAPTER 3

Polishes

The years between 1920 and the present have probably seen greater changes in the way furniture is polished than in the preceding four hundred years. Today, virtually all furniture is finished with one or other of several synthetic resin lacquers, while from 1920 to 1950 the most widely used finish was cellulose lacquer. The only change remotely comparable was when French polish was introduced around 1825; previously, from about 1500 onwards, wax polishes and oil and spirit varnishes were employed.

The painting of furniture was widespread in medieval times and continued to be so, alongside wax and oil finishes, until about 1650 when it was superseded by varnishes and japanning. It reappeared about 1770 and continued to be in vogue until about 1810, when the use of brass (and other metal) inlays, plus French polishing, finally rendered it unfashionable.

It is not always easy, even for experts, to tell one antique finish from another, particularly when the piece has been polished and re-polished over many years. The best way is to apply the appropriate solvent to an out-of-the-way part of the piece; thus, methylated spirits will dissolve French polish and the spirit varnishes, while turpentine or turpentine substitute (white spirit) will dissolve oil varnishes and wax polishes. There is no need to make a big issue of the test; the best way to apply it is to damp a wad of cotton wool with the solvent, rub it lightly on to the chosen part and see what, if anything, comes off.

The following notes give details of the principal types of polish.

Regency-style rosewood, carved-and-gilt serving table c1815. With a marble top, supported by four carved-and-gilt scrolled legs united by a base with a mirror back

French Polish

This type of spirit varnish was introduced (as the name suggests) from France. In composition it differs little from other spirit varnishes and is distinguished by the method of application.

It consists of shellac dissolved in methylated spirits. The colour of the polish can be varied to suit the wood by using different types of shellac and by adding dyes, such as alkanet or dragon's blood if an authentic antique colour is required.

The polish is applied with a fad, which is a piece of folded wadding, and when the finish has reached a certain stage a few drops of linseed oil are first applied, and later taken off, with a rubber. This is, again, a piece of wadding covered with a piece of lint-free rag – as a matter of interest, in the trade this rag could be bought by the sackful from polish suppliers, and consisted mainly of men's wornout white shirts!

Properly applied the polish gives a deep lustrous finish; unfortunately it is easily marked by heat and water but it has the advantage that it can be revived easily from time to time. One cannot readily assume that any piece that is French polished must neces-

Pair of George III elbow chairs c1777, in carved-and-gilt wood with fluted legs, oval upholstered backs, and the arms upholstered with pads

sarily have been made after 1825, as the Victorians had an exasperating habit of tinkering with antiques to 'improve' them, and many pieces were stripped of their original finish and French polished – this applies particularly to eighteenth-century mahogany furniture.

Gilding

Gilding has been known since time immemorial and has always been practised by highly skilled craftsmen. There are two principal methods of applying gold leaf, namely oil gilding and water gilding, and both were used on furniture; the choice depended on whether or not the gilding needed to be burnished. Oil gilding cannot be burnished, but water gilding can, and the latter was often employed in both burnished and matt finishes on the same piece.

Dating and identifying gilt work is a job for professional experts and is so complicated that even

Queen Anne double-domed bureau c1710, with mirror-glazed doors. These carry hinged panels which enclose a fitted interior with numerous pigeonholes and drawers. The bureau section contains eight drawers around a central cupboard. The whole piece is in bottle-green lacquer

they have trouble. Their task is not made easier by the fact that some gilding contains no gold but only bronze and copper alloys, or consists of other metals coated with a varnish called *auripetrum*.

If any reader has gilt or parcel-gilt (partially gilded) furniture, he would be well advised to ask an expert to see it. As a last word on the subject, never attempt to repair or restore gilding, or try to remove the valuable patina that has built up over the years.

GRAINING AND MARBLING

Dealing first with graining, it can be defined as a way of painting woodwork to imitate the grain and colour of a more costly or attractive timber. During the middle and later years of the Victorian period it was widely used on cheap furniture and was, in most cases, quite crudely done; the Arts and Crafts Movement of the time abhorred it. During the Georgian period, however, it was commonly employed and, provided it was executed skilfully, was regarded as both legitimate and acceptable. It was also applied towards the end of the sixteenth century to such woods as pine to imitate oak or walnut, particularly for wall panelling, but was ousted by veneering from about 1670 onwards.

The process involved applying scumble glazes to the wood and manipulating them with various brushes and tools to resemble the colour and grain of the desired timber. The scumble glaze could be either oilbound or waterbound (although in the latter, oatmeal stout or beer was considered better); powder colours were then added to it to give the basic ground colour.

The tools recommended for obtaining the grained effect were a very mixed bag and included: combs made from steel or leather, some with teeth cut out at regular intervals; mottling and veining brushes; an assortment of rags of various textures for wiping out; and a pigeon's wing, which gave a realistic interpretation of figured walnut!

Marbling was accomplished by methods and tools very similar to those used for graining and, in fact, many of the stately pillars in the grandest country houses are made of wood which has been marbled. It was also used to decorate woodwork and furniture generally, and table tops particularly, from the early seventeenth century until the 1870s and 80s, when the influence of the Arts and Crafts Movement discouraged the use of imitative materials. Historically, it can be traced back to at least the thirteenth century in England, when Henry III ordered that the posts in his bedroom should be marbled.

JAPANNING AND LACQUERING

Like marquetry and inlaying, these two terms are often regarded and used as though they were interchangeable. They are not; in fact, japanning is an inferior imitation of lacquering. The raw material is the basic difference between the two, as japanning utilises shellac, while lacquering employs the sap of the 'lacquer' or 'varnish' tree, *Rhus vernicifera*, a member of the Sumach family, which is widely grown in Japan. The tree also grows quite happily in England but is usually confined to collections of unusual trees as the sap can cause severe irritation if it touches the skin.

Shellac is derived from the incrustations of lac insects which feed on the sap of trees in India and Thailand; the incrustations are processed to produce different forms of shellac. Lacquer, on the other hand, is sap which has been collected from lacquer trees tapped for the purpose; when the sap emerges it is transparent but soon turns black after exposure to the air.

Japanning was fashionable throughout the first half of the Victorian period and was applied not only to furniture (generally small occasional pieces) but also to papier-mâché and metalwork such as trays, jugs, etc. There was no attempt to imitate the Oriental motifs of earlier work, and the decoration often included very British flowers such as roses, forget-me-nots, etc; the quality varied widely, too, from very accomplished work down to the crudest. At this period japanning was an art form on its own, and had abandoned all pretensions to being an imitation of lacquer work.

The seventeenth and eighteenth centuries were the heydays of both japanning and lacquering, and in the eighteenth century some pieces of European lacquering were produced that were equal, or superior in quality to, the lacquered pieces from China and Japan then being imported. This situation arose because the demand grew so large that Oriental craftsmen had to hurry their work, with the inevitable result that the quality suffered (it takes about a year to lacquer one piece); also, they tended to scamp the construction and preparation of the work to be lacquered. To remedy this, some European cabinet makers were sent to the East to supervise the construction; also, some Chinese lacquer craftsmen were brought over to Europe probably in the hope (never actually realised) that they would impart their trade secrets. Sometimes the pieces were made in Europe and sent to China by ship for lacquering.

In all this to-ing and fro-ing it is not surprising that

there was a wide variety of styles and qualities, which makes it difficult for anyone other than an expert to decide on authenticity. However, it is possible to give some pointers, as follows:

(a) genuine Japanese lacquer almost always had a predominantly black background as this was the only colour acceptable to the ruling class. The designs tended to be sparse, stylised, and uncluttered, with the pattern exquisitely detailed. The design was always deliberately assymetrical.

(b) in Oriental lacquer work the colours used most frequently were black, brown, dark green, light brown, ochre, purple, red, vermilion, and yellow; in England black, blue, bistre (transparent brown), chestnut, olive, and red; in France blue, green, reddish orange, white, and yellow.

(c) English, and for that matter, all European interpretations of Oriental designs fell short of the originals in that the craftsmen found it difficult to depict truly Oriental faces, dress, and gestures – sometimes they showed a reasonably accurate representation of a Chinese or Japanese landscape and then spoiled it by including English figures, dogs, and cottages. Also, they seemed unable to grasp the Japanese principle of assymetry in design, which was that although the main elements may be disproportionate, the design as a whole should appear as a balanced composition. Similarly, English craftsmen frequently included perfectly symmetrical borders that would never have appeared on Oriental work.

(d) during the late seventeenth and early eighteenth centuries japanning became a popular pastime for young ladies with time on their hands. Today large quantities of indifferently japanned pieces remain, most of them of small size, such as trinket and jewel boxes, and various kinds of little tables. The hobby was greatly stimulated by the publication in 1688 of John Stalker and George Parker's *Treatise on Japanning and Varnishing*, which included both instructions and designs for reproduction by amateurs.

PAINTED FURNITURE

There hardly seems to have been a time when furniture has not been painted in one way or another – unless it was during the first half of the eighteenth century when japanning and varnishing replaced it – and the style and extent of the painting is what concerns us.

The leading exponent of all-over painted furniture during the last years of the Victorian period was C. R. Mackintosh, who was fond of white and pastel colours for his furniture; his hallmark was a stylised tightly furled rose; his style is discussed more fully elsewhere.

Many of the Arts and Crafts Movement designers also used paint, either all-over (as with much of the Liberty style furniture), or to pick out the salient features (as with Baillie-Scott, Philip Webb, Bruce Talbert, and others). The most notable exception was Charles Eastlake, who disliked hiding the natural appearance of wood and so preferred oil or wax polishing. William Morris, Rossetti, Burne-Jones, Madox-Brown, and Holman Hunt all collaborated enthusiastically in producing furniture decorated with panels, which were often painted in the pre-Raphaelite manner.

The Regency styles frequently combined painted backgrounds with gilt decoration; the paint was usually black, white, ivory, or *en grisaille* (that is, paints of grey, olive green, or buff colours which simulated objects in relief). Robert Adam and his successors, Hepplewhite and Sheraton, all used similar techniques and included painted panels and medallions with classical subjects.

As we have seen, japanning and lacquering were so popular for the hundred years following the Restoration in 1660 that painting furniture was indulged in only spasmodically. Between about 1500 and 1660 wax or oil finishes, or oil varnishing, were the usual finishes. Before the earlier date, in medieval times, most furniture was painted. This was done for the very good reason that chimneys, as such, had not been invented and the smoke from the fire escaped eventually through a hole in the roof, having first deposited a layer of soot and smuts on everything. This coating was washed off every spring (hence spring cleaning) and painted finishes allowed this to be done easily. The paints were lead-based and on this really early furniture you can sometimes see where the lead has turned the oak figure black, once the paint has been stripped off.

VARNISHING AND OIL POLISHING

Two types of varnish were used as finishes for furniture – spirit varnish, and oil varnish – the latter being the earlier one.

Spirit varnishes consist of gums or resins dissolved in methylated spirits; the gums or resins include shellac (or seed lac, which was the old name), copal resin, gum damar, and gum sandarac.

Oil varnishes are made by dissolving such resins and gums as copal, damar, and fossil resin in an oil of some sort; linseed oil was the most common, but

Two 17th-century oak joined stools. Such examples are difficult to date as similar designs were made over an extended period of time – probably they are c1640–1680

hazelnut and walnut, juniper, poppy, and sweet oil (olive oil) were also utilised.

Much of the furniture found in ordinary homes in the Victorian period was spirit-varnished, and most of the varnishing left much to be desired as it was either dark and treacly, or so thin that it soon cracked or wore off. What was called China varnish (shellac dissolved in alcohol) began to be used at the end of the seventeenth century and throughout the eighteenth until it was supplanted by French polish.

In the sixteenth and seventeenth centuries, an early method of preserving wood (apart from painting) was to rub some oil into the surface – nut, poppy, and linseed oils were all employed. It was soon found that dissolving a resin or gum in the oil made the job easier and gave a better finish that did not have to be constantly renewed.

Sheraton described a method of oil polishing which he said was 'the general mode of polishing plain cabinet work' (*Cabinet Dictionary*, 1803). It consisted of applying a coat of linseed oil (which could contain a colouring agent such as alkanet root) and leaving it to soak into the wood surface for two to seven days, depending on its hardness. Some brickdust was then sprinkled on and rubbed with a cloth to form a putty with the linseed oil; the continual rubbing of this putty along the grain of the wood brought forth the shine.

WAX POLISHING

This type of polish was made by dissolving beeswax in turpentine, sometimes with the addition of a little linseed oil; a later mixture recommended by Sheraton was beeswax, turpentine, a few drops of copal varnish, red lead, and a powder colour all mixed together and moulded into a ball.

Furniture of the type designed by the Cotswold School and the Arts and Crafts Movement was often wax polished, as it was a point of honour not to hide the natural grain and figure of the wood. Sheraton outlined a wax-polishing method in his *Cabinet Dictionary*, which involved rubbing hard wax into the wood with a piece of cork. The wood was then scoured with powdered brickdust on a cloth and, if repeated often enough, the process would bring the desired finish. The beeswax and turpentine polish was among those which replaced the practice of painting furniture from about 1500 onwards.

CHAPTER 4

Veneers

One of the most useful methods of dating a piece of furniture is by studying the thickness of the veneers, remembering that in England the practice of veneering was not introduced until about 1660. This technique consisted of gluing a thin sheet of wood (the veneer) on to a thicker piece (the groundwork); the veneer was chosen because of the attractiveness of its grain or figure and not, as is often thought, to cover up bad workmanship.

Until the early years of the nineteenth century, probably about 1820, sheets of veneer were cut by hand-sawing: the illustration in fig 20 shows clearly how it was done, and comes from *L'Art du menuisier ébéniste*, Paris, 1774. When veneers were sawn like this it was virtually impossible to cut them much less than 5mm (³⁄₁₆in) thick, if only because the saw would often wander along the grain. However, the cabinet maker would further reduce the thickness by planing it first with a scrub plane to make the thickness uniform, followed by a toothing plane that produced a series of grooves which acted as a key for the glue. The conclusion is, then, that veneers which are about 3mm (⅛in) thick (or thicker) date the piece to between 1660 and 1830.

The historical chart on page 176 shows that Sir Marc Isambard Brunel patented a circular saw in 1806. Most of his activities were with civil engineering, and it would have taken some years for the invention to filter through to the furniture trade – although almost certainly veneer sawing had become a separate trade during the early years of the eighteenth century. It is probable, then, that veneers cut by means of a circular saw (called saw-cut) date back to about 1830, and were cut with large saws up to four or five feet in diameter; Spear & Jackson exhibited one of about 1.5m (5ft) diameter at the Great Exhibition of 1851. This method produced veneers from 1mm (¹⁄₃₂in) to 2mm (¹⁄₁₆in) thick, which were used until the advent of knife and rotary cut veneers about 1900 to 1914. The latter types of veneers are both paper thin – about 0.7mm – and are the only ones used today.

The craft of veneering was brought to England by immigrant craftsmen who followed Charles II across the Channel, and their numbers were further augmented by Huguenot refugees fleeing religious persecution in 1685, and by Dutch craftsmen who came over from Holland during the reign of William and Mary (1689 to 1702) – William was, of course, Dutch.

English craftsmen took up the craft with, at first, more enthusiasm than circumspection and this led them to make mistakes. First, they did not appreciate that any faults in the groundwork would eventually

Satinwood writing cabinet c1795, with bookshelves, suitable for a lady. Decorated with marquetry, the bureau section has a curved tambour front. Note the wire-mesh panels to prevent papers and books from falling out

show through, or cause the veneer to split. Thus, in early examples (late seventeenth century) where through dovetails were used to join the drawer fronts to the drawer sides (see fig 9), the veneer was laid over the ends of the tails. This inevitably led to splits or stress marks in the veneers due to the slight movement of the joints with the opening and closing of the drawer; further, as the glue was soaked up by end grain, there was every chance that adhesion would gradually be lost and the veneers would lift.

Second, they often used quartercut oak as a groundwork. Now, straightgrained mild oak is perfectly sound as a groundwork and can be found used for that purpose on furniture in the eighteenth century; however, quartercut oak when sawn exposes the ray figuring, which is harder than the surrounding wood and is less liable to shrink. This meant that as the oak shrank over the years the rays stood proud of the surface and eventually showed through the veneers – also the rays were harder and less amenable to gluing so, once again, there was a danger of the veneers lifting.

Third, they tended to overdo the veneering and to use it in unsuitable locations. Consider fig 21; note how the mouldings above the bracket feet, and the feet themselves, were crossveneered and therefore extremely vulnerable. The illustration is of a William & Mary chest of drawers, dated about 1700, in Bristol Museum.

Fourth, the craftsmen (and their successors) rarely veneered both sides of the wood except where appearances called for it – for example, on the inner faces of doors. The risk of damage was greatest with table tops and extending leaves or flaps because when the glue was applied, the water in it caused the veneer to swell. As the veneer dried out it shrank and tended to pull the groundwork on which it was laid into a hollow shape. So the situation arose where the groundwork, for example a table top fixed to a frame, was trying to resist the shrinking of the veneer, and over a period of years something – the table top, the veneer, or the glue – had to go.

Fifth, the veneer should always be laid on the heart side of the groundwork as wood warps away from the heart and thus counteracts the pull of the veneer. Fig 22 explains the term heart side. This kind of danger was probably found out the hard way by trial and error by seventeenth-century craftsmen. In my opinion, it

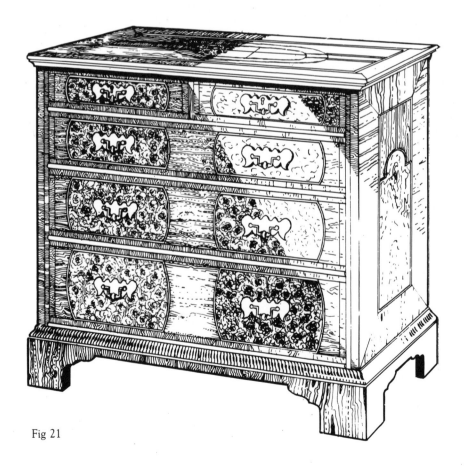

Fig 21

Walnut chest of drawers c1720, the drawer fronts being decorated with herringbone bandings and the top having quartered veneers. Note the carrying handles – quite normal for this period

Walnut side table c1705, with a quartered-veneer top inlaid with herringbone banding. The legs are typical Queen Anne style with club feet.

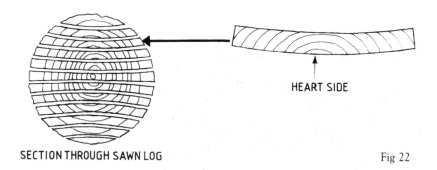

SECTION THROUGH SAWN LOG — HEART SIDE — Fig 22

is likely to be the reason why table and cabinet tops of the Queen Anne and William & Mary periods were invariably quartered or laid with a pattern based on the graining of the veneers running in opposing directions to minimise the risk of splitting or wrinkling.

Sixth, when veneer was cut by a saw, inevitably grooves or score marks were left by the saw teeth. These had to be removed so that the underside of the veneer was fairly smooth, otherwise excess glue remained in the grooves and shrank and pulled down the veneer over the years. This resulted in a surface marred by a series of ridges which can be felt with the fingers or seen when the piece of furniture is viewed against the light.

The remedies for all these faults had to be learnt painfully, and by the middle of the eighteenth century the technique of veneering had been perfected, at least as far as the best makers were concerned; later veneered work in the nineteenth century was of the highest quality, as indeed was the cabinet making.

It has been stated that, in the late seventeenth century, oak was often used as a groundwork, but pine was used as well. When mahogany arrived about 1730, most veneering was laid on a mahogany groundwork – a purpose for which most varieties of the timber were ideally suited. Towards the end of the eighteenth century, when upholstered seating came into its own, beech was used for the frames and was veneered on the show-wood parts, but only in comparatively small sizes.

Inlays, Intarsia, Marquetry

These three terms are often regarded as interchangeable but, in fact, are not. The nomenclature can best be clarified by quoting from William A. Lincoln's authoritative book *The Art and Practice of Marquetry* (Thames & Hudson):

There are two popular misconceptions, both in Britain and America, about the meanings of the words 'marquetry' and 'intarsia' . . . I have discovered that in practically every country in the non-English-speaking world, with the single exception of France, the word 'marquetry' is not used. The work is described everywhere as 'intarsia', with slight variations in spelling in different languages . . . For clarity, it is best to use 'intarsia' to describe the pictorial inlay work practised in fourteenth-century Italy, and particularly that showing scenes in perspective . . . In the English-speaking countries the word 'intarsia' means inlay – a design or pattern of wood or other material inserted into groundwork which has been suitably [prepared] to receive it . . . But the use of the word 'intarsia' in this sense is actually wrong; there is no such word in the *Oxford Dictionary*, neither is it in common usage among the people who practise the craft . . . To describe any form of decoration which is actually sunk into a solid base, the correct English word is 'inlay'.

The word 'marquetry' is used to describe a pattern or design of wood veneers, assembled together and overlaid with glue, to completely cover a surface . . . the veneers are not sunk into the groundwork, but are overlaid on a flat surface.

From about 1820 onwards, almost every furniture style used inlay; the Gothic Revival, the Arts and Crafts Movement, and Art Nouveau in particular. Although different woods were utilised to create the desired effects, there was also plenty of metal inlay (often in the form of *repoussé* copper panels) together with semi-precious stones.

Brass inlay was popular in the last decade of the eighteenth and the early part of the nineteenth centuries; thus we find Sheraton saying in his *Cabinet Dictionary* (1803): [inlaying with wood is] 'an expensive mode of decorating furniture used in the cabinet-making of twenty and thirty years back: the present mode of inlaying with brass is more durable, and looks well into the black woods of any kind.'

Card table c1790, in sycamore and satinwood with tulipwood crossbanding. The flutes and central decoration on the frieze rails are simulated in marquetry

Before this, from about 1670 to 1770, inlaying was overshadowed by marquetry, and we must go back to the sixteenth and seventeenth centuries to find it widely used as decoration, when hardly a piece of furniture was made which did not have its full complement. The technique was simple enough; the outline of the pattern was marked on the surface and then the wood was wasted (cut away) to form recesses for the different shapes and kinds of wood. They included: ash, bog oak, ebony; fruitwoods such as apple, cherry, mulberry, and pear; holly, sycamore, and yew. Other materials such as bone, ivory, mother of pearl, and tortoiseshell were also employed. Incidentally, bog oak is found in Eire, and is oak which has become fossilised by having been buried in a peat bog for several centuries. It is jet black and

extremely hard; it can usually be distinguished because the inlaid pieces were cut across and not with the grain. The holly wood was boiled before being used in order to preserve its whiteness.

You may come across the term 'markatree' applied to inlaid work in records of the sixteenth and seventeenth centuries, but it was nevertheless usually inlay as opposed to marquetry.

MARQUETRY

From the late nineteenth century back to its introduction in the late seventeenth century, marquetry was used, in one form or another, to decorate furniture. There was a period between about 1790 to 1810 when painted decoration was preferred, but the

Victorians soon revived the fashion for marquetry and it remained popular throughout the era.

In the years around the middle of the eighteenth century marquetry fans, shells, swags, pendant husks, and floral motifs were used on even the most humble workaday furniture, while the more presumptuous pieces had panels displaying allegorical or classically antique subjects.

In 1780 the 'French horse' or as it was known in England, the marquetry cutter's 'donkey', was invented in Paris. Prior to its introduction, the veneers for marquetry pieces had been sawn by means of the same wooden-framed bowsaws which had (since their arrival about 1562) been used to cut inlays. Before 1562 cutting the inlays was a difficult and laborious task as the craftsmen used knives with enormously long handles reaching to the shoulder so that the whole weight of the body could be applied. With the advent of the donkey, up to a dozen versions of the same pattern could be cut at one time, thus increasing output which in turn made the product cheaper and stimulated interest. The appliance was in general use until well into the twentieth century.

Engraving marquetry does not seem to have been introduced until the second half of the eighteenth century, and consisted of cutting fine lines in the surface of the veneers and filling them with a black composition. Arabesque, or seaweed, marquetry was in vogue about 1690 and was so called because the intricate scrolls and curlicues resembled the fronds of seaweed. Two woods were normally used, often box or holly for the pattern and walnut for the ground-work; this exacting work demanded precise sawing to the line with the saw blade held at a slight angle so that the gap made by the sawcut (or kerf) was taken up and was practically indistinguishable.

Floral marquetry was fashionable from about 1670 to 1700, and included many varieties of wood, some of them scorched in hot sand to achieve the desired effect of shading. The designs were often so complicated that they were divided into sections; the veneers for each section were chosen according to colour, grain, etc, and were stuck down on to a piece of paper. The corresponding part of the design (on paper) was then glued on top and, when dry, the pieces were sawn out, the paper removed and the cut out parts kept in separate trays.

BANDINGS (fig 23)

A banding is a strip or band of veneer or inlay, normally between 12mm and 38mm wide (½in and 1½in), that is used as a decorative motif – most often as a border to a panel. There are four types: (A) straight banding, when the grain runs parallel to the edge; (B) crossbanding, when the grain runs crosswise at a right angle to the edge; (C) feather banding, when the grain runs obliquely across; and (D) herringbone, which has the pattern divided centrally along the banding, with the grain on each half opposed at about right angles to the other to achieve a continuous chevron pattern.

Mahogany sideboard c1785, with satinwood bandings and floral marquetry decoration. The spandrels carry marquetry shell ornaments

A Carlton House style of writing table c1790, in satinwood with rosewood bandings. The fretted gallery is brass

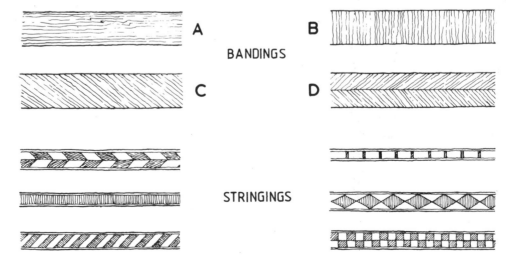

A

B

BANDINGS

C

D

STRINGINGS

Fig 23

46

Typical Pembroke table c1780, in satinwood with rosewood crossbandings

Crossbandings of veneer have been used since the introduction of marquetry, and are still commonly employed today. Inlaid bandings, usually of feather or herringbone pattern, were one of the most popular forms of decoration in the Tudor, Elizabethan, and Jacobean periods; the bandings were often enlivened by being formed of strips of contrasting coloured timbers which gave a chequered effect, and the pattern almost invariably ran clockwise.

Stringings (fig 23)

These are also sometimes called strings; and are thin strips of patterned wood, ranging from lines, only as thick as a piece of stout paper, up to 3mm (⅛in) square. There is a wide variety of patterns, some of which are shown; their use and popularity were contemporary with bandings.

Boulle

Often spelt Buhl, this form of inlay was perfected by the French craftsman, André Charles Boulle (1642 to 1732); he did not invent it but developed it from the mosaic type of inlay that was in fashion in Italy and France throughout the seventeenth century and which utilised such materials as wood, ivory, silver and tortoiseshell.

Briefly, this technique involved laying sheet brass (or, at a later date, silver) into a tortoiseshell background; and the converse, which was to lay tortoiseshell into brass, fig 24. The former was called *première-partie*, and the latter, *contre-partie*, the *première-partie* being the more sought after. On some pieces both *parties* were displayed, generally on an ebony background, and this was known as counter-change Boulle. As one would expect, the effect was one of magnificence, and Boulle enhanced it even more by underlaying the tortoiseshell with red or green paper, silk, or paint, so that the colours glowed through the more transparent parts of the shell. He went even further and embellished the brass with engraved patterns, which were filled with a paste of contrasting colour.

The technique was introduced into England at the end of the seventeenth century, and although Gerreit Jensen (working 1685 to 1715) practised it while he was the royal cabinet maker, and Peter Langlois (another cabinet maker) used it in the middle of the eighteenth century, it did not find favour with the English cabinet makers of the time. However, in 1815 a Frenchman, Louis Gaigneur, opened a Buhl factory off the Edgware Road, London, and among his customers was the Prince Regent whom he supplied with an inlaid writing table. About the same time, a firm called Town and Emmanuel of New Bond Street, London, were also advertising themselves as makers of Buhl, etc. Thus interest was revived and Buhl was used intermittently in the first half of the nineteenth century.

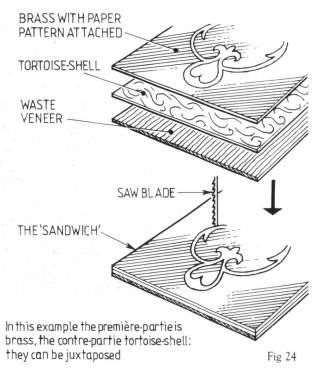

BRASS WITH PAPER PATTERN ATTACHED

TORTOISE-SHELL

WASTE VENEER

SAW BLADE

THE 'SANDWICH'

In this example the première-partie is brass, the contre-partie tortoise-shell: they can be juxtaposed

Fig 24

A late 18th/early 19th century Dutch burr walnut and ash crossbanded bureau-bookcase. The upper part with a moulded arched cornice has foliate scroll cresting and is fitted with shelves and drawers below enclosed by a pair of glazed panel doors, with foliate scroll headings, having candle slides below. The sloping fall encloses a fitted and graduated interior with a well and slide, containing three long graduated drawers of undulating outline between canted angles, terminating in scroll feet

Inlaid satinwood sofa table with rosewood crossbandings c1800. Note the absence of a cross stretcher

COMPO

This was more correctly known as composition, and consisted of whiting, resin, and size mixed together and heated. It was pressed into a mould while still plastic and, when set, was removed and glued or pinned in place.

Robert Adam used it extensively during the second half of the eighteenth century, not only for furniture decoration but also for ceilings and fireplaces, and it was similarly employed by many other cabinet makers. As a matter of historical interest, Adam's original moulds are still used by a London firm of plaster workers.

GESSO

This is a kind of thin paste made by mixing hot parchment size (or rabbit skin glue) and whiting, plus a few drops of linseed oil. When cold it is spread on to the wood, coat on coat, until the required thickness is obtained (unlike compo, it was not pressed into a mould). When set it can be carved, incised, or gilded; the foliage, tendrils, icicles, etc, seen on Rococo designs were made by applying gesso to wire framework. It was also used on the carved and gilt furniture of the Restoration period.

Gesso has been used for thousands of years, and was favoured in ancient times as a ground for tempera painting. In England it was employed during medieval times as a base for painted or gilt work, and for incised or punched decoration – as an example, the Coronation Chair (c 1300) in Westminster Abbey is covered in gilt gesso, decorated with lines of punched dots. By about 1730 such decoration had largely gone out of fashion.

ORMOLU

The original French term *or moulo* (ground gold) was used in that country from the sixteenth century

onwards to describe gold leaf that had been ground and prepared ready for gilding metal mounts, which were usually bronze. It is now called *bronze doré*.

The word ormolu has been employed in England since the middle of the eighteenth century to describe mounts and other metal fittings made of brass or gilt bronze. The creator of British ormolu was Matthew Boulton, who opened a factory in Soho, Birmingham, in 1762 for its manufacture and that of brassfoundry in general. Ormolu became popular in Britain from the 1760s during the Neo-Classical period; such ormolu as there was before then was imported from France and was generally of inferior quality.

The following is a brief description of how it was made. The first step was to produce an original pattern in wood or wax and well known sculptors were often employed on this work. The pattern was then cast in bronze and tooled and chased to a superfine finish, and finally gilded or dipped in acid and lacquered.

OYSTERS

These are slices of veneer obtained by sawing across the smaller branches of a tree; if the sawcuts are made at an oblique angle, the result is oval shaped slices;

Regency rosewood table c1810, with brass mounts, a drawer on either side, and the legs with Egyptian masks and winged brackets, terminating in paw feet

if cut at right angles, more or less circular slices. The exposed patterns of end grain have a vague resemblance to oyster shells, hence the name. Laburnum was one of the most favoured woods for the purpose, but kingwood, olive wood, and walnut were also employed.

This form of veneering has been used intermittently since its introduction in the late seventeenth century until the present day; however, its greatest popularity was from about 1670 to 1710, when it was overtaken by the craze for japanning.

PARQUETRY

This consisted of mosaics of differently coloured woods glued on a groundwork to form geometrical patterns; chequered or diamond shapes were the most widely used. The mosaic could be inlaid or in the form of marquetry, or an inlay combined with marquetry. It was most fashionable in walnut furniture from 1670 to about 1715, and has been very little used since.

CHAPTER 5

Styles and groups

These notes are not clues as such, but are included to fill in the historical background and to explain the various influences that cause a new furniture style to develop.

AESTHETIC MOVEMENT

The chief exponent of the style was William Godwin, and the designs of Charles Eastlake and Bruce Talbert also contributed to its influence.

In general terms the movement advocated pastel colours in decoration, and light, almost flimsy construction; there was a strong emphasis, too, on Japanese motifs and Godwin, in particular, was fond of using Japanese leather paper, bamboo, and ebonised wood. Eventually the style came to include Arab and Moorish fashions, and the London firm of Liberty & Co was instrumental in promoting the designs to such an extent that they were often referred to as the Liberty style. The fashion was comparatively short lived, however, as it appealed mainly to an intellectual elite and was, in any case, too expensive for most people.

ART NOUVEAU

The name derives from that of a shop opened by Siegfried Bing in Paris in 1895, but the first designs pre-dated this as they appeared at the Paris *Exposition Universelle* in 1889. A Belgian architect, Victor Horta, is recognised as the original creator of the style.

The designs employed flamboyant, sinuous curves not only in the decoration but in the constructional parts as well, and almost every design included a theme of foliage or flowers with the stems and leaves prominently displayed; often they were worked in copper or other metals, embossed on leather, or etched on glass. Fumed oak was also popular, as was wood which had been stained green.

Some French designers, such as Guinnard, Vallin, and Majorelle, took the style to its limits, but in Britain its influence was more restrained and is

exemplified by the work of such designers as C. F. A. Voysey and C. R. Mackintosh. The furniture manufacturing trade produced its own version in the late 1890s which was known as the Quaint style; by 1914, however, Art Nouveau in all its manifestations was no longer fashionable.

ARTS AND CRAFTS MOVEMENT

In 1888 a master-bookbinder named T. J. Cobden-Sanderson suggested the formation of an Arts and Crafts Exhibition Society. The Society was associated with several kindred groups such as The Century Guild, The Guild and School of Handicraft, and the Cotswold School. Its aims were to promote the production of furniture and other artefacts such as printing, wallpaper, metal work, crockery, lamp shades, etc, which were simple and honest in design, the emphasis being on sound construction and fitness for purpose. As one of its exponents, William Morris wrote, 'Art is the expression of man's pleasure in labour' and 'Have nothing in your houses that you do not know to be useful and believe to be beautiful' – sentiments that were also expressed by John Ruskin.

In the case of furniture, this meant that the joints used in construction were left visible and sometimes even accentuated; indigenous woods were used rather than imported exotics (particularly oak, which was often left natural colour); and great emphasis was laid on metal work, notably hinges, handles, and flat decorated panels, often of copper.

The philosophy behind the movement spread to the USA where several communities were formed which developed it into a life-style – one of the most distinguished adherents being the architect, Frank Lloyd Wright.

The movement had a profound effect on the design of British furniture, although at the outset it was too expensive for any but a wealthy elite; the Cotswold School style was, however, carried on by Sir Gordon Russell into the 1950s and was probably one of the primary factors in the design of Utility Furniture during and after World War II.

THE ART WORKERS' GUILD

An association, formed in 1884, amongst whose members were William Morris, C. F. A. Voysey, and W. R. Lethaby. The aims were to foster better standards of decoration and construction than those produced by the contemporary manufacturers of popular furniture, and to form a nucleus for other artist-craftsmen with similar views.

BAROQUE

The name derives from an Italian word meaning irregular pearl, and the association with oyster shells is particularly apt, as this kind of shell was often one of the principal decorative motifs. The style originated in Italy and soon spread to become the most dominant throughout Europe.

It arrived in England in the last quarter of the seventeenth century, and was undoubtedly encouraged by the Dutch craftsmen who followed Charles II after he became king in 1660. It was also helped by large numbers of French Huguenot refugees who arrived in England having fled the religious persecution following the Revocation of the Edict of Nantes in 1685. William Kent (c 1686 to 1748) used the style extensively in his designs, as did Grinling Gibbons, the woodcarver (1648 to 1721), and Daniel Marot (1663 to 1752), the French Huguenot designer who worked for William III. Chief characteristics of the style were gilding, gesso, scagliola, carved shells, wreaths, swags, festoons of flowers, amorini (cherubs), caryatids, human masks, and trophies of musical instruments or weapons. By about 1740 the influence of the Baroque had waned, although early Georgian furniture retained some of its features; by 1750 it had been virtually replaced by the Rococo.

THE CENTURY GUILD

Founded by Arthur Heygate Mackmurdo (1851 to 1942), this was a brotherhood of artist-craftsmen described by him as 'those workers (who) band together who dearly love their art, not as a means of a living but as a fulfilment of life.'

In 1887 The Century Guilds Inventions Exhibition was held in London, and in 1889 Mackmurdo and a fellow-designer, Herbert Horne, set up in business to 'design complete interiors to the highest ideals and yet with reasonable economy'. Their interest in the business soon waned as they were more artistically than commercially minded and, as the firm's products were far beyond the pockets of any but the wealthy, it did not last long.

Some critics have called their designs proto-Art Nouveau; and, indeed, Mackmurdo believed that the inspiration for a designer's work should come from the appreciation of natural forms in flowers, foliage, trees, etc. His early work tended to be heavy and stolid, but he gradually transformed it by including painted, inlaid, or copper panels, with the addition of fretcut patterns of swirling, sinuous foliage. He was very partial to incorporating an inscription somewhere on his designs, and almost every piece of cabinet furniture he designed carried a classical cornice.

CHINESE STYLE (*Chinoiserie*)

From about 1660 Chinese style decoration appeared in England, although it was by no means new in France. The rule of the Council of State and Parliament under the Cromwells from 1649 until 1659 had effectively stopped decoration either being introduced from abroad or becoming fashionable.

The style reached its peak between 1745 and 1760, when it can best be described as a craze – so much so, that a contemporary writer complained 'Chairs, tables, chimney-pieces, frames for looking-glasses, and even our most vulgar utensils, are all reduced to this new-fangled standard: and without doors [outdoors], so universally has it spread that every gate to a cow yard is in Ts and Zs and every hovel for cows has bells hanging at the corners': (William Whitehead writing in *The World*, March 1753). The designer of the pagoda in Kew Gardens, Sir William Chambers, also contributed when he wrote a treatise entitled *Designs of Chinese Buildings, Furniture, Dresses, Machines, and Utensils* (1757), and later bitterly regretted having been responsible for both the building and the treatise. Chinese decorative motifs were widely used by many eighteenth-century designers and makers, notably Thomas Chippendale, senior; Ince and Mayhew, John Linnell, and Robert Manwaring.

CROMWELLIAN STYLE

This refers to the plain but sturdy furniture made during the years from 1649 until 1660 when the country was ruled by the two Cromwells, Oliver and his son Richard. The religious beliefs of the Puritans regarded any but the simplest decoration as idolatrous, and no doubt it was the removal of this excessive restraint that caused the outburst of rich and varied ornamentation which followed the Restoration of Charles II in 1660.

Mahogany armchairs in the Chinese style c1765, with caned seats for use with loose cushions

George III sofa c1770 with a mahogany frame and legs, upholstered in cream wool with appliqué wool embroidery of birds and flowers

GEORGIAN STYLE

A term used to describe the furniture, architectural, and decorative styles prevalent in the years from 1714 until 1830. The era can be divided into three periods, namely: early Georgian from 1714 to 1730; mid-Georgian from 1730 to 1770; and late Georgian from 1770 to 1830. The most apt comment to sum up the basic characteristic of the styles is that, rather than relying on the whims and caprice of fashion (as did the French), they were founded on well understood and recognised rules of classical proportion.

GOTHIC AND GOTHICK STYLES

The only connection with the Goths is in a pejorative sense, as when Giorgio Vasari (1511 to 1574) dismissed all pre-Renaissance furniture as Gothic in much the same way as we would use the term 'vandal'. Interestingly, the American author Washington Irving used the word in just the same sense when, in 1822, he described the Coronation Chair in Westminster Abbey as 'rudely carved of oak, in the barbarous taste of a remote and gothic age'. The term was used in the seventeenth century to distinguish the medieval from the classical style of architecture.

The craze for Gothic architecture and furniture from about 1720 was satirised by William Whitehead in 1753 when he wrote that 'our houses, our beds, our bookcases, and our couches, were all copied from some parts or other of our old cathedrals'. At first the style was a mixture of the Baroque and the Gothic, but this later changed to a Rococo Gothic which in turn became Strawberry Hill Gothick. Several eighteenth-century designers, particularly Thomas Chippendale, senior and Robert Manwaring, combined the Gothic and Chinese styles on one piece of furniture.

The Gothic Revival of the first half of the nineteenth-century was a more literal transference of original medieval styles to architectural and furniture designs, and lacked the lightness and delicacy of the eighteenth-century fashions.

GOTHIC REVIVAL

In her book, *The Victorian Home*, Jenni Calder writes, 'One of the most significant features of Victorian art and interests was medievalism, and Morris and his associates the pre-Raphaelites encouraged and even exploited this . . . they did not create it . . . we have to go further back and look at literature, architecture,

the Gothic novel and the Gothic cathedral, and, pre-eminently, the historical novels of Sir Walter Scott'.

It seems improbable, not to say ridiculous, that a particular fashion in novels could have affected architectural styles so much as to give us the hallowed edifices of the Houses of Parliament (designed by Charles Barry and decorated by A. W. N. Pugin), and St Pancras Station (by Sir Gilbert Scott), but it seems to have provided the origins of the style. The last-named architect pointed out the irreconcilable difference between his and his colleagues' philosophy and that of William Morris, when he wrote 'Providence has ordained the different orders and graduations into which the human family is divided, and it is right and necessary that it should be maintained' – from his book *Secular and Domestic Architecture* (1857). In his opinion the Gothic style, when properly interpreted and executed, was a tangible expression of religious faith.

The trend towards this Gothic genre probably started with the publication in 1764 of a book by Horace Walpole called *The Castle of Otranto*. It was a pseudo-historical novel and was followed in the early nineteenth century by the books of two lady novelists, Jane Porter and Ann Radcliffe. Their stories contained all the necessary ingredients of ruined and haunted castles, sinister monks, and beauty and innocence rescued in the nick of time by heroic deeds. Sir Walter Scott admired Ann Radcliffe enough to call her 'this mighty enchantress' and to write a preface to her collected works in 1824.

It was, however, Sir Walter more than anyone else who inspired the fashion, and in fact the Gothic furniture of the period came to be called Abbotsford furniture, after the name of his house. A. W. N. Pugin succinctly summarised the style in his book *The True Principles of Pointed or Christian Architecture* (1841) as follows: 'Hence your modern man designs a sofa or occasional table from details culled out of Britten's *Cathedrals* . . . We find diminutive flying buttresses about an armchair; everything is crocketed with angular projections, innumerable mitres, sharp ornaments, and turreted extremities . . . There are often as many pinnacles and gablets about a pier-glass frame as are to be found in an ordinary church' and then he admits that he had 'perpetrated many of these enormities in the furniture I designed some years ago for Windsor Castle'.

Oak cabinet c1836, in the Gothic Revival style of A.W.N. Pugin

Guild of Handicraft

Established by Charles Robert Ashbee in the East End of London and moved to Chipping Camden (Glos) in 1902. He designed most of the furniture himself and it was made up by J. W. Pyment, his chief cabinet maker. The designs were basically rectangular and decorated with veneer or metal panels, often incorporating restrained Art Nouveau motifs. Two of his best-known associates were M. H. Baillie Scott (1865 to 1945) who designed several upright pianos for Broadwoods, and Sidney Barnsley, who later set up his own workshop at Sapperton (Glos).

Jacobean

A term which should, strictly speaking, be applied only to the furniture made during the reign of James I (1603 to 1625), but which today refers to the general style from about 1590 to 1630.

'Jacobethan' Furniture

The modern name given to furniture made during the first half of the nineteenth century which purported to be Elizabethan in style, but was actually a mixture of Tudor and Jacobean styles laced with what the manufacturer or designer considered were 'improvements'.

Neo-Classicism

Just as the Rococo style was a reaction against the Baroque, so Neo-Classicism was against Rococo. Its origins lay in the excitement of the public at the result of the archaeological excavations at Herculaneum and Pompeii that extended over a period of years from about 1748 to 1792; although Pompeii had first been discovered about 1594 the site had not been systematically unearthed at that time. The discoveries led to Rome becoming a Mecca for architects, artists, and designers of most of the European nations, among them Robert Adam, and it was he who introduced the style to Britain.

Characteristics of the style are: the use of gilding, the introduction of painted furniture, and the employment of compo built up on a wire matrix to form filigree or tracery patterns. Decoratively, the style used the anthemion (honeysuckle) motif, rams' heads, urns, swags, festoons, and paterae: these were applied judiciously to well proportioned and elegant carcases or frames, which contrasted strongly with the assymetrical fantasies of the preceding Rococo.

Robert Adam was undoubtedly the chief exponent of the style in England, but it was adapted and modified by such well known designers as Gillow & Company, Hepplewhite, and Sheraton.

Queen Anne Period

A term that today refers to furniture made in the opening twenty years of the eighteenth century – Queen Anne reigned from 1702 to 1714. The era saw the introduction of the type of cabriole leg that bears her name, and also the vastly increased use of veneers as a decorative feature; veneering was also ideal for finishing the curvilinear shapes of chairs and cabinet pieces which were introduced.

Rococo (or Rococco)

The name derives from the French word *rocaille* meaning rock work, and the term was originally used to describe the rock and shell ornament in the grottoes at Versailles.

The style included such unconventional decoration as C-scrolls, simulated rocks, shells, trees festooned with creepers, dripping water, and sometimes included Chinese pagodas, peasants, and lattice work. Such *Chinoiserie* (see Chinese style) first appeared in France during the late seventeenth century, and French wood carvers soon realised that it was ideally suited to the Rococo style, particularly because of the assymetry which was one of its main characteristics.

Rococo reached England in the middle of the eighteenth century but never reached the same heights of fantasy and exaggeration that it did in France. It was taken up by such contemporary craftsmen as Thomas Chippendale, senior, Ince and Mayhew, Vile and Cobb, and Thomas Johnson. By about 1790, however, the fashion was replaced by Neo-Classicism, which was itself a reaction against the fripperies of Rococo, just as the latter was the antithesis of the heavy and ponderous Baroque. In the middle years of the nineteenth century there was a revival of interest in Rococo but it was soon absorbed and transformed into the vague and florid decoration loved by the Victorians.

Sleeping chair c1670, in oak, upholstered in red brocade. The back is fixed, unlike some examples in which the angle can be adjusted on a ratchet

STRAWBERRY HILL GOTHICK

In 1747, Horace Walpole (1717 to 1797), son of the famous politician Sir Robert Walpole, and himself later Earl of Oxford, bought a house at Strawberry Hill, Twickenham, Middlesex. He transformed what was a modest Georgian house into a Gothic villa, and furnished it accordingly. Although the design and decoration were based on authentic medieval Gothic examples, the whole thing was interpreted in a Rococo manner and executed with a light touch. It was a great success, and Walpole found himself conducting guided tours, which he had to limit to one a day! As one would expect, the style was anathematised and rejected by the Gothic Revivalists of the nineteenth century – note the addition of the final 'k' to differentiate it.

WILLIAM AND MARY

William was Dutch and many Dutch craftsmen followed him to England, bringing with them superlative skills in the arts of veneering and marquetry. It was during this period that quartered, halved, and crossbanded veneers were introduced; also oyster veneers. The practice of using pegs to pin tenons fell into disuse, and better glues and handmade screws replaced them. Tea drinking became fashionable and led to the designing of small tables, tea caddies, etc. The principal designer of the time was Daniel Marot, a Frenchman, who was employed by William as artistic adviser between 1694 and 1698.

STUART PERIOD

This extends from the accession of the first Stuart, James I, in 1603 until the end of James II's reign in 1688. It is, however, subdivided into Jacobean (James I), Early Stuart (Charles I), Carolean (Charles II), Restoration (Charles II and James II), and Cromwellian (1649 to 1660)

TUDOR PERIOD

Strictly speaking, the term Tudor style should only be applied to furniture made between 1485, when Henry VII became king and the death of Mary Tudor in 1558. However, the style is considered today to cover the periods 1500 to 1558 (Early Tudor) and 1558 to 1603 (Late Tudor or Elizabethan).

VICTORIAN PERIOD

Queen Victoria came to the throne in 1837 and her reign lasted until 1901. It may conveniently be broken down into three periods, namely early Victorian from 1837 to about 1850; mid-Victorian 1850 to 1880; and late Victorian 1880 to 1901.

Early Victorian furniture was largely dominated by the Gothic Revival, although the designer J. C. Loudon also influenced furniture styles by his books in which the designs were often left-overs from the preceding Regency period, but which also included some prototypes of the Victorian Vernacular style.

The mid-Victorian period was notable for the Great Exhibition of 1851, at which several examples of the Victorian Vernacular were displayed; they were, however, more ponderous and coarser than earlier examples of the style, and led to the kind of furniture which, in our time, has been disparaged as Victoriana and could be called the Victorian version of Rococo. There was also considerable interest in French styles, particularly as there were close links between the British and French royal families.

The late Victorian era included several conflicting trends. There was the 'back to medieval craftsmanship' school led by William Morris; the Art Nouveau style; the craze for Japanese furniture; and the demand for reproduction furniture of the Adam, Hepplewhite, and Sheraton periods.

VICTORIAN VERNACULAR

The name given to a style popular from about 1830 to the 1880s. It was based at first on the Neo-Classical style, and included designs of new balloon- and spoon-back chairs, chiffoniers, and davenports. The style gradually became debased, mainly by manufacturers who wanted to exploit it commercially, and by the time of the Great Exhibition (1851) it had become a vulgarised and coarsened Rococo.

CHAPTER 6

Tables

In this chapter and those which follow, up to and including Chapter 15, illustrations of pieces of furniture are grouped together in types – for instance, tables form one group, chairs another, and so on. You can look through them to see which illustration most nearly matches your antique; or, if you are buying, to find the piece that most appeals to you. As far as possible everyday vernacular pieces have been chosen in preference to what one might call museum or classical examples, and a short history is supplied for each group.

This chapter contains illustrations of card, credence, dining, extending, gate-leg, pedestal, Pembroke, and Sutherland tables; also constructional details relating to them.

CARD AND GAMING TABLES

Tables specifically designed for playing cards and gaming did not appear in any great numbers until the end of the seventeenth century. The lining of the tops was first done in velvet or needlework, but baize (or 'bayes' as it was then called) became popular from the early eighteenth century onwards. It was first introduced into England by Huguenot refugees about 1600.

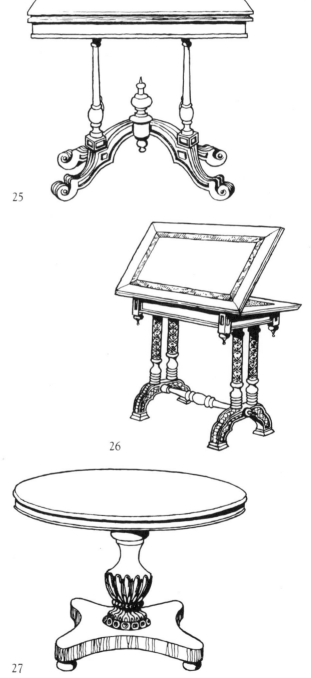

25

26

27

FIG 25: a card table with a folding top veneered in burr walnut supported on four turned pillars; the underframe consists of diagonally curved stretchers (called a saltire) and four splay feet. The saltire is crowned by the bulbous turned finial beloved of the Victorians, while the feet are vaguely reminiscent of the French Neo-Classical style. c1870.

FIG 26: a Gothic Revival design of card table in oak, with a folding top. Typically, the original medieval motifs have received the exaggerated treatment which many Victorian designers delighted in. c1860.

FIG 27: 'loo' table with the top veneered in rosewood, as are the frieze rail and the curved base; the turned and carved pillar and the feet are of solid rosewood. As with all loo tables, the top can be tilted upright and the table stood against a wall. c1835.

The name derives from the card game 'Lanterloo', popular from the middle of the 18th century to the early 19th century.

28

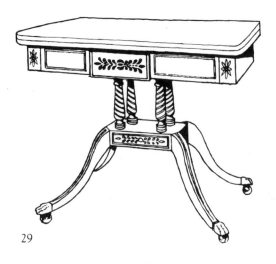

29

30

31

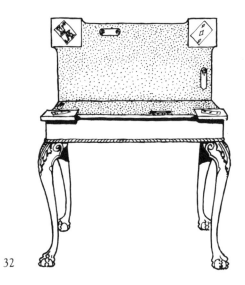

32

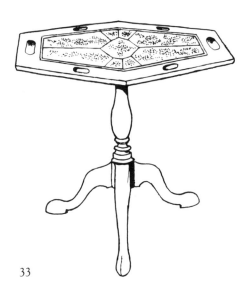

33

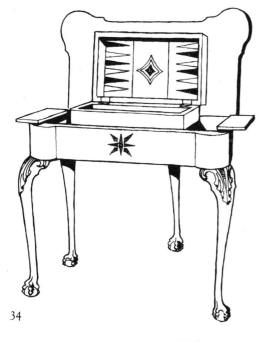

34

35

36

FIG 28: folding top card table, veneered in walnut; with a pedestal base. The feet show French Empire influence. c1835.

FIG 29: a Regency style folding top card table in mahogany, supported on four turned pillars which are, in turn, mounted on four claw feet. The embellishment on the panel in the frieze rail is brass inlaid into ebony. c1820.

FIG 30: folding top card table, Regency style, in mahogany. Note the reeding on the curved supports and the claw legs. c1810.

FIG 31: semicircular (or demi-lune) card table in mahogany and satinwood inlaid with various woods. The legs are square-tapered with block toes, sometimes called 'plinth' feet. c1790.

FIG 32: the paragon of card tables! Made in mahogany with cabriole legs and claw and ball feet, with acanthus foliage carved on the knees. The top has a baize lining, a playing card inlaid at each corner, and guinea-pits, (depressions for counters or money). The flap folds over to rest on an extension framework called a concertina side; c1760.

FIG 33: a charming little tripod card table in walnut, the hexagonal top being covered with a needlework centre; guinea pits are sunk in the borders. c1750.

FIG 34: a gaming table, in walnut. Fitted with an inner compartment which houses dice, chess, and backgammon accessories; it could also be used as a card table. It is notable because it incorporates a cabriole leg at the back that is joined to a hinged rail which swivels outwards to provide a support for the flap when it is open, and this was a common feature of card tables of the period. c1720.

FIG 35: one of the earliest gaming tables is this walnut piquet table with the top mounted on a hexagonal pillar and tripod scrolled feet. The playing surface is lined with velvet, there is a small drawer in the frieze, and the faces of the flaps, when closed, are decorated with scrolled marquetry. c1695.

FIG 36: another early card table veneered in walnut with a square foldover top, which is inlaid with stylised inlay. The turning on the legs is interesting, as it contains several motifs such as the ball and reel, the bobbin, and (at the bottom) balusters. Note that the edges of the top are veneered, as are the top rails and leg squares of the gate-leg frames. A craftsman's touch, this – the back frame rail of the table is veneered and recessed out to house the top of the gate-leg frame, and so a consistent surface is achieved.
  Veneering like this was often laid on an oak groundwork, which led to splits and kindred troubles when the oak shrank or swelled at a different rate from the veneer. c1690.

FIG 37: a typical credence table. A name for what is, essentially, a fold-over-top table. They were sometimes used in churches to support the vessels for the Mass and no doubt this explains the name (which was not contemporary); they were also used as tables on which to place food before tasting it to find if it was poisoned. Although this one is three sided, they were often semicircular. When open, the top was supported by a leg which swung out from the back, as described in Fig 34. c1610.

FIG 38: a late Victorian dining table of which there must be many still in existence. The more expensive ones were made in mahogany while cheaper ones were in birch stained to a mahogany colour, but both had the massive turned legs typical of the Victorian era. c1890 to 1914.

FIG 39: extending dining table in mahogany – the extension is a pull-out one at one end only. The ball and vase shaped turning of the legs is more exaggerated and finer than the equivalent designs used later and this piece was probably made in the 1840s, but the basic design carried on until the end of the century. c1845 to 1875.

FIG 40: a circular expanding table made in two connecting halves, each with three legs. The two halves could be separated and up to four loose flaps inserted. Note the turned and reeded legs – this variation of an 18th century style was popular throughout the century. c1830 to 1880.

FIG 41: an extending dining table with D-shaped ends, made in mahogany. The reeded legs and edges around the table tops indicate that it is a late Regency design. c1815.

FIG 42: mahogany extending dining table mounted on two turned pillars, each fitted with four claw feet and brass paw castors. Although not intentionally, it answers almost exactly to the description of a dining table given by Thomas Sheraton in his *Cabinet Dictionary*, 1803: he writes: 'The common useful dining tables are upon pillar and claws, generally four claws to each pillar, with brass castors. A dining table of this kind may be made to any size, by having a sufficient quantity of pillars and claw parts, for between each of them is a loose flap, fixed by means of iron straps and buttons so that they are easily taken off and put aside.' c1800.

FIG 43: a typical mid 18th century dining table with semicircular flaps, carved knees, and claw and ball feet. In mahogany. c1750.

FIG 44: a mahogany dining table with rectangular flaps and cabriole legs with claw and ball feet. Flaps of this shape were uncommon, as they were very heavy to lift in use. c1750.

FIG 45: mahogany dining table with semicircular flaps; the legs are cabriole with scrolled ears and hoof feet, sometimes called '*pied-de-biche*' or hind's foot. c1720.

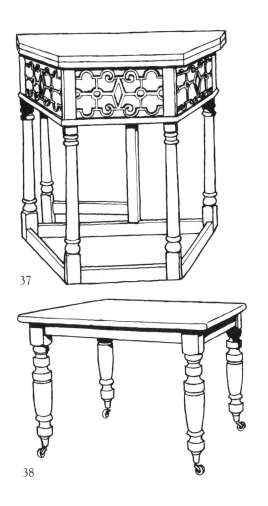

37

39

38

40

41

42

43

44

45

FIG 46: a country-made dining table in elm with matching stool. Chairs for dining did not appear until the 17th century, and this piece dates back to the late 17th century. The style of turning on the legs is called gunbarrel or cannon for obvious reasons.

FIG 47: a magnificent example of an oak draw table: that is, one with a pull out leaf at each end; the leaves are contained under the centre bed when not in use – exactly the method used on modern tables of the type. The legs are called cup and cover, or melon bulb; the cover for the bulb is carved with

heavy gadrooning, and the bulb itself is quartered with acanthus leaf carving. Note the Ionic capitals at the tops of the legs – these were commonly used at the end of the 16th and the beginning of the 17th centuries. c1600.

FIG 48: long joined table in oak, nearly 3.5m (11ft) long, with pegged joints, square-turned legs (except for the central back leg), and ogee-shaped brackets. c1550. This kind of table is often called a refectory table: as monasteries were abolished during the Reformation (1536 to 1539), the term is not historically correct – long table was the contemporary name.

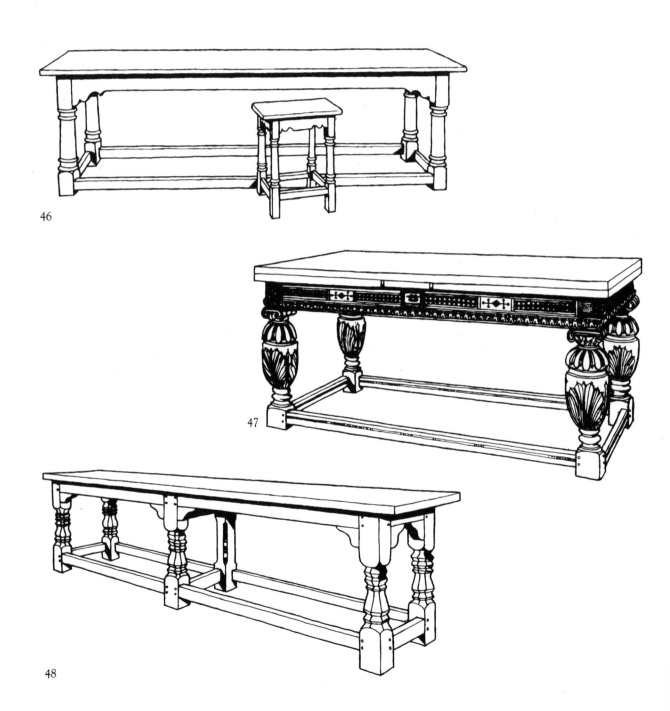

46

47

48

PEDESTAL TABLES

Pedestal tables appeared in the late eighteenth century and remained very fashionable throughout the nineteenth. As with gate-leg tables, they were designed for the smaller rooms of contemporary houses but (unlike the gate-leg) they were designed to give an air of opulence and solidity and to be something of a status symbol.

They could be put to many uses such as a general purpose table or a dining table, or used for writing or card playing. The tops were always given special treatment, either in the form of fancy veneers, or inlays and marquetry.

FIG 49: a popular design of centre pedestal table with a fixed (that is, non-tilting) circular top supported on a pillar base which itself rests on four scrolled legs. The latter are a modified form of the reversed S-scroll pattern used at the turn of the 17th and 18th centuries; (see fig 199). They were a characteristic of this type of leg during the Victorian era, and the scrolling on the knee grew heavier, and the carving more ornate, as the period progressed. Note the central finial on the base – another Victorian device.

This table was made in walnut with a veneered top, but many table tops were covered with intricate 'seaweed' marquetry, inlays, or veneered patterns. c1880.

FIG 50: circular pedestal table with its top veneered with burr figured walnut, a nulled (gadrooned) pillar support, and tripod claw feet with Rococo style scrolled toes. c1870.

FIG 51: an octagonal table in oak with four turned columns supporting the top; all in the Gothic revival style. c1865.

FIG 52: another octagonal table displaying even more marked signs of the Gothic Revival to the point of over-indulgence. This table has four drawers and was probably intended for writing. c1860.

FIG 53: circular table with a triangular pedestal support rising from a three point base: the feet are a plain bun design. A very popular design, it was made in mahogany, rosewood, and walnut. c1835.

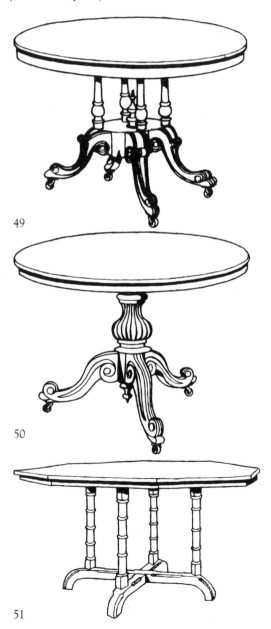

49

50

51

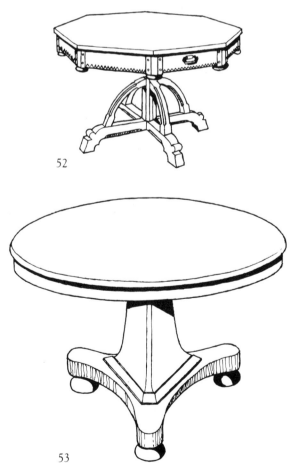

52

53

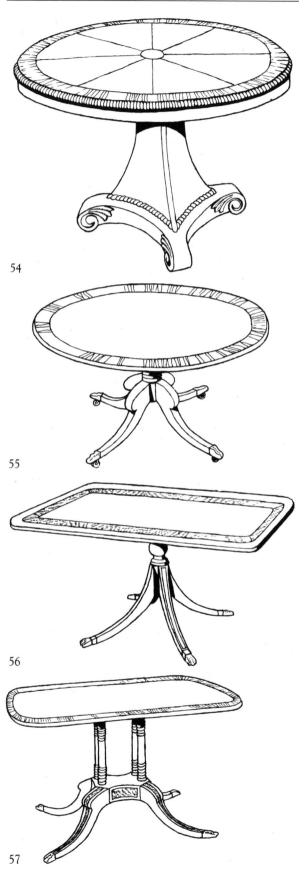

54

55

56

57

FIG 54: a walnut veneered pedestal table with a circular top and three point base, the toes being scrolled. The banding around the top is brass inlay. The design is reminiscent of one of Thomas Hope's from his book *Household Furniture* (1807); as is fig 53. c1825.

FIG 55: circular pedestal table in mahogany with a cross-banded edge to the top; the legs are an exaggerated form of a characteristic Regency style with shaped knees. c1825.

FIG 56: mahogany pedestal table with oblong top; a banding of satinwood is inserted near the edge of the top. The claw legs terminate in carved paw feet. c1800.

FIG 57: pedestal table in mahogany, the top being oblong with curved ends and crossbanded edges. Note the neat inlaid ebony stringing on the legs and base – indicative of good class Georgian work. c1800.

HISTORY OF FLAP AND GATE-LEG TABLES

The history of dining tables with flaps, and also of gate-leg tables, is intriguing because it illustrates how designs can come into being as a result of social changes rather than the vagaries of fashion.

By the year 1500 the medieval customs of feudalism were in rapid decline, and this was hastened during the reign of Henry VII (1485 to 1509) who not only curbed the brutal rule of the barons but also forbade them to build castles. The new era of peace in the countryside led to the building of many manor houses. One result of this was that, instead of communal meals in the great hall, the local lord and his family took to dining in a separate room: in 1526 this 'eating in corners and secret places' was denounced by Bishop Grosbeake, but with little effect.

Smaller dining rooms meant smaller dining tables and from 1550 onwards all kinds of extending flap and gate-leg tables proliferated. Such tables were found useful, too, in the eighteenth century as they could be kept in an ante-room and only brought out for meals, thus leaving space for the 'company' (as it was then called) to circulate – bearing in mind the voluminous skirts of the period, the ladies certainly needed room to move!

Gate-leg tables were introduced in the early sixteenth century and, like the dining tables already discussed, filled a need for a table which could be easily set up and removed for meals and yet seat up to eight persons.

The contemporary name was falling table; the term gate-leg seems to have been applied from the mid nineteenth century onwards. In early specimens the flaps were fastened to the beds with iron hinges fixed with nails; often the gate-leg section was pivoted on wooden hinges. The joint between the flaps and the bed (the fixed section of the top) could be one of three kinds – square, bead and groove, or rule; the rule joint was used almost invariably in tables after about 1750. About the same date the tops of the beds began to be secured to the frame rails with screws instead of the pegs formerly used.

PEMBROKE TABLES

A Pembroke table is a small flap-table in which the flap is always supported by a hinged bracket (or fly) and never by a gate-leg. The flap can be hinged to either the long or the short sides of the bed; the table invariably has a small drawer or two beneath the top.

It is not certain whether the name of the table derives from the Countess of Pembroke (1737 to 1831) or from the ninth Earl (1693 to 1751) – the Earl being a talented amateur architect. The tables begin to be mentioned in accounts, letters, etc, from 1750 onwards, and were intended for use as breakfast tables or ladies' writing tables.

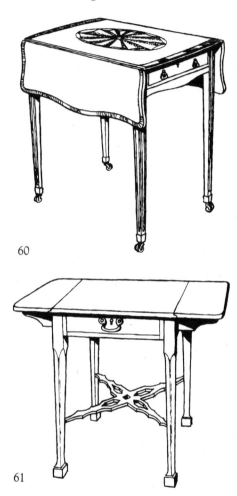

60

58

59

61

FIG 58: a mahogany Pembroke table with shaped flaps which, when raised, combine with the bed to form a circle. The edge of the top, the drawers, and the legs all have inlaid satinwood stringing. c1800.

FIG 59: mahogany veneered table with painted decoration and, unusually, a solid underframe. Embellished with satinwood bandings. c1790.

FIG 60: an elegant example in satinwood with kingwood crossbandings. Note the delicate serpentine shaping of the flaps and the apron beneath the drawer, and the fan marquetry in the centre of the bed. c1790.

FIG 61: one of the earliest designs of Pembroke table. The tapered legs are chamfered and terminate in plinth feet, and the diagonal stretchers are pierced. Made in mahogany and based on a design for a breakfast table in Chippendale's *Director*. c1755.

62

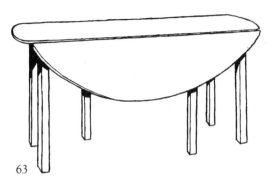

63

64

65

FIG 62: Sutherland table. This is a gate-leg table with a very narrow 'bed' (that is, the central portion of the top between the leaves), and very deep leaves. It was, and still is, a popular design. It was named after the Duchess of Sutherland, a Mistress of the Robes to Queen Victoria. c1860. This was the only new design of gate-leg table to appear since the 18th century: the original examples, which first came into being during the 16th, 17th and 18th centuries, have survived virtually unchanged until the present day.

FIG 63: a gate-leg table in mahogany with a long, narrow bed up to 2m long by 460mm (6ft 6in by 1ft 6in), and shaped flaps. Sometimes called a wakes table, as the long, thin shape made a suitable support for a coffin; after the funeral the same table was used for the wakes meal. Whether this was actually the case, or merely apocryphal, is not known. c1770.

FIG 64: mahogany gate-leg table with single flap and turned cylindrical legs known as spider legs; note the curved spandrels in the underframe. c1765.

FIG 65: mahogany gate-leg table, again with spider legs, and club feet. Note the small drawer under the bed for cutlery, etc; this kind of table was popular for light meals such as breakfast or supper. c1760.

FIG 66: what one might call a standard pattern of gate-leg dining table; in mahogany with turned tapered legs and club feet. c1760.

66

67

68

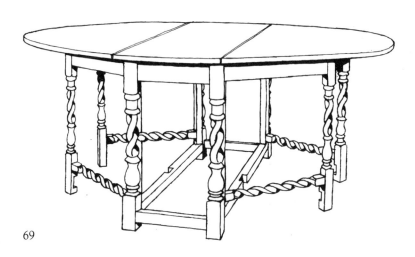

69

70

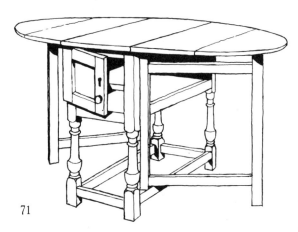

71

FIG 67: an elegant gate-leg table in mahogany. The most notable feature is the style of leg – cabriole with small scrolled ears and hoof foot. c1740.

FIG 68: an oak gate-leg table with semicircular bed which opens to a full circle when the single flap is raised. There is a small drawer under the top. c1690.

FIG 69: a walnut gate-leg table, with double gates to ensure stability. The legs are twist-and-turned baluster pattern, as are the bottom rails of the gate. c1680.

FIG 70: small gate-leg table in oak. The special feature about this table is that it has virtually no bed: when the gates are closed the top hangs vertically. c1680.

FIG 71: a country-made gate-leg table; a door encloses two drawers under the top of the bed. The design is simple and functional and the turned legs and stretchers are well within the scope of any village turner. All in all, a piece very reminiscent of the Shaker furniture in America. c1670, although the design is practically ageless.

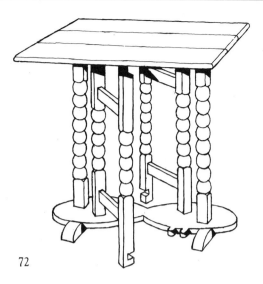

72

FIG 72: an unusual gate-leg table with a square top about 680mm (26in); such a small table would be for occasional use only. The specially attractive feature is the shaped baseboard into which one's feet fit. c1670.

SOFA TABLES

Sofa tables were a development of the Pembroke table and first appeared in the late eighteenth century; they became popular in the first quarter of the nineteenth but the design does not seem to have been taken up by the Victorians.

Both the Pembroke and the sofa tables had their flaps supported by flys; the sofa table was, however, more elongated and always had flaps across the ends. It was (as the name implies) intended to stand near a sofa and in many examples there were drawers on one side only, the drawer fronts and handles on the other side being dummies. Some tables were made with the top containing a chessboard panel, which was revealed by raising a flap; others included a rising desk for writing or drawing.

Early pieces from 1790 onwards usually had end standards acting as supports for the top, often without a stretcher rail but with an iron strapping fixed to the underside of each standard as reinforcement. Later designs from 1810 frequently had a central pedestal consisting of pillars resting on a platform which was, itself, supported on four shaped legs.

73

FIG 73: another gate-leg table in oak; the shaped uprights are a deliberate imitation of twisted legs in silhouette. Note the pierced-lyre-shaped ends; this must be one of the earliest times that this motif was employed – it is normally found on late 18th and early 19th century sofa tables.

74

FIG 74: mahogany sofa table with pedestal platform support. The most notable feature is the shape of the legs, which follows the Greek *klismos* style (see fig 175c); the decorative paterae on the corners of the platform presumably cover the constructional wedging of the tops of the legs where they penetrate it. The platform itself is veneered all over – the grain of the veneer on the edges runs vertically, which it could never do if the platform was solid. c1830.

75

76

FIG 75: a mahogany sofa table with end supports. A clean and elegant design with shaped legs that have a restrained form of the humped knee so characteristic of the Regency style. The stringing lines are ebony. c1825.

FIG 76: another mahogany example with twist pillars in the end supports – note how the angle of the lines is reversed so that the thread or swash slopes inwards – obviously, the maker was concerned to get things just right. The claw legs have typically Regency style knees and each is inlaid with a brass strip; the drawers and top have satinwood stringing around the edges. c1820.

FIG 77: sofa table veneered in rosewood with satinwood crossbanding around the top: serpentine legs form the support and are fixed to a central collar. c1810.

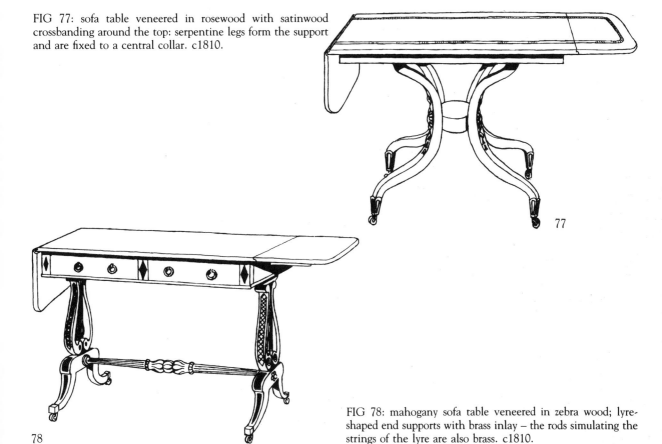

77

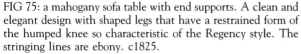

78

FIG 78: mahogany sofa table veneered in zebra wood; lyre-shaped end supports with brass inlay – the rods simulating the strings of the lyre are also brass. c1810.

79

FIG 79: a painted and parcel gilt (partly gilded) sofa table. It is in the Egyptian style, which originated in France during the reign of Louis XVI. It disappeared over the period of the French Revolution, and resurfaced following Napoleon's expedition to Egypt in 1798. Several Egyptian style designs were included in Thomas Hope's *Household Furniture and Interior Decoration* (1807), and in George Smith's two books, *Collection of Designs for Household Furniture* (1808) and *The Cabinet-Makers' and Upholsterers' Guide* (1826)

The Egyptian motifs on the table are: the X-shape of the legs; the capitals at the upper ends of the legs beneath the frieze rail; the inset lion masks; and the representation of a lamp on the drawer front. c1800.

Here are some illustrations of period table legs that may act as clues.

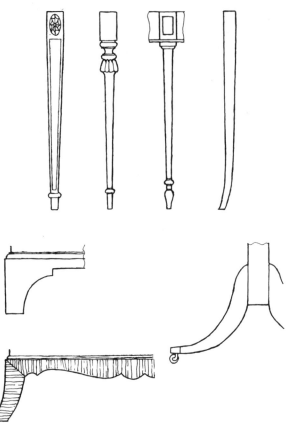

FIG 81: table legs and bracket feet of the Sheraton period, 1790 to 1805.

80

FIG 80: what one could call an archetypal sofa table, in mahogany with satinwood bandings and inset veneers on the legs. The end standards and the sweeping splay legs are an example of restrained elegance and, indeed, the whole piece is characteristic of the late Georgian period. c1790.

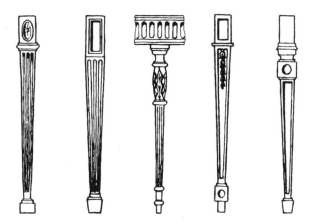

FIG 82: table legs and bracket feet of the Adam period, 1762 to 1790.

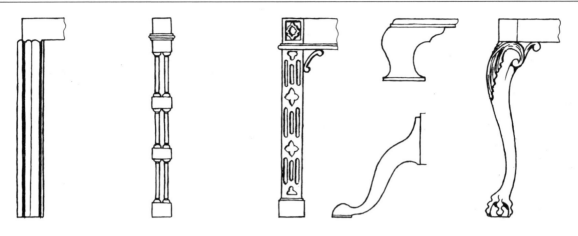

FIG 83: table legs and bracket feet of the Chippendale period, 1750 to 1775.

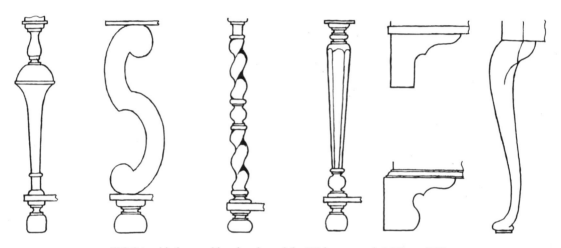

FIG 84: table legs and bracket feet of the Walnut period, 1660 to 1730.

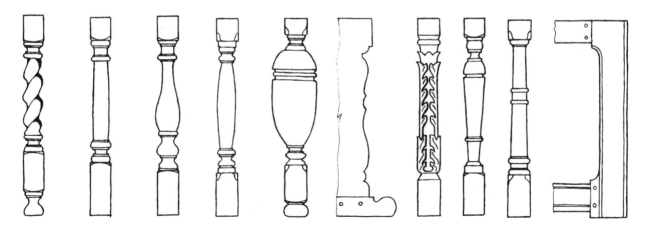

FIG 85: table legs of the 17th century and Jacobean period, 1600 to 1645.

FIG 86: table legs and feet of the Tudor period, 1558 to 1600.

CHAPTER 7

Special purpose tables

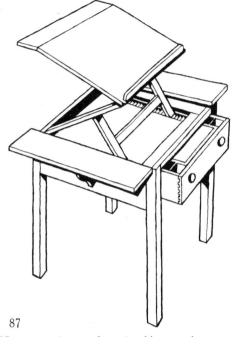

87

FIG 87: an artist's or architect's table in mahogany with an extendable top that rises on a ratchet and can be adjusted to any desired height. Narrow flaps supported by flies are provided at each side of the top, and the centre drawer is fitted out with compartments for brushes, pens, etc. c1760.

Here are illustrated examples of special-purpose tables, such as artists', breakfast, console, dressing, and drum tables; nests of tables; also night, side, tea, tripod, work, and writing tables.

ARTISTS' TABLES

The two features which distinguish an artist's from an architect's table are: (1) the architect's table is more robustly built of thicker timber; (2) the legs of the main frame of the architect's table have extra turned column legs (with castors) fitted inside them for extra stability. Presumably this was needed to support the heavy weight of reference books, ledgers, etc.

BREAKFAST TABLES

Tables such as those illustrated were no doubt designed to meet the needs of ladies who, at that time, entertained their friends to a late breakfast. The custom seems to have died out by the end of the eighteenth century, and breakfast tables disappeared with it.

88

FIG 88: another artist's table having a pull-out front with an adjustable drawing board fitted in the centre, and wing drawers which contain brushes, pens, inks etc and swing out. Drawers for reference books, portfolios and the like are fitted in the end. In walnut. c1760.

89

FIG 89: breakfast table in mahogany with shaped flaps supported by flies. It is similar to one illustrated in Chippendale's *Director*, and has Gothic touches in the C-scroll brackets and underframe. This design of underframe in the form of St Andrew's Cross is called a 'saltire'. c1760.

Tables specifically used for breakfast were known as early as medieval times and are often referred to in Tudor records. They were, however, almost always small flap, or gate-leg, tables.

FIG 90: breakfast table in mahogany in the Chinese Chippendale style. The fretted panels at front and back are concave to form recesses for the knees and to allow the doors to open; their function (apparently) was to stop domestic pets eating the food. c1760.

Usually the frets were made of wood, but were sometimes brass wire. As a single thickness of wood sometimes proved too fragile to be fretcut, an early form of plywood was used, consisting of three thicknesses glued together with the grain of the centre sheet running at right angles to the outer ones.

90

DRESSING TABLES

Dressing tables as such made their appearance about the middle of the seventeenth century. Before that date, toilet accessories were laid out on ordinary tables, although in Elizabethan and Stuart times special caskets were in use. These contained small drawers and were covered in embroidery or stump work – a kind of needlework with the ornament raised in relief on a foundation of wadding or wool. It was not long before these were raised on legs to develop into the dressing table proper.

Mid-eighteenth-century kneehole and pedestal-type dressing tables were often made as dual-purpose pieces for toilet and writing. Applying the multiplicity of powders, pastes, and patches was a long business (and indulged in by the men as much as the women), and the bedroom was recognised as a place for gossip, socialising, and writing confidential letters.

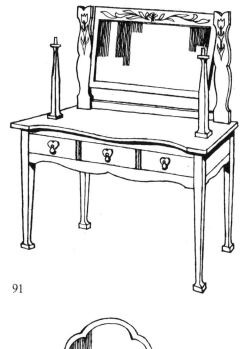

91

FIG 91: an English interpretation of the Art Nouveau style; a dressing table in mahogany with decorative inlays at the tops of the mirror supports, and behind the handles. Note the inclusion of Quaint style candlesticks at each side of the mirror. c1900.

FIG 92: a pedestal, or kneehole, dressing table in birch with black stringing around the drawers and mirror, and ebonised knobs. A very popular design of the time. c1870.

92

93

94

95

96

FIG 93: oak dressing table in the Gothic Revival style, although the treatment is restrained. The stretcher (which pierces the solid ends), the lancet-shaped mirror, and the frieze rail with lightly carved arcading, are the appropriate characteristics. c1870.

FIG 94: a kneehole dressing table in satinwood with rosewood bandings. The lyre-shaped supports for the mirror are an attractive feature but the undershelf could be hazardous! c1810.

FIG 95: mahogany kneehole dressing table with serpentine front, plain tapered legs, and cockbeading around the drawers. The mirror and the two side pieces flanking it fold down to cover the assortment of small boxes containing toilet requisites. c1790.

FIG 96: commode dressing table with serpentine front, in satinwood with mahogany banding. The end drawers swing out and are fitted with mirrors and compartments for toilet accessories; the centre drawer contains a bookrest, which can be set up on a ratchet. The design has affinities with 'Rudd's Table or Reflecting Dressing Table' illustrated in George Hepplewhite's book *The Cabinet Maker and Upholsterer's Guide* (1794) which he describes as '. . . the most complete dressing table made, possessing every convenience which can be wanted, or mechanism and ingenuity supply'. The 'Rudd' referred to was Margaret Caroline Rudd, a notorious courtesan of the time. c1790.

FIG 97: kneehole dressing table in burr walnut, with a cupboard at the back of the kneehole section. The top rises to reveal a mirror and fitted compartments. c1730.

97

98

FIG 98: dressing table in walnut with three drawers, a shaped apron, and claw and ball legs with acanthus leaf carving on the knees. A toilet mirror (fig 98A) would have been a necessary adjunct to the table, which could have an alternative use as a writing table. c1730.

This design is called a lowboy in the USA, and the term is also frequently used in Britain. It is interesting also to note that a bureau in the USA is a kind of dressing table and bears no resemblance to the British version.

99

FIG 99: a classical William & Mary style of dressing (or side) table in walnut; the shaped apron, finials, faceted legs, and shaped stretcher are all typical of the period (1689 to 1702). As with Fig 98, when used as a dressing table it would have required a separate toilet mirror. c1690.

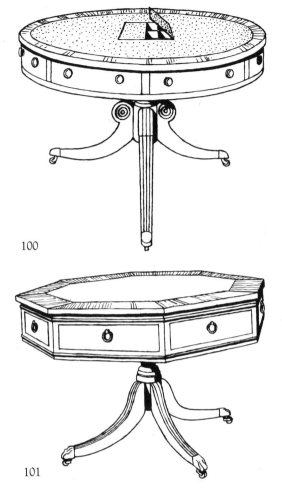

100

101

DRUM, CAPSTAN AND RENT TABLES

Rent tables (also called drum or capstan tables when the top is circular) were used on large estates during the eighteenth and early nineteenth centuries. They usually have four (one for each quarter year) or seven (one for each weekday) drawers, and a till for money. Often, the drawers would have monograms on their fronts to identify the tenants – this is particularly the case where the number of drawers do not correspond with any time interval (eg daily, monthly, or quarterly).

The design is basically so useful that it was not confined to rent tables, but was used for library or writing tables. The description rent table (which was not contemporary) has come to apply to any table of the type.

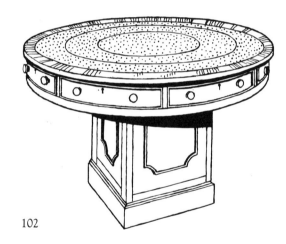

102

FIG 100: a circular-topped rent table in mahogany with, apparently, eight drawers; however, four only are actual drawers, the others being dummies. The leather-lined top has two flaps in the centre, which open to disclose a till tray: as there are only four drawers the table would probably have been used for quarterly rents. Note the scrolled knees on the claw legs – they have turned paterae applied to them. c1820.

FIG 101: an octagonal-top table in mahogany with satinwood stringing and crossbanding around the top. As there is no provision for a till it was probably used as a library table. Four of the drawers are dummies. The claw legs are worth noting as, in the best convention of the period, they taper in their thickness down to the toes and the reeding tapers similarly, which involved hours of painstaking benchwork with a scratchstock. c1800.

FIG 102: mahogany circular-topped library table, the top being lined with leather tooled in concentric ring patterns. All drawers are operative, but of necessity they are not very deep. The square support has a door enclosing a cupboard with shelves for books, pens, inks etc. c1795.

FIG 103: a true rent table with a heptagon top and seven drawers – one for each day of the week; the central panel is satinwood and can be lifted out to disclose a till. The piece is in mahogany with a leather-lined top. c1770.

103

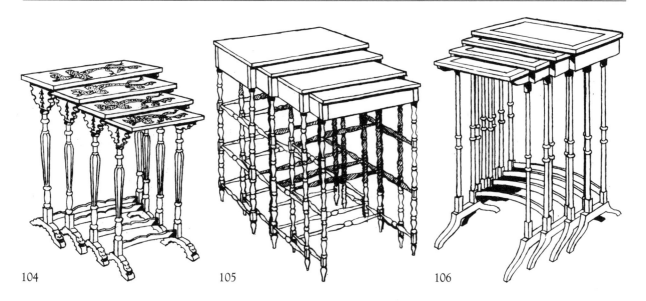

104   105   106

NESTS OF TABLES

Nests of tables were introduced in the early eighteenth century and are still produced today. The difficulty of confining three or four tables in a small space means that the basic design cannot be radically altered and the same two or three variations on the one theme have persisted over the years – in any case, they were never popular in the Victorian era.

They were originally made as occasional tables for needlework or, as George Smith puts it in his *Household Furniture*, 1808, 'they prevent the company rising from their seats when taking refreshments.' The tops were invariably decorated in some way, from fancy veneers and crossbandings to the most exquisite japanning.

A nest of three tables was called a trio; of four, a quartetto (although in the records of Gillow & Co, they are referred to as quarto); and of five, a quintetto.

NIGHT TABLES

Night tables first appeared about 1750 and replaced the old fashioned and rather crude close stools, which were enclosed stools or boxes containing chamber pots. They were frequently embellished with inlays or marquetry which led one writer in 1769 to declare that night tables intended for 'genteel bedrooms are sometimes finished in satinwood and in a style a little elevated above their use'.

They are sometimes called commodes – a term which is of recent origin and one to be avoided as it

FIG 104: a nest of four tables in painted wood with dragon motifs decorating the tops, which are japanned. This feature, plus the dragon's head feet and ends, continue the Oriental style, fashionable in the middle of the 18th century, but unusual in the early 19th. c1830.

FIG 105: a rare example of a nest of four tables favoured by Richard Gillow, of Gillow & Co. Note the three tiers of stretcher rails which make the design so individual; similar nests were produced, some of which had a tray fitted between the lowest stretchers on the smallest table. This was presumably to hold chess or draughts pieces since this table top was a chequer-board. c1810.

FIG 106: the classic design – a nest of four tables with turned column legs ornamented with rings. It is similar to one shown in Sheraton's *Cabinet Dictionary*. c1810.

107

FIG 107: a mahogany night table with a tambour shutter that slides horizontally across the front and reveals a small cupboard. The gallery around the edges of the top is called a tray top, and enables the whole table to be lifted and carried easily: the two drawer fronts are dummies as they enclose the compartment for the chamber pot. c1800.

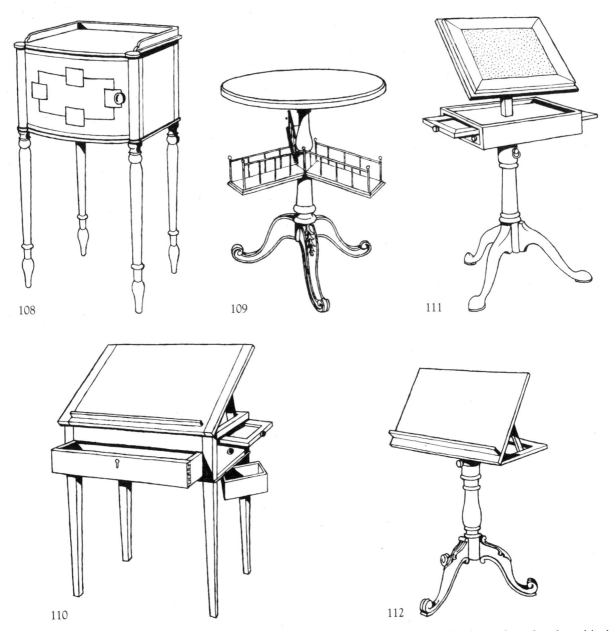

108

109

111

110

112

FIG 108: another night table in mahogany with a bowfront and turned tapered legs with tulip feet; the legs project at the front. c1800.

FIG 109: a late Victorian reading table with a circular top and book trays halfway down the supporting pillar – these trays revolve around the pillar. c1880.

FIG 110: a mahogany reading table with plain tapered legs (called Marlborough legs); the top is adjustable to give a convenient angle for reading. The pull-out slide could be used to support a candle or a note pad, and the swing-out box pivoted on the frame held pens, inks, etc. There is also a drawer beneath the slide. c1790.

FIG 111: an attractive thoughtful design in mahogany. The book support is lined with leather and can be adjusted both for slope and height; when not in use it drops into a recess to become a rectangular-topped tripod table. It also incorporates the usual slides for candles or other accessories: beneath each slide is a shallow drawer. Note the gunbarrel turning on the pillar. c1770.

FIG 112: a more basic design of reading table in that there are no slides or drawers, merely the reading slope. This is adjustable for height as its support rises or falls in a hole bored out of the supporting pillar (as does fig 111); the angle of slope is adjusted by a rack and a series of notches, rather like those on a modern deckchair. The feet terminate in scrolled toes, and are in the French Rococo style, which was fast going out of fashion at this time. c1760.

can lead to confusion. A French chest of drawers was originally called a *commode*, and the word gradually came to mean (to eighteenth-century English cabinet makers, at least) any piece of furniture, including chairs, with a serpentine front.

READING TABLES

Reading tables were a mid-eighteenth-century innovation brought about by the increased number of books, pamphlets, etc, being published. During Victorian times the tables were supplanted by many and varied designs of combined music/reading stands.

SIDE, CONSOLE, AND PIER TABLES

Side tables date back to the fifteenth century and were a development of the chests then in wide use. They were probably used originally as an adjunct to dressers, and were handy at mealtimes to hold food, additional cutlery or utensils, etc. In Stuart times they were also used to support ornaments, vases, and what Pepys in his *Diary* called a 'bowpot' (that is, a large vase for the display of sprays of foliage or cut flowers). Many of the tables were only decorated or carved on their fronts and ends, indicating that they were intended to stand against a wall.

Later, at the end of the eighteenth and the beginning of the nineteenth centuries, they blossomed into magnificence with ornate carving and gilding, and often with marble or scagliola tops. Scagliola was a composition of plaster of Paris, isinglass, coloured pigment powder, and marble chips, mixed to resemble marble – much of it was imported from Italy, or made in England by Italian craftsmen brought over for the purpose. Obviously, such grand pieces were intended to impress visitors with their opulence.

113

114

115

FIG 113: a mahogany side table with plain squared tapered Marlborough legs and a single drawer. The gallery board at the back of the top is surmounted by a swan neck broken pediment with painted decoration. c1900.

FIG 114: a small side table which, although plain, has an elegance of its own. It is in mahogany; and only the details of the legs, particularly the turned bulbs near the tops and the slim tapered feet, indicate that it was made at the turn of the 18th and 19th centuries. c1800.

FIG 115: semi-elliptical pier table made in mahogany with inlaid satinwood stringing and drawer fronts; the whole piece is very much in the Sheraton manner. c1790.

The principal characteristic of a console table was that it was supported by legs at the front and fixed to the wall at the back; in more elaborate examples the support was provided by an eagle with outspread wings or dolphins intertwined. The tables were introduced from France in the eighteenth century.

Pier tables, as their name suggests, were intended to stand against the wall of a pier – that is, the wall between two openings such as windows. One of their chief uses was to support candelabra so that the candle-light was reflected by a mirror (a pier glass) fixed above the table. The alternative contemporary name was clap table, and Celia Fiennes (a lady who travelled all over England in the latter half of the seventeenth century and kept a diary of her journeys) refers to clap tables under the large looking glasses between the windows at Windsor Castle.

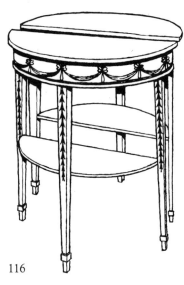

116

117

FIG 116: a pair of pier tables, each top being semicircular. In mahogany with inlaid satinwood; the husks and swags are in the Neo-Classical style introduced by Robert Adam and espoused by both George Hepplewhite and Gillow & Co. c1785.

FIG 117: mahogany console table; with veneered top. The legs are turned and tapered, and both the legs and the frieze rail are reeded. Again, a Neo-Classical design. c1780.

118

119

FIG 118: a serpentine-fronted side table in mahogany with cockbeading around the drawer rail; the legs are square and tapered with small blocks towards the bottom – characteristic of the period. c1780.

FIG 119: Georgian style side table in mahogany. The cabriole legs have carved scrolls on the backs of the knees and pointed pad feet: the drawer fronts have cockbeading around them. c1750.

120

121

FIG 120: walnut side table with veneered and quartered top; the cabriole legs are slightly hocked and terminate in pad feet. Note the crossbanding around the drawer front – a decorative detail typical of the period. c1715.

FIG 121: a walnut side table embellished with arabesque (seaweed) marquetry, as much furniture was at this time. The popularity of marquetry was due to the magnificent work done by craftsmen from the Low Countries who either followed Charles II after his restoration to the throne (1660), or as craftsmen-refugees from the Revocation of the Edict of Nantes (1685) which withdrew freedom of worship from the Protestant Huguenots in Roman Catholic France.

Note that the twist legs diminish in diameter from bottom to top to give the effect of entasis; the shaped stretchers are veneered both on their faces and their edges. A beautiful example from the period, embodying high craftsmanship. c1690.

122

123

FIG 122: walnut side table decorated with floral marquetry. The S-scroll legs, and the shaped underframe, are all veneered. c1680.

FIG 123: an early design of oak side table. The upper spandrels are carved in low relief; note the scratch moulding on the edges of the legs and on the bottom edge of the undershelf rail. c1525.

TEA TABLES

Tea tables with oblong tops were contemporary with pillar and claw tables, and usually the teapot, cups, etc, were brought in on a silver tray, the whole thing being set on the table top. In fact, some contemporary references mention that the tray itself was called a table and the actual table on which it stood was called a stand.

Tea was introduced into England from Holland in the middle of the seventeenth century and was (we are told) on sale in every street by 1659. At first it was regarded as a herbal medicine but by 1725 many tea gardens had been established in and around London. By 1750 these had acquired a doubtful reputation and it became fashionable to drink tea in one's own house rather than in public: hence the popularity of the small tea table.

124

TRIPOD TABLES

Tripod tables (the contemporary names were claw table, or pillar and claw table) first appeared early in the eighteenth century, and were obviously developed from the candle stands that were in use from the date of the Restoration (1660) onwards – these almost invariably had some kind of tripod support.

The accepted method of fixing the legs to the base of the pillar was by means of a slot-dovetail: although this is as strong a joint as can be obtained, a circular metal plate with three extended arms (each arm was screwed to the underside of a leg) was sometimes screwed to the bottom of the pillar to give extra strength. Without such a reinforcement, legs could very easily be torn off.

125

FIG 124: a mahogany tea table with slender cabriole legs, which have claw and ball feet and acanthus leaf carvings on the knees. A pierced brass gallery surrounds the top. Such a table was not only used for tea drinking but also for the display of china. c1750.

FIG 125: an early example in walnut with a tray top, cabriole legs, and club feet. c1715.

FIG 126: a tripod table in walnut, the top veneered in walnut and having a scalloped edge simulating the piecrust edge. The claw legs have pad feet; the two features that mark the design as Victorian are (1) the ugly bulbous turning on the supporting pillar, and (2) the small turned finial at the lower end. c1870.

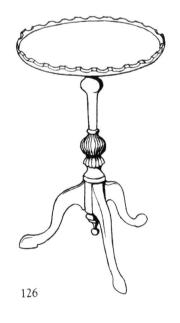

126

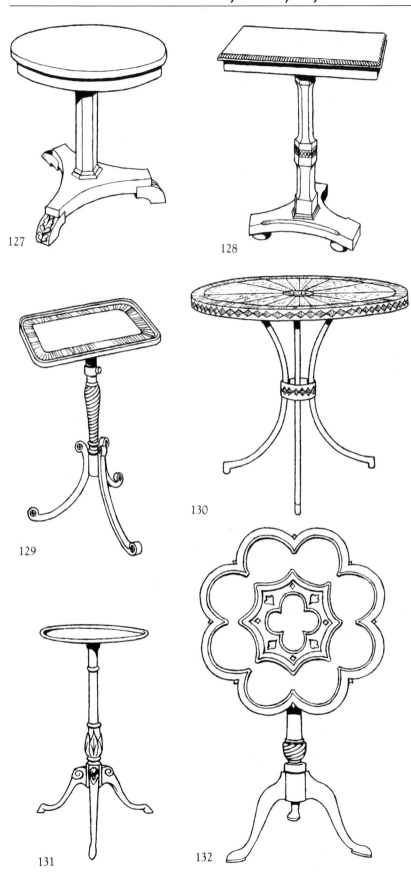

FIG 127: a design which was quite long lived – from about 1830 until 1880. It was made either in mahogany or walnut, and from top to toe was veneered all over. The small scrolled feet are carved with stylised acanthus foliage. c1830 to 1880.

FIG 128: made in oak, this square-topped tripod table is vaguely in the Gothic Revival style with an octagonal pillar. c1830.

FIG 129: a delicate design in mahogany with scrolled legs, a square top with rounded corners, and the pillar turned and twisted in an elongated vase shape. Small brass paterae decorate the leg scrolls; the top can be adjusted to move up or down. c1810.

FIG 130: mahogany and inlaid satinwood tripod table with bent curved supports tied with a collar. The top is expertly veneered with radiating veneers of satinwood. c1790.

FIG 131: small tripod table, which was used either for tea or wine drinking. In mahogany; the legs are decorated with carved rams' heads on the knees and have hooved feet. c1780.

FIG 132: a tripod supper table of a type distinguished by the carved circular recesses on the top; in mahogany, with satinwood inlaid embellishment. Note the spirally twisted bulb (or knop) – a feature of the Georgian period, although such bulbs were often alternatively carved with acanthus foliage. As can be seen, the top tilts into a vertical position. c1760.

127

128

129

130

131

132

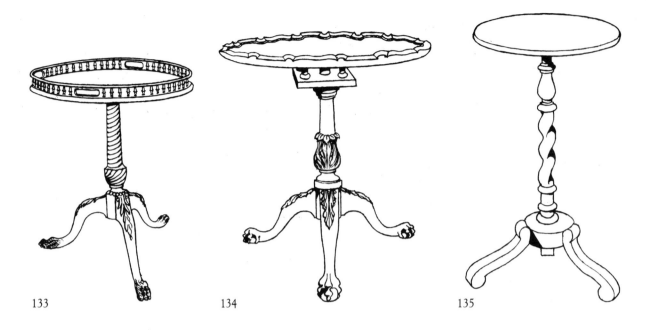

133   134   135

FIG 133: a mahogany tripod table, with the same kind of bulb as fig 132, plus carved lion's paw feet and acanthus on the knees. The top is fixed and is surrounded by a turned spindle gallery, all in wood. c1755.

FIG 134: the classic Georgian style tripod table with a true piecrust top, birdcage tilting movement, carved bulb, acanthus foliage on the knees, and claw and ball feet. c1750.

FIG 135: an early circular-topped tripod table in walnut with a yew top, S-scrolled feet, and a twist pillar. c1680.

FIG 136: many tripod tables had tilting tops, and were called snap tables; they could be left in a vertical position when not in use. To achieve this, late 18th and 19th century designs often used a metal fitting called a banjo catch (fig 136A) while earlier pieces incorporated a birdcage movement (fig 136B).

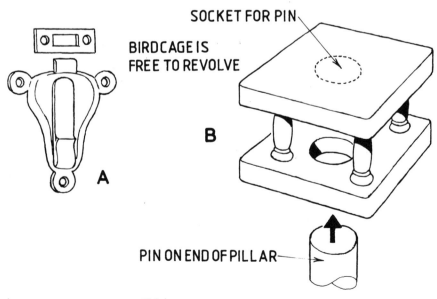

SOCKET FOR PIN

BIRDCAGE IS
FREE TO REVOLVE

A

B

PIN ON END OF PILLAR

136

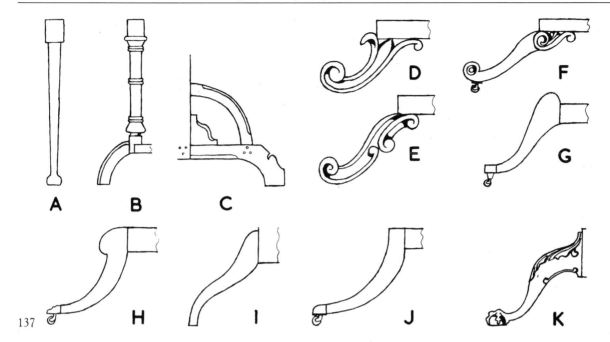

A B C D E F G H I J K

137

WORK TABLES

Needlework and embroidery were both popular in Tudor and Stuart times, when the various accessories were kept in small chests or wooden stools with lift-out lids. Most of the beads, silks, etc, were imported from Holland and Italy, and it was not until the 1650s that the production of needles in England gave the crafts a boost.

Work tables, such as those described, did not appear until about 1770 and were of two principal types – those that resembled a small table with a drawer divided into compartments, and those with some kind of pouch suspended from the top. The first type often had a fire screen resembling a picture-frame filled with canvas, located along the back edge of the top; this could be erected to protect one's face from the heat of the fire. Some of these screens were simply hinged to the edge and dropped down behind the table when not in use, while others dropped between the back legs of the table.

The second type had a pouch made either of fabric or of wood, and in many cases, the pouch could be pulled forward on runners so that the work could be taken out or put away without disturbing the drawer. The alternative, when the pouch was fixed, was to have a lift-out tray (sometimes called a skibbet) with compartments for threads, wools, thimbles, etc, and this was taken out to give access to the pouch. Many of these work tables had hinged flaps on the top which could be opened to reveal backgammon and/or chess boards.

FIG 137: legs used on tripod and pedestal tables. (A) Art Nouveau, 1880 to 1910; (B) and (C) legs used on popular designs of centre pedestal tables of the Gothic Revival style, about 1865; (D), (E), and (F) are the vaguely Rococo style which was fashionable from about 1850 to 1880; (G) and (H) are in the Regency style, 1810 to 1820; (I) and (J) date from about 1770 to 1790; (K) is a typical mid 18th century leg with an acanthus leaf carved on the knee, and claw and ball feet.

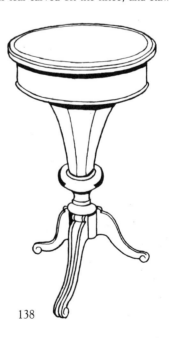

138

FIG 138: a late 19th century design in walnut with a circular drum top to contain needlework accessories; the 'work in progress' was stored in the trumpet-shaped support (earlier examples had an urn-shaped support). The legs have neatly scrolled feet – a characteristic of the period. c1870.

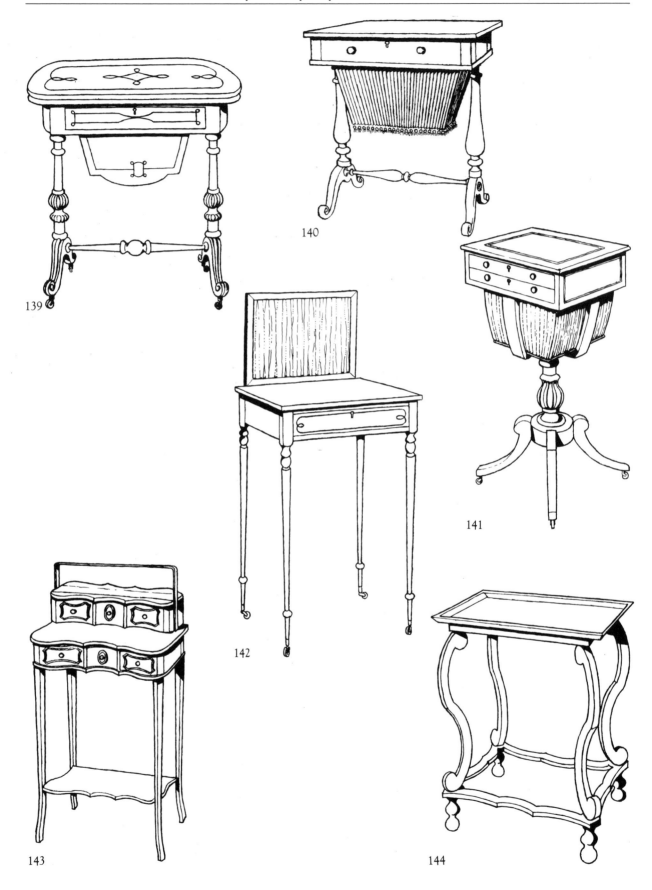

139

140

141

142

143

144

FIG 139: an excellent example of a combined work and games table (this combination was very popular in Victorian times). The top is double, and swivels and opens out to reveal a backgammon board on one half and a chequerboard on the other. There is a drawer for accessories and the work in hand is contained in the wooden box. Made in walnut, it has beautifully matched and figured veneers and boxwood marquetry. The 'French' style legs with volutes on the scroll feet are typical of good-class pieces of the period. c1860.

FIG 140: a mahogany work table similar to one designed by J. C. Loudon in 1833. With reeded pillars and legs with scroll feet. c1840.

FIG 141: walnut work table with curved supports mounted on claw legs; the feet carry brass castors. The drawers are dummies, as the top lifts up to reveal the storage compartment and the interior of the pouch. c1825.

FIG 142: not all work tables had pouches, which were a 19th century addition. This satinwood table has a drawer with a division inside and a pull-up screen to protect the lady's face from the heat of a fire. c1810.

FIG 143: mahogany work table with a pouch and two tiers of drawers with serpentine fronts – the upper tier could be carried separately by means of the handle. The front edge of the top is curved to follow the line of the drawers (the shape is actually called an *arc en arbalète* – that is, the curve of a crossbow), and the low shelf has the same outline. The ornamentation is inlaid ivory. c1785.

FIG 144: an oak table with a tray top which may have been used as a tea table but was more likely to have been a bead table. Such tables were used for the coloured bead work that became popular after the Restoration (1660); the raised rim would have prevented the beads rolling off the top. Note the elongated S-scroll legs and hourglass-shaped feet – typical of the period. c1690.

WRITING TABLES

It is difficult to categorise writing tables as virtually any kind of table can be used for the purpose, particularly library tables, which are often described as library-writing tables. Bureaux and bureau-bookcases are dealt with separately.

Writing tables did not appear until the end of the seventeenth century and the original designs were borrowed from the French. Early examples (up to 1700) often had dual purposes, being both card and writing tables, with fold-over flaps and gates. The monumental kinds of pedestal, writing-cum-library tables have been omitted, as such designs were only found in the enormous libraries of the rich.

Bonheurs-du-jour were French designs, which became fashionable in the eighteenth and nineteenth centuries, and were writing and dressing tables combined, with drawers and small cupboards for trinkets.

Another writing table of French origin was the cheveret. This was intended for ladies' use, and can be identified by the sets of drawers and/or cupboards situated at the back of the top; they are often movable and are fitted with carrying handles for the purpose.

The Carlton House table received its name from an entry in Gillow & Co's cost books in 1796, and is thought to have been supplied for the Prince of Wales's (later George IV) bedroom at Carlton House. However, Thomas Sheraton gave such a design in his *Cabinet-Maker and Upholsterer's Drawing Book* (1794) and he called it a 'Lady's Drawing and Writing Table'.

FIG 145: a mahogany cheveret in what one might call the Edwardian-Sheraton style which was popular from the last years of Queen Victoria's reign until the outbreak of World War I in 1914. Most of the pieces are beautifully made, using fine timber and veneers, as the Empire could supply the best of timbers, and hand craftsmanship was still much in evidence although machinery had taken over the hard, slogging work.

This example has patterned veneers on the doors, with various motifs of foliage in marquetry. There is a flap in front of the cupboards and drawers which unfolds outwards to form an extra leather-lined writing surface. Usually, such flaps are supported by lopers but in this case the drawer is pulled partly open to act as a support, its upper edges being covered with baize to prevent marking. c1900.

145

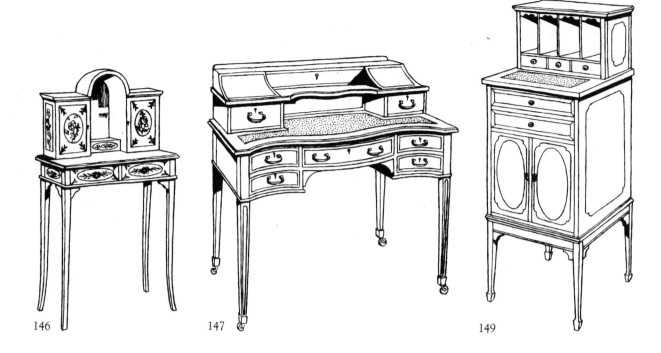

146   147   149

FIG 146: lady's *bonheur-du-jour* in satinwood with marquetry decoration. The space between the two cupboards is backed by a mirror and capped by a semicircular arch. c1900.

FIG 147: a Carlton House writing table in the Edwardian-Sheraton style already referred to in fig 145.
   It is in mahogany with satinwood stringing; the top is leather-lined and has a flap covering a well between the two sets of drawers. c1900.

FIG 148: walnut *bonheur-du-jour* with marquetry decorations; the drawers flanking the mirror give the effect of a Carlton House table. The mirror is hinged and is opened by pressing a concealed catch to reveal secret shelving. c1870.

FIG 149: satinwood cheveret, with ebony stringing, vaguely Sheraton in style. c1850.

FIG 150: mahogany writing table on standard-type legs, with scrolled feet. The top is leather-lined with a crossbanded mahogany veneer surround. c1830.

FIG 151: a rosewood writing table; the top has a brass gallery around three sides, and the edges of the drawers carry brass beading. The X-shaped legs with lions' head masks and paw feet are reminiscent of Thomas Hope's Neo-Egyptian and Greek furniture designs in his book *Household Furniture and Interior Decoration* (1807). c1805.

FIG 152: a mahogany Carlton House table of characteristic design. The top is leather-lined with a brass gallery around it; the stringing lines are in satinwood. c1795.

FIG 153: Sheraton style writing table, the top in figured mahogany veneer with rosewood crossbanding around the edge. The standard ends are connected by a curved stretcher. c1795.

FIG 154: a satinwood cheveret, with tray under shelf. The nest of drawers with a book trough above is movable, the handle being used to carry it. c1790.

FIG 155: a walnut writing table of the kneehole type; on bracket feet, and with boxwood stringing. The kneehole contains a cupboard: the top, the end posts of the carcase, and the feet all have canted corners. c1720.

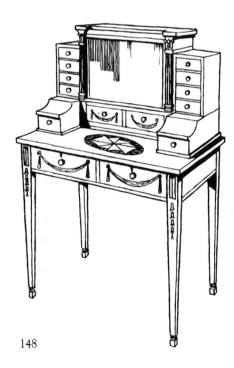

148

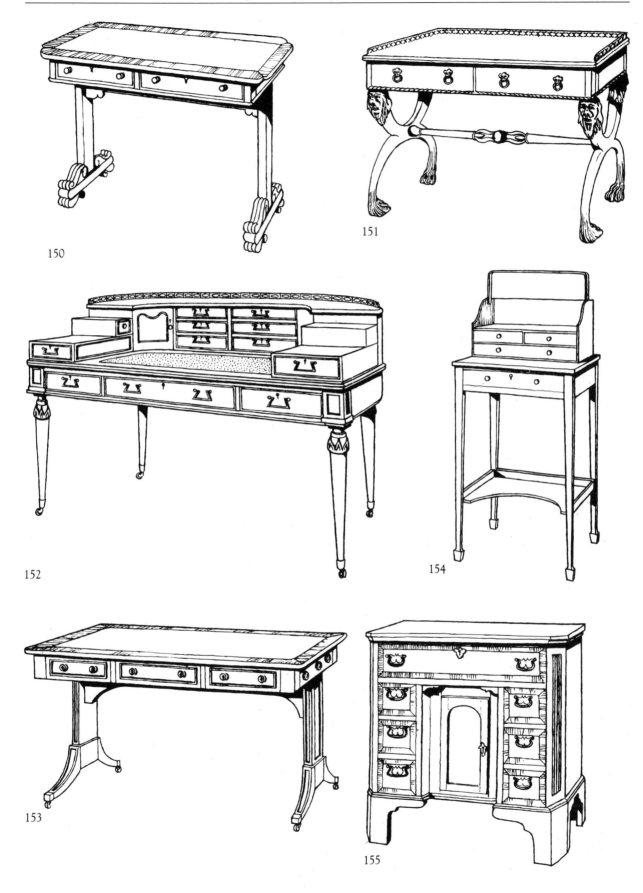

150

151

152

154

153

155

CHAPTER 8

Chairs

Historical and constructional notes on all kinds of chairs except Windsor and upholstered chairs appear in this chapter, together with illustrations of typical examples.

HISTORY

Of all the many different pieces of furniture, chairs have probably been subjected to the vagaries of fashion more than any other, and the total number of chair designs must run into a hundred or two. Space is too limited for more than a judicious selection, and those which are included are meant to be examples of the predominant styles of their respective periods.

Chairs have existed for thousands of years and from contemporary sources such as wall paintings, vases, and other artefacts we know that they were used in Ancient Egypt, about 3000BC, and also in the Assyrian, Greek and Roman civilisations. Many of the classical designs appear familiar and this is no flight of fancy, because they were translated bodily into fashionable use during the Classical Revivals in the late eighteenth and nineteenth centuries. These revivals were not confined to Britain, but also affected French and American furniture styles, and Thomas Hope's book *Household Furniture and Interior Decoration* published in 1807 is a good example of this historical plagiarism. See also figs 175A, B, and C.

From the earliest times until the seventeenth century, chairs were status symbols and were for the sole use of royalty, the nobility, or the head of the household. Thus, when the Constable of Castile was entertained by James I at Whitehall in 1604, records state that, 'Their Majesties sat at the head of the table on chairs of brocade with cushions, and at the Queen's side sat the Constable, a little apart, on a tabouret (stool) of brocade with a high cushion of the same', and Prince Henry was also provided with a similar stool. As might be expected, the Church followed the royal example and reserved chairs for the use of its highest dignitaries.

Not until the eighteenth century did chairs come to be recognised as seating for all and sundry, and thereafter different types of chair proliferated. As well as Windsor chairs there were barbers', cockfighting, drunkards', gouty, hunting, kneeling, library, nursing, portable, porters', sewing, shaving, writing, and many other types.

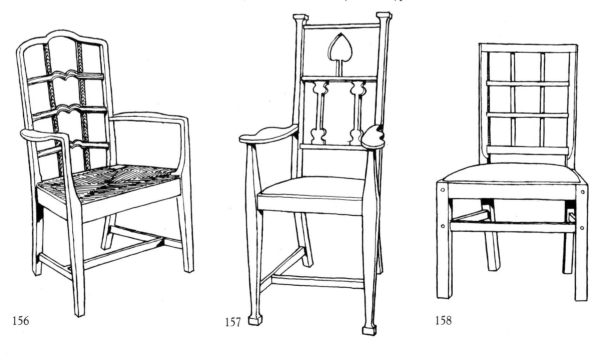

156   157   158

FIG 156: lattice back armchair designed by Ernest Gimson. It is a well thought out chair and combines gracefulness and lightness; note the bevelling on the inside edges of the backfeet and the tapering on the front legs, which is also only on the inside edges. The vertical stays are inlaid with box and ebony stringing. Gimson was fond of the lattice back not only for chairs but also for some of the sideboards he designed; the rush seat was almost obligatory for any chair designed by a member of the Arts and Crafts Movement, as he was.

The values of chairs like this, and of those that follow up to and including fig 165, are greatly enhanced if the chairs can be proved to have been designed or made by a known participant in the Arts and Crafts Movement, the Art Nouveau style or the Century Guild. In other words, provenance is (almost) everything. c1915.

FIG 157: a commercial rendering of Art Nouveau, this armchair has the heart-shaped motif and the tapered legs with block-shaped feet typical of C. F. A. Voysey's designs – although A. H. Mackmurdo introduced this style of foot in the 1880s. c1900.

FIG 158: a side chair, probably designed by Ernest Gimson, to accompany a massive bow fronted sideboard he designed for Ernest Barnsley. Note, as in fig 156, the lattice back and chamfered backfeet, plus the pegged tenons on the front legs – all characteristics of the Cotswold School of the Arts and Crafts Movement. c1895.

FIG 159: a high-backed chair by Charles Rennie Mackintosh. He was an architect in Glasgow and a leading designer in the British version of the French Art Nouveau style. This chair, and others like it that he designed, must have been uncomfortable as the low seat and high back (up to 1.5m (5ft) tall) make no concessions to comfort. But we must remember that he designed them to fit into large interiors such as restaurants and mansions where they were as much objets d'art as furniture. He was particularly fond of having his chairs painted in white or soft pastel colours, and they were frequently decorated with a stylised, tightly closed rose which was one of his hallmarks. At the time they were regarded as 'quaint' and this quality was admired by those who considered themselves avant-garde, although the style never became remotely popular. c1895.

FIG 160: an Arts and Crafts style armchair in which a simpler, cruder country design has been adapted and refined. The slim proportions are good, as are the tapered and turned backfeet (above the pummels), and the front legs. The pierced heart shape in the back panel (which serves as a hand hole), and the rush seat are both typical of the style. 1890 to 1910.

FIGS 161 A and B: two classical ladderback armchairs by Ernest Gimson, both of them beautifully proportioned and graceful. The graduated sizes and shapes of the ladder rails in (B) are similar to those in fig 165, and both are based on the Yorkshire ladderback chairs used between 1730 and 1800.

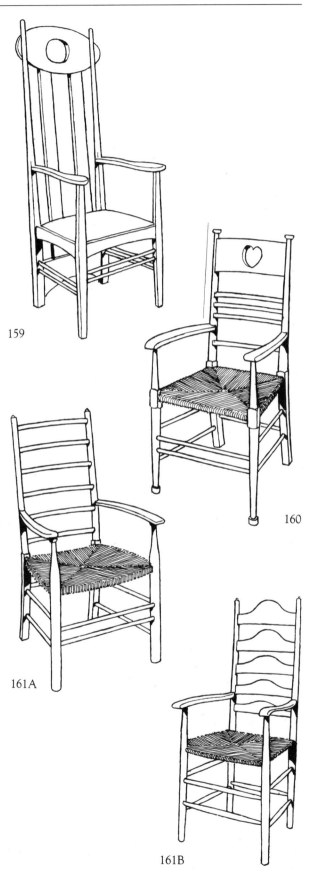

159

160

161A

161B

During the Middle Ages chairs were made by joiners, coffer makers (who made chests), and wood turners: it was not until 1632 that disputes as to which craftsmen should be granted a monopoly of chair making were settled by a Court of Aldermen who decided that it should be the joiners. However, the rival faction of carpenters ignored the decision; and in 1633 the turners were complaining that 'the joiners assume unto themselves the art of turning'. It all sounds rather topical and depressing and the matter was never officially settled. Sheraton wrote in 1803, 'Chair making is a branch generally confined to itself; as those who professedly work at it seldom engage to make cabinet furniture. . . . The two branches [cabinet making and chair making] seem evidently to require different talents in the workmen to become proficient.' Which is just as true today as it was then.

The earliest chairs (apart from the throne-like designs used by the uppermost classes of society) were known as back stools and, as their name implies, were simply stools with an added back. Their chief characteristic was that the backfeet (the trade term for the back legs) had no rake backwards (as in later chairs) and from the seat downwards extended vertically to the floor. Because they had no arms, the name back stool also served to denote that they were single or side chairs. The term was still being used in this sense when Ince and Mayhew referred to them in their *The Universal System of Household Furniture* (1759 to 1762); remember that until about 1580, all chairs were arm chairs.

FIG 162: a well known and often illustrated side chair that exemplifies English Art Nouveau in its early years. It was designed by Arthur Heygate Mackmurdo (1851 to 1942) for the Century Guild in 1882 and was made by Collinson and Lock; it is now in the William Morris Gallery, Walthamstow, London.
FIG 163: taken from an illustration in the book *Decoration and Furniture of Town Houses* by R. W. Edis, FSA, FRIBA; he also wrote *Healthy Furniture and Decoration*, published in 1884. The decoration consists of incised rings on the turned legs – this feature, plus the rush seat and the shaped side pieces, appear to be a deliberate attempt to revert to rustic simplicity. c1881.
FIG 164: this chair is typical of many designs of the period which were described as being in the Eastlake style. He was an architect and designer who was an exponent of the revived (and revised) Early English style. In 1868 he published *Hints on Household Taste* which was immensely popular in England and the USA, and undoubtedly the designs were adapted by manufacturers to suit their customers.
The features that are typical of his style are the arcading below the back panels, the overlapping roundels (sometimes called money carving) on the faces of the backfeet, the incised rings on the front turned legs, and the space nailing round the upholstered parts. 1880 to 1890.

162

163

164

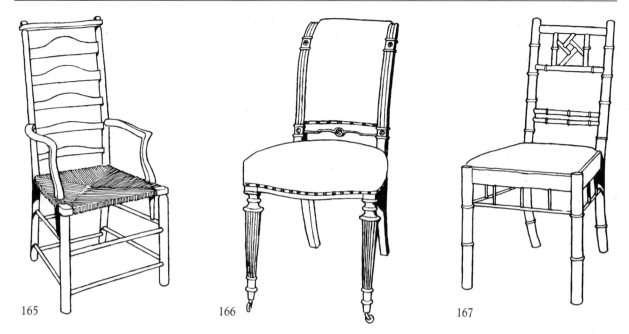

165   166   167

FIG 165: a ladderback armchair manufactured by Morris, Marshall, Faulkner & Co a firm founded in 1861 by William Morris in association with Madox Brown, Burne-Jones, Rossetti, and Philip Webb. It is very doubtful whether Morris ever designed any furniture, most of it being designed by Philip Webb.

This particular design proved very popular and was usually made from beech with an ebonised finish; the seat is, of course, rushed. Note the graduated ladder rails (see also fig 161B), and the characteristic way the arm stump extends down to the underframing. 1865 to 1890.

FIG 166: an upholstered dining chair of a type popular in the 1870s although it was rather too expensive for ordinary working people, who preferred either the ubiquitous balloon-back chair, or mass-produced 'repro' designs. c1865 to 1880.

FIG 167: a typical 'bamboo' chair of the late 19th and early 20th centuries. Until 1854 Japan was closed to trade from the West, but in any case, Japanese influence on Victorian culture was slow in growing. One architect, E. W. Godwin, was enamoured of all things Japanese and designed a considerable amount of furniture in the fashion.

This chair, however, is an example of how the style was taken up by manufacturers and mass-produced. The woods used were beech, birch, or ash, turned and painted to imitate bamboo. c1875 to 1914.

FIG 168 A and B: two bentwood chairs of the Thonet type. Michael Thonet, who was born in Germany, opened a factory for the manufacture of such chairs in Vienna in 1849. Although the fact that some woods when saturated with steam became pliable and would retain a bent shape, had been known for many years, he exploited this to the full in his beechwood rocking chairs and small chairs. He exhibited them at the Crystal Palace Great Exhibition of 1851 and was highly successful; so much so that he opened a London factory, and in 1870 he was reputed to be turning out 1,200 daily.

They remained popular until well into the 20th century and were widely imitated. Thonet's own chairs can be recognised, however, by the subtle swelling and shaping of the curves – niceties that other mass-producers did not bother with. c1855 to 1915.

168A   168B

169A

169B

169C

170

171

FIG 169 A, B, and C: three balloon-back chairs of a type which had a long run of popularity from about 1830 until the late 1870s. There were many and varied variations on the shapes of the back and legs but the chairs are always recognisable as balloon backs. Illustrations (A) and (C) are of dining chairs; (B) is of a drawing room chair with the French style cabriole legs at the front, introduced about 1850. Many chairs were made of solid rosewood and the amount of timber cut to waste in shaping the curves must have been enormous. Those used in the bedroom were usually lighter in weight and were made of beech or birch.

FIG 170: a chair reminiscent of the Abbotsford chair (fig 171), with vaguely medieval motifs in the decoration of the back and the caning of the seat and back. Despite the fact that it

was a grotesque mixture of styles it remained popular for many years. c1840 to 1890.

FIG 171: the well known Abbotsford style of chairs, which derives its name from Sir Walter Scott's house in Scotland; the term was not contemporary and was not, in fact, used until 1901 (see Gothic Revival, page 54).

The design is more a relic of the Restoration period than the Elizabethan, and in any case the decorative details are Victorian interpretations of the originals and bear only a passing resemblance to them. The upholstered panels are sometimes embellished with embroidery, but more often with Berlin woolwork; this was needlework based on squared off paper patterns originally introduced about 1805 from Berlin. c1840 to 1870.

FIG 172: one of the last of the classical chair designs, this piece has a curved tablet top back rail, with a carved back stay, and with thurmed front legs.

Thurming (or therming) is a process for creating the facets on this kind of leg and was used before the introduction of mechanical saws. A drum was mounted in a lathe and the legs fixed temporarily to it; as the drum revolved the wood turner would form one facet on each leg. The lathe was then stopped and each leg would be rotated to expose another facet to be turned, and so on. As one can imagine, the process was fiddly and laborious.

Such chairs were made in either rosewood or mahogany, or a combination of both. c1835.

FIG 173: Thomas Hope, a connoisseur and amateur arch-aeologist, published his book *Household Furniture and Interior Decoration* in 1807, and this design of chair is typical of his preoccupation with classical Greek and Roman designs. It was made in beech, and painted with Etruscan style motifs. c1807.

FIG 174: a ladies' chair with the back and seat in one continuous curve, and no arms. Although it first appeared in Regency times, similar designs were still being made well into the middle of the 19th century. c1820 to 1870.

FIGS 175 A, B, C: two Regency period small chairs, both with sabre-shaped front legs. This kind of leg derives from the ancient Greek *klismos* chair shown in (C). The purchase of the Elgin Marbles in 1816 greatly stimulated classical influence on all kinds of furniture. Design (A) circa 1820; (B) circa 1810.

172

173

174

175A

175B

175C

176

177

178

179

180

181

182

183

184

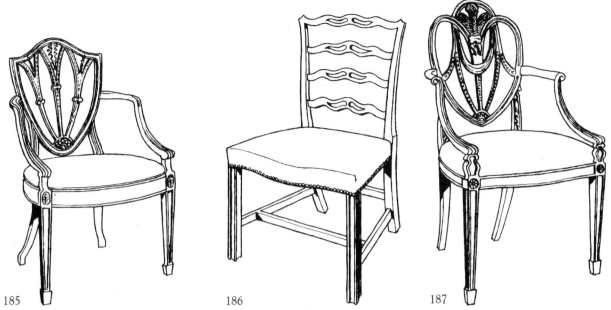

185   186   187

FIG 176: a Regency Trafalgar armchair with double curved backfeet and a back stay known as a cable twist. This latter feature, with similar nautical motifs such as anchors, dolphins coiled ropes, and the like, led pieces so adorned to be known as Trafalgar furniture; it is also common to find that furniture made shortly after the date of the battle (1805) carries a black emblem of mourning of some kind for the death of Nelson. c1805 to 1810.

Thomas Sheraton also designed what he called Trafalgar chairs to commemorate the victory; some of the last he designed (he died in 1806), were grotesquely decorated with anchors, dolphins tied together with ribbon, and similar motifs. They were, sadly, obvious signs of his declining powers.

FIG 177: a Sheraton style armchair, in beechwood which has been japanned, and gilt. The trellis lattice work in the back and the caned seat are typical of the period: loose cushions were used on them. c1800.

FIG 178: another Sheraton style armchair, with the seat rails, the front leg squares, and the tablet in the top back rail all veneered with satinwood. Note the reeded decoration – characteristic of the period. c1795.

FIG 179: a carved and gilt armchair in one of Hepplewhite's styles, which he called a cabriole chair and which (he said) ought to have a stuffed back. Not that he was consistent about it – on the facing page of his book *The Cabinet-Maker and Upholsterer's Guide* (1794) he showed one with an upholstered seat and a wooden back. Sheraton also used the term 'cabriole' in his *Cabinet Dictionary* (1803) to describe a French easy chair, stuffed all over.

The chair illustrated has what is called a tablet back referring to the top back rail; often the painted parts were *en grisaille*, a French term which describes painting in a monotone colour such as grey, olive green, or buff, with the subject in simulated relief. c1790.

FIG 180: Hepplewhite style armchair in mahogany; the backfeet are reeded on the front face, while the arms, stumps, and front legs are channelled out; these two forms of decoration were frequently used on late 18th and early 19th century chairs. The back uprights and top rail have carved motifs of stylised wheatears and husks (a chain or succession of buds or small flowers) – again, these are typical of the period. c1790.

FIG 181: a classical Hepplewhite style chair of the shield-back style, also called a 'camel back', due to the pronounced hump-like curve of the top back rail. The paterae have a circular fan motif and are inlaid in boxwood; the front faces of the back and the backfeet are channelled, and the front legs are fluted – all characteristic features. c1788.

FIG 182: a Sheraton style chair, with a Prince of Wales' feather design in the splat, combined with a vase shape – both favourite motifs of Hepplewhite's, but used by Thomas Sheraton as well. c1783.

FIG 183: an anthemion-back armchair, also called a honey-suckle-back – anthemion is the Greek word for honeysuckle. The description is applied to any chair back that includes the motif, even if only in a small degree. Note the padded arms with the small paterae where they meet the stumps; this is a characteristic of the period. c1775 to 1790.

FIG 184: a shield-back cabriole armchair, Hepplewhite style. Note the padded arms, which terminate in paterae. c1780.

FIG 185: a beautiful example of a wheatear shield-back armchair. The wheatear refers to the carving in the banisters of the back. c1775.

FIG 186: this is sometimes called a fiddleback chair because the pierced openings in the ladder rails of the back resemble the sound holes of a violin in shape. See fig 194 for the other design of fiddleback chair. It is a Chippendale style chair, with the channelling on the front legs and the outward splaying of the backfeet at the top being typical. Note, too, that for the first time in about a hundred years here is a chair with an underframe; this was no doubt rendered necessary to impart strength because the seats of Chippendale's chair designs were broader and more capacious than those designed by Adam, Hepplewhite, and Sheraton. c1775.

FIG 187: Hepplewhite armchair with a heart-shaped back incorporating the Prince of Wales' feathers, which, as previously noted, was one of his favourite devices (see also fig 182). c1775.

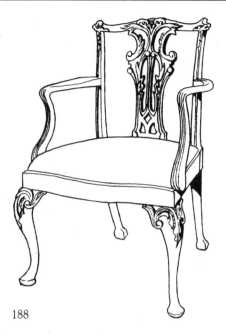

188

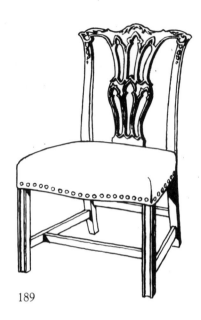

189

FIG 188: a Chippendale armchair in mahogany; the design of the splat is similar to one in his book *The Gentleman and Cabinet-Maker's Director* (1754). The cabriole legs terminate in club feet, which is an unusual feature for a Chippendale chair and were not illustrated in his book – but then, nor were claw and ball feet and they are recognised as typically Chippendale. c1755.

FIG 189: another Chippendale small chair; this one shows Gothic touches in the cusped ends to the pierced openings in the splat. c1755.

190

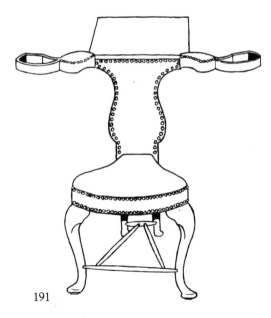

191

FIG 190: a writing (or corner) chair in walnut. The cabriole legs have acanthus carving on the knees and terminate in claw and ball feet; the serpentine-shaped front seat rail is veneered, and the back uprights are fluted. c1740.

FIG 191: a reading chair in mahogany; alternatively called a library chair. The occupant sat astride the chair, back to front, so that a book could be placed on the hinged and adjustable board, and the reader's splendid coat tails would not be creased. The trays contained pens, inks, and candle holders. It is sometimes known as a 'cockfighting' chair in the belief that spectators used it to see the proceedings. So they may have done; but the primary purpose of the chair was for reading. Another name was 'horseman's chair', presumably because the occupant appeared to be riding the chair rather than sitting in it. c1720.

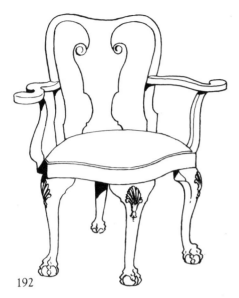

192

193

FIG 192: often referred to as a writing chair doubtless because the central front leg enabled the chair to be drawn close to a table or desk for the occupant to be in a comfortable position for writing. Sometimes called a corner chair. This one is in walnut, with the splat and serpentine seat rail veneered. The carved shells on the knees, the cabriole legs, and the claw and ball feet, are all typical of the period. c1720.

FIG 193: an elegant armchair with upholstered seat and back (often in silk). The front legs are turned and tapered, with club feet: the main shaft would have been turned off-centre, and the foot shaped by hand – an operation called benching in the trade. The arm shape is known as a scroll-over or shepherd's crook. c1720.

FIG 194: a walnut chair that is interesting because it exhibits some special features. The splat is the vase shape typical of the style of the chair; the design is called a fiddleback because the

outline of the back with the concave curves at the waist resembles that of a violin. Further, the front legs have three peculiarities, as follow: (a) the tops of the legs are hipped – that is, they lap around the corners of the seat frame; (b) the shape of the cabriole legs is called hocked; and (c) the feet are a stylised form of the hoof foot that dates back to Assyrian times. So, with unintentional alliteration, the legs can be described as 'hipped, hocked, and hoofed.' c1720.

FIG 195: a bended back chair in walnut, with hocked cabriole front legs, and a shaped stretcher rail. c1710.

FIG 196: like fig 195, another bended back chair. Armchairs like this are often called Hogarth chairs; not because he designed them but because he showed himself sitting in one in a self-portrait. The term was not contemporary, but bestowed by the Victorians, who loved historical allusions. c1710.

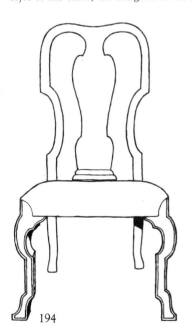

194

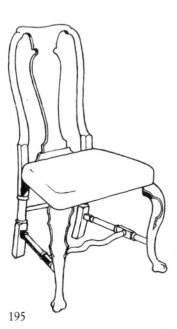

195

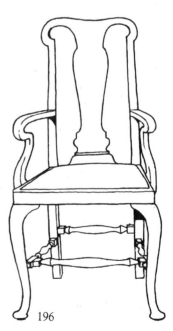

196

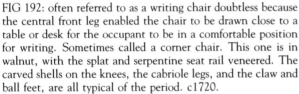

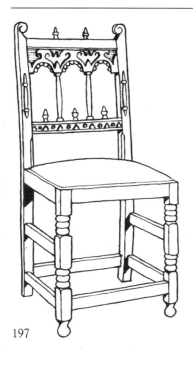

197

199

198

200

201

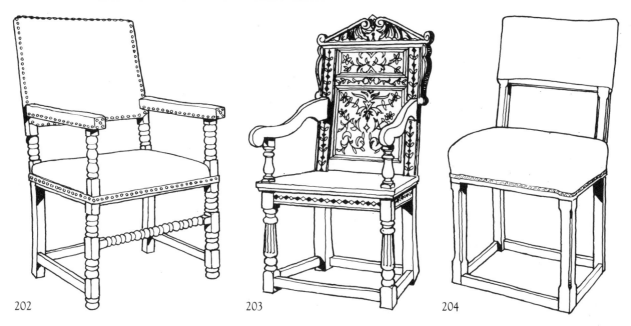

202   203   204

FIG 197: a Derbyshire back stool in oak, so called because the backfeet are vertical from the seat level downwards, and have no backward splay. The distinguishing features are: the scroll ends on the backfeet, the acorn-shaped finials on the top back rail and back stay, the arcaded back with turned column banisters, the split turnings used as decoration on the backfeet, and the low height of the underframe from the floor. c1680.

FIG 198: another oak example, called a Yorkshire back stool. Its characteristics are the heavy back rails which are carved and punched with stylised ornamentation (mainly scrolls), the acorn finials, and the low underframing. c1680.

FIG 199: a Restoration armchair in walnut, with caned panels, representative of a large number of armchairs made at this time; Charles II was restored to the throne in 1660. Cane began to be imported from the Malay Peninsula by the East India Company shortly after that date; the cane furniture makers reaped a rich harvest from those who lost all their belongings in the Great Fire of 1666, as they could supply replacement furniture quickly.

Almost all such chairs have some royal emblem, usually some form of the Crown incorporated in the carving, together with Flemish S-scrolls: the front underframe rail was also always heavily carved. Although walnut was the timber in vogue, some chairs were made in beech stained to imitate walnut, while others were in oak. c1680.

FIG 200: a walnut armchair with twist turned members, and a caned seat and back. Twist turning, or spiral turning as it is sometimes called, is a misnomer because although the basic cylindrical shape is turned on a lathe, the bines (the ridges of the twist) are marked out, cut with gouges, and rasped, all by hand. As a matter of historical interest twist turning lathes are mentioned in 1677 and 1686, but such lathes were the exceptions rather than the rule until the middle of the 18th century. English twist turning normally had a thin bine, which is accentuated by deep hollows, while the Dutch equivalent had a thicker bine and the twist (or swash – the angle at which the bines sloped) was more acute and rapid. c1665.

FIG 201: oak mortuary back stool. A combination of the Derbyshire and Yorkshire designs (figs 197 and 198). It derives its name from the small carved representation of a man's face with a beard which appears in the centre of the upper back rail; it is said that this commemorates Charles I who was executed in 1649. c1650.

FIG 202: an oak armchair with the seat and back upholstered in leather; the turned pattern is called ball and ring. The design is included to illustrate the austerity of furniture during the Commonwealth which was from 1649 to 1658. c1650.

FIG 203: an armchair called a panel-back or wainscot chair. The latter term was the contemporary one used in letters, wills, etc of the time; 'wainscot' was actually a Dutch word describing quartered oak, and this was often the timber used to make the chairs.

It is a lighter and more sophisticated development of the joined chair (fig 208) as the sides are left open, the arms are shaped, and the lower stool part is no longer enclosed and is replaced by an underframe more or less at floor level. The most striking difference is in the architectural style capping rail that laps over the back, and its attendant ear-pieces. Such chairs were often beautifully and intricately decorated with inlaid designs as well as carving. c1630.

FIG 204: oak farthingale chair, also called an imbrauderer's or upholsterer's chair, possibly because they were often hired from upholsterers when needed. The term farthingale was not contemporary but was coined during Victorian times.

Such chairs, without arms (and all chairs before about 1580 had arms) allowed ladies wearing farthingale skirts to sit down without disarranging the whalebone hoops that supported them. The fashion was remarkably long lived, although when Catherine de Braganza arrived to marry Charles II in 1661 her attendant ladies wore them and were criticised for being out of fashion. The King regarded them with his usual dry humour as being a kind of chastity belt. c1580 to 1660.

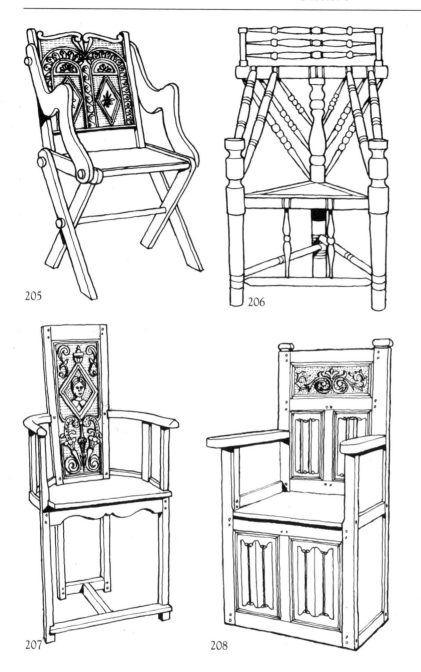

205

206

207

208

three legs, there are four-legged examples (a good one is in the Welsh Folk Museum, Cardiff). Pegs are turned on the ends of each part to enter sockets on the fellow part and make the joint; note how the side lists of the underframing are set one above the other into the back post so that the holes do not weaken it. The seat was fitted with a loose cushion. c1500 to 1650.

FIG 207: *caquetoire* or *caqueteuse* chair, the name deriving from the French word *caqueter* to chatter – hence it is sometimes called a gossip chair.

The original design was French, and the first chairs appeared in England towards the middle of the 16th century. The narrow back usually contained a lozenge-shaped panel which framed a female head, the background being filled with carved foliage; all of it very much in the Renaissance style. The chairs were made in oak or walnut. c1535 to 1600.

FIG 208: a joined or joyned chair (compare with fig 203). Probably the design is a development of a chest fitted with a back and, in fact, the seat of such a chair often lifts to disclose a storage space for clothes, linen or household articles, when it is called a close chair. Some were also used as commodes. Note the infilling of the side under the arms and the panels all round the legs. The joints between the stiles, rails, and muntins were mortised, with the tenons pegged; the panels were often adorned with linenfold carving. c1500 to 1600.

FIG 205: an oak armchair with folding framework. It is more commonly known as a Glastonbury chair; this name was given to it in 1836 in a book called *Specimens of Ancient Furniture*, written by Henry Shaw. This shows a grand disregard for history, as the last Abbot of Glastonbury was executed in 1539 and the abbey destroyed by Henry VIII during the Reformation, and the chair did not appear until the last years of the 16th century in Elizabeth's reign, which was from 1558 to 1603.

Most examples are found in churches and are almost always early 19th century. c1590.

FIG 206: an oak thrown or throwne chair. Obviously, most of the parts were turned (or thrown, as it used to be called) on a lathe, hence the name; almost certainly it was made by the local turner or wheelwright.

The design is a very old one and can be traced back to the Byzantine era (395 to 1453), and illustrations appear in 13th and 14th century manuscripts. Although most thrown chairs have

SOME CONSTRUCTIONAL DETAILS

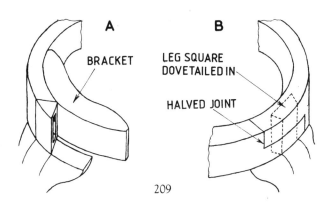

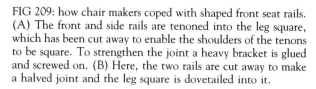

209

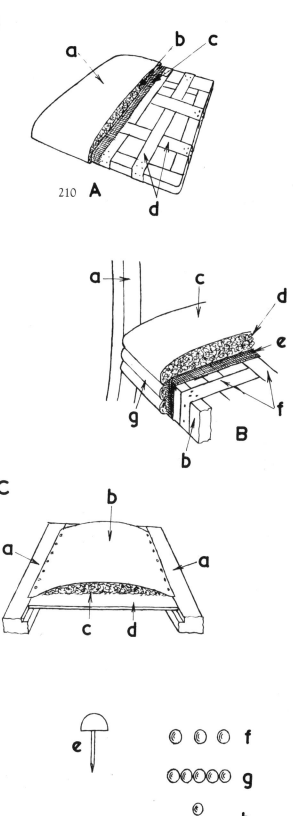

210 **A**

FIG 209: how chair makers coped with shaped front seat rails. (A) The front and side rails are tenoned into the leg square, which has been cut away to enable the shoulders of the tenons to be square. To strengthen the joint a heavy bracket is glued and screwed on. (B) Here, the two rails are cut away to make a halved joint and the leg square is dovetailed into it.

FIG 210: upholstering chairs for comfort began about 1645, and here are three ways of upholstering chair seats. A loose drop-in seat is shown at (A) and (a) is the linen undercover over which the outer fabric was laid; (b) is the horsehair or wool stuffing; (c) the canvas platform stitched to the webbing; (d) the webbing; the webs were taken right round the seat rails and tacked underneath. The bottom of the seat frame was then often covered with black canvas. This type of seat was introduced from Holland during William and Mary's reign (1689 to 1702).

FIG 210 (B) shows a stuffover seat in which the upholstery hides the seat rails completely. It was one of the first styles to be used and has continued until the present day. (a) the backfoot; (b) the side seat rail; (c) linen undercover; (d) horsehair or wool stuffing; (e) a canvas platform stitched to the webbing; (f) webbing; (g) rolls formed by stitching and tacking with gimp pins. The heads of these were covered by gimp, which was a narrow braid.

FIG 210 (C) shows a pin cushion seat where the upholstery lies on top of the seat; the seat rails are often arranged horizontally so that there is a border of polished wood. (a) seat rails; (b) final cover, with an undercover; (c) horsehair or wool; (d) wood base; (e) dome-headed nails (called antique nails today) which were often used. Alternatively, the cover could be tacked down and gimp nailed over to hide the tack heads; (f) the nails could be space nailed about 25mm (1in) apart, as shown; or close nailed as in (g); or cluster nailed (h) which was popular in the 16th and 17th centuries.

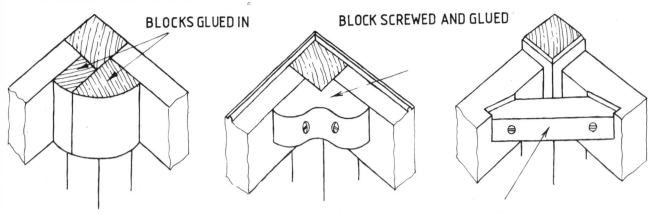

BLOCKS GLUED IN   BLOCK SCREWED AND GLUED

FIG 211: three ways of fitting seat brackets to strengthen the chair frame.

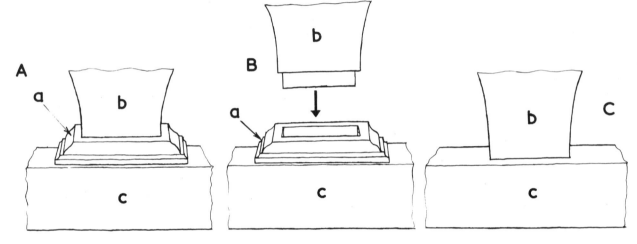

A

a   b

B

b

a

C

b

c   c   c

FIG 212: (above) the shoe (a) housed the lower end of the splat in splat-back chairs; the splat (b) was not glued or fastened in, so that it was freee to shrink or swell across the grain without splitting. Sometimes the shoe was integral with the back seat rail (c), or it could be composed of separate pieces fitted around it and mitred and glued to each other to the seat rail.

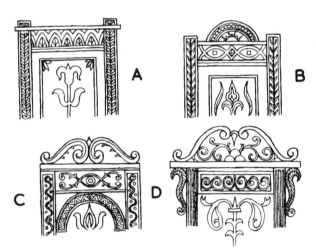

A

B

C   D

FIG 213: the changes in chair backs that took place during the century 1550 to 1650. (A) c1550, the top rail is mortised and tenoned between the backfeet; (B) a small pediment is mounted on the top rail by about 1600, and this is followed by (C) with a larger pediment c1625. (D) is the wainscot chair back in all its glory – the top rail now laps over the backfeet and has supporting ears; and a scrolled pediment surmounts the whole thing.

FIG 214: (right) the changing styles of chair front legs. (A) Art Nouveau, 1880 to 1910; (B) Victorian Rococo, 1850 to 1880; (C) a tapered, turned, and reeded design by George Smith. Used on many Victorian chairs, particularly balloon backs, 1840 onwards; (D) sabre leg, c1810; (E) tapered leg, with spade toe, c1785; (F) the Marlborough tapered leg – the foot was sometimes left plain, c 1785; (G), (H), and (I) are all c1775 and in the Adam style; (J) c1770 – the faces are fluted with a reeded return at the bottom; (K) c1760; (L) the traditional cabriole leg with an acanthus leaf carved on the knee and a claw and ball foot, c1755; (M) cabriole leg with carved shell on the knee, c1715; (N), (O), (P), and (Q) are typical of the Walnut period 1660 to 1730; (R) reversed scroll leg c1690; (S) double scroll leg c1675; (T) mid 17th century leg, made either in oak or walnut; (U) oak leg c1600.

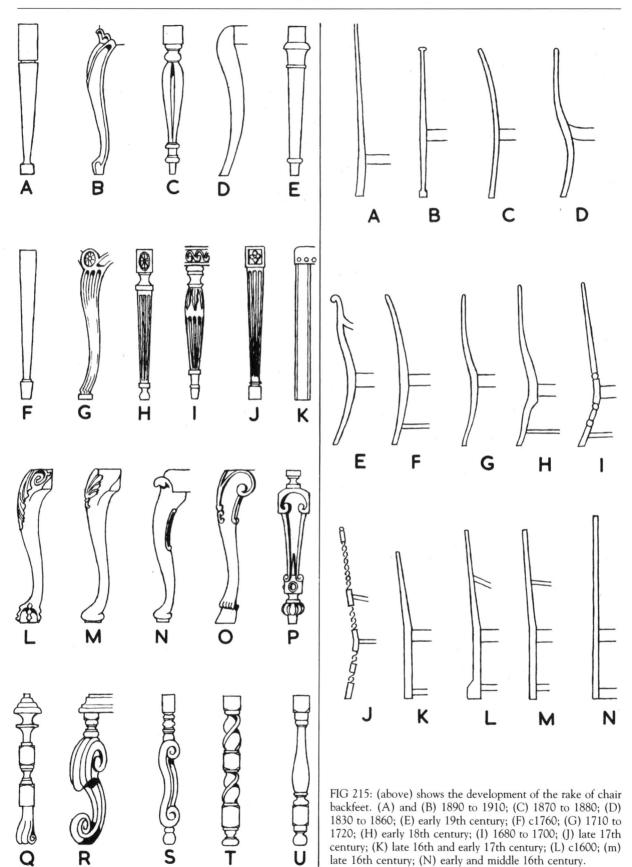

FIG 215: (above) shows the development of the rake of chair backfeet. (A) and (B) 1890 to 1910; (C) 1870 to 1880; (D) 1830 to 1860; (E) early 19th century; (F) c1760; (G) 1710 to 1720; (H) early 18th century; (I) 1680 to 1700; (J) late 17th century; (K) late 16th and early 17th century; (L) c1600; (m) late 16th century; (N) early and middle 16th century.

CHAPTER 9

Upholstered chairs

This chapter deals with upholstered armchairs, plus the intriguingly named Cosy Corners, and couches, day beds, love seats, settees, and sofas.

The upholstering of chairs seems to have begun during the reign of Elizabeth I (1558 to 1603), for towards the end of the sixteenth century we have Sir John Harington exclaiming, 'The fashion of cushioned chayres is taken up in every merchant's house'. He must have been a gentleman worth knowing; he was Elizabeth's godson and was banished from court for lampooning one of her favourites. He settled at Kelston in Somerset and there astonished his neighbours, if not the world, by inventing the water-closet.

From that time until the end of the eighteenth century, the only way to provide any kind of resiliency or springiness was by stuffing the upholstery with a soft filling. Wool was obviously a prime candidate owing to its availability, but down, feathers, dried hops, and straw were also used. In 1740 a Mr Henry Marsh invented a form of metal coiled spring which was used in a chamber-horse, but upholsterers had to wait until 1828 when a Mr Samuel Pratt patented his coil spring. Bed mattresses were often supported on ropes or leather straps fixed to the frame, and leather was also used as a support for loose cushions, being replaced after (about) 1660 by cane work. Webbing of more or less the same kind as the present day article was certainly in use at the end of the eighteenth century as Sheraton mentions it in his *Cabinet Dictionary* (1803).

The upholstery covers were magnificent. Many were of needlework, others of exotic velvets, brocades, silks, and damasks; the last named sometimes incorporated gold or silver threads, when it was known as 'damassin'.

Now for more detailed descriptions of the various types of upholstered chairs. It should be noted that the terms settee and sofa (sometimes spelt 'sopha') were interchangeable.

The Albany couch was advertised under that name by Heal & Son Ltd of London (the firm is still well known today) in the 1870s and it was an early Victorian form of day bed. It was included in J. C. Loudon's *Encyclopaedia* of 1846.

Bergère chairs and settees originated in France and were large chairs or settees with low seats, loose cushions, upholstered backs and the space under the arms filled and upholstered. When made in the form

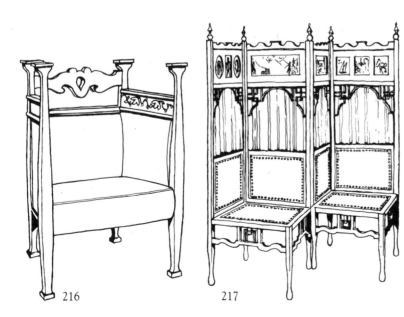

FIG 216: an Art Nouveau style of chair bordering on the Quaint style; the small block feet and capped uprights are motifs often used by C. F. A. Voysey. c1900.

Fig 217: screen settee in the Quaint style. It could be used with the screen in two positions, either to form a settee with a screen at each end, or to form two corner seats side by side (as shown). c1895.

216   217

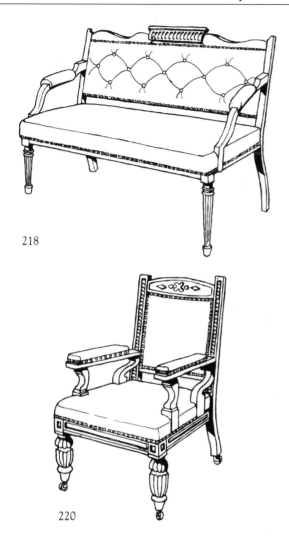

218

219

220

FIG 218: an open armed mahogany settee in the Edwardian-Sheraton style, with an upholstered and buttoned back. Such Sheraton influence as there is, is provided by an inlay of boxwood and ivory in the centre of the top back rail and in the reeded legs. c1895.

FIG 219: a typical late Victorian Cosy Corner seat in the Quaint style. Some were decorated with oriental motifs and described as Moorish or Turkish. Display cabinets appear to have been compulsory. c1895.

FIG 220: an easy chair in the Victorian Vernacular style with a heavy frame which was usually in mahogany; the upholstery was either leather or, in cheaper models, leathercloth or American cloth. c1890.

of a two-seater settee, it was called a *marquise*, a *confidant* or a *tête-à-tête*; the last name was also given to another piece of furniture in England: see fig 238. The basic requirements of an English *bergère* chair or settee was that the seat, back, and the spaces beneath the arms should all be cane work which acted as a support for loose cushions.

Chaise-longue was the French term for, literally, a chair with an elongated seat and an inclined back and arms, all of which were upholstered, and which first appeared in the late eighteenth century. By the middle of the eighteenth century the arms had disappeared and it became a reading seat or Albany couch; see fig 242.

Cosy Corners were introduced in the 1880s and continued to be popular during the 1900s. As opposed to earlier corner seats, which were fixed to or built into a wall, they were free-standing although their weight made them a virtual fixture. They were usually made in the Quaint style and were always

fitted with numerous shelves and cabinets for the display of bric-à-brac. At the time they were often regarded as the preserves of courting couples, and in at least one song of the 1900s the singer referred to his 'Cosy Corner girl'. There was a Moorish variation of the design, called a corner divan seat, which was frequently attached to the walls – like the Cosy Corner; this also became adorned with various shelves and fitments of pseudo-Moorish design.

Day beds were introduced in the sixteenth century and must have been fairly well known as Shakespeare mentions them in his plays. Our example (fig 259) shows a design with an adjustable headboard but fixed headboards were equally common: the adjustment was usually accomplished by dropping the link of a chain on to a hook, or by means of a ratchet. Our drawing is of a simple country-made piece; many day beds, however, were quite sumptuous, with gilt or painted decoration and luxurious upholstery: at the other extreme, day beds of plain design and inexpen-

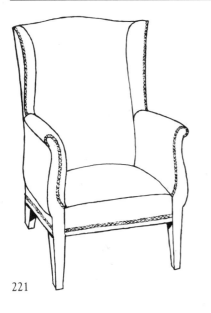

221

222

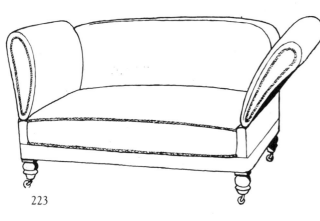

223

sive wood were often burnt with the mattresses once the latter had worn out. There seem to have been two distinct lengths – those with six legs had a length of between 1.52 and 1.67m (5ft to 5ft 6in) long; the others, with eight legs, were nearly 2m long (about 6ft 6in).

'French chair' was the term used by chair makers of the mid eighteenth century to describe an elbow chair (that is, a chair with open arms that do not extend the full depth of the seat) with an upholstered back, seat, and pads on the arms. Today, they are sometimes called Gainsborough chairs, presumably because he included them in his paintings.

Ladies' chairs were low chairs without arms and with the seat and back formed in one continuous curve. The absence of arms allowed ladies wearing voluminous skirts to sit down without creasing them. The design had several alternative names such as: Spanish, fancy sewing, tea, and tatting chair – tatting was a kind of fancy knotted lace work. Ladies' easy chairs were slightly different; although they had low seats, they had small, vestigial arms, and were known as Pompadour or Prince of Wales' chairs.

Sleepy Hollow chairs are, of course, named after Washington Irving's story, *The Legend of Sleepy Hollow*, and in the USA were as illustrated in fig 246. They had the alternative name of gondola chairs.

FIG 221: a late Victorian easy chair with vestigial saddle-cheek wings. It is a good reproduction piece in the Sheraton style, although a similar design is in Heppelwhite's *Guide*, 1788. Original chairs c1790; this repro piece is c1890.

FIG 222: an open-arm easy chair made in mahogany by Morris & Co. It was designed by George Jack, who had originally trained as an architect, for Philip Webb. The design was known as the Savile, and was usually upholstered in a William Morris chintz. c1890.

FIG 223: a Chesterfield style settee with drop-ends. Similar designs are still being produced today. See also fig 232. c1880.

FIG 224: Victorian version of what is called today a hammock chair – the contemporary 1880s name was Spanish chair. Classed as a lady's chair it had no arms and could equally well have qualified as a nursing chair. c1880.

FIG 225: lady's easy chair, sometimes called a Prince of Wales' chair owing to the pattern of fluting and buttoning in the back; or a Pompadour chair. c1880.

FIG 226: a divan easy chair characterised by its high back, rollover arms, and the long seat that extends well beyond the arms, and which has a bow front. c1880.

FIG 227: mahogany club chair; the back and seat are deeply sprung and buttoned, and the upholstered arm pads are extra wide and also buttoned. Almost always upholstered in leather. c1880.

224

228

FIG 228: a typical *chaise-longue*, which was popular from 1870 onwards. Upholstered in leathercloth, the frame was probably beech or birch stained to match the show-wood – in this case, mahogany. c1870 to 1910.

FIG 229: easy chair in mahogany in the Victorian Vernacular style – ornate and ponderous with a heavily built frame and massive legs. The turned spindles filling in under the arms were a common feature. Upholstered in leather, with a buttoned back and a tight seat. c1870.

FIG 230: an easy chair with an adjustable back, commonly known as the Morris chair, and made in ebonised wood. The design was adapted from a traditional Sussex chair, although it also bears a resemblance to the chair shown in fig 247. c1866.

225

226

229

227

230

Screen-settees made their appearance in the 1890s and were, indeed, folding screens with seats attached and decorated in the Quaint style of the time. The *Cabinet Maker and Art Furnisher* magazine in July 1896 wrote: 'It is intended that the whole structure shall be about the height of an ordinary four-fold screen, which article it resembles in general outline. It is, indeed, designed for service in the dual capacity of screen and settee, and takes the form of two corner seats, hinged together, and available for use under varied conditions.'

The Turkish style was popular in the middle years of the nineteenth century but was mainly confined to men's smoking rooms, which were often called Divans. As the best tobacco came from Turkey, enterprising shop owners opened these Divans or Cigariums, which were often decorated in the Turkish style.

The ottoman was also popular (although not illustrated) and consisted of a low, long seat with or without a back upon which several persons could sit with extra cushions to provide comfort.

Wing easy chairs were introduced in the second half of the seventeenth century, and were known as easies, sleeping, cheeked, or saddle-cheeked; at the end of the nineteenth century they were sometimes called grandfather chairs.

Up to the nineteenth century, upholsterers were often referred to as upholders; actually, upholders supplied everything for house furnishing including furniture, carpets, curtains, etc, and some were undertakers as well.

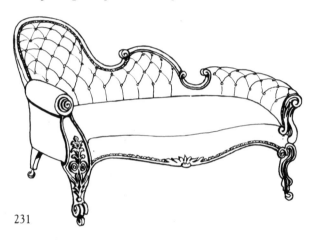

231

232

FIG 231: settee in the Victorian French Rococo style; the frame is in lavishly carved walnut. c1860.

FIG 232: a true Chesterfield settee identified by its large size, having two roll-over arms, deep stuffed upholstery, a tight seat (no loose cushions) and a back which is the same height as the arms. Usually, but not invariably, the upholstery is buttoned. Whether the name derives from the town or one of the Earls of Chesterfield is not known. See also fig 223. c1860.

FIG 233: an easy chair with an extra-deep seat and bolster arms, and with a deep fringe hiding the legs – the contemporary name was Turkey or Turkish chair. The upholstery cover was often velvet with a panel of oriental style carpet in the back. c1860.

FIG 234: a couch in the Victorian French Rococo style with buttoned head and arm rests. The frame is in walnut and incorporates the long sweeping curves of the Rococo style which appeared in France about 1730. The curves were eagerly adopted by the Victorians, to whom they represented opulence and a vicarious sensuality. Indeed, such couches are sometimes called Love seats in the USA as well as in Britain: however, the true English version is shown in fig 256. c1850 to 1890.

FIG 235: spoon-back armchair in the Victorian Rococo style. The best examples were in mahogany or rosewood but, as with many other popular designs, beech or birch stained to a mahogany or rosewood colour was used for cheaper models. c1850 to 1880.

FIG 236: fully upholstered (called stuffover in the trade) *chaise-longue*, no wood being visible. c1850.

FIG 237: a smoking room chair in mahogany with buttoned leather upholstery. Some examples have a pull-out drawer housing a spittoon under the seat. c1850 to 1880.

FIG 238: an *Indiscret* or conversation sofa, which originated at the court of Napoleon III (1848 onwards); an even more complicated example was shown at the Great Exhibition of 1851. Also called a *tête-à-tête* or sociable. 1850.

FIG 239: lady's spoon-back chair in a restrained Victorian Rococo style; such chairs were often supplied en suite with larger matching armchairs. c1850.

FIG 240: an Oxford easy chair with a high back and a long seat that projects beyond the open arms, which are fully padded. The back is padded and has what is called in the trade a roll-top. c1850.

233

234

235

236

238

237

239

240

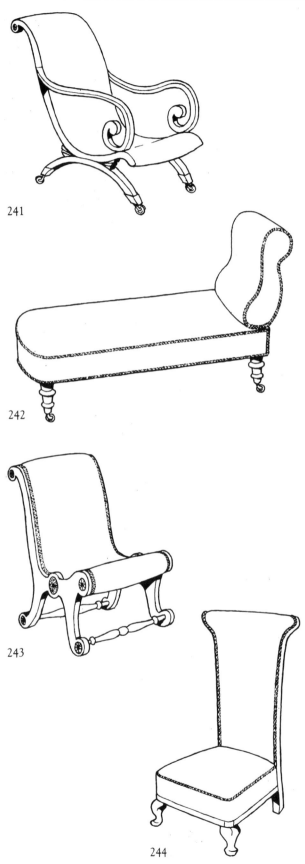

241

242

243

244

FIG 241: a reclining easy chair from J. C. Loudon's *Encyclopaedia*. With open scrolled arms, and the seat and back made in an uninterrupted curve. In profile, the design vaguely resembles an X-chair. This is sometimes (incorrectly) called a Sleepy Hollow chair – the British version is shown in fig 246. c1845.

FIG 242: reading seat, known as an Albany couch. J. C. Loudon included a similar design in the supplement to his *Encyclopaedia*, 1846. c1840 to 1880.

FIG 243: a chair design that became fashionable in the Regency period and continued to be so until the 1880s; the one illustrated was japanned black with gilt wire inlays and gilt paterae. This type of arm-less chair with the seat and back made in a continuous curve was known at the time as a Lady's chair, subsequently they were called tatting, fancy sewing, or tea chairs. c1840 to 1880.

FIG 244: a *prie-Dieu* chair (also called a kneeling, praying, or devotional chair). The characteristics were a low seat and a high back with a wide upholstered arm-pad at the top. The chairs were a boon to ladies wearing crinolines as they could kneel down comfortably without crushing their dresses. c1840 to 1870.

FIG 245: lounge or lounging chair with loose seat and back cushions and padded arm rests. The bobbin turnings are characteristic. c1840 to 1860.

FIG 246: described by the manufacturers, William Smee & Sons, as a Superior Lounge chair, this is the British version of the American Sleepy Hollow chair. With buttoned upholstery (the seat cushion is loose), and walnut show-wood. c1840.

FIG 247: one of the earliest club chairs. It retains the influences of the Regency style in the carved arms, the scrolls and the feet of the front legs. The position of the arm in relation to the back was determined by a brass rod which could be inserted in one or other of the holes in the rear end of the arm. The upholstery was stuffed, not sprung, and the design first appeared in a book called *The Modern Style of Cabinet Work*, 1832.

FIG 248: *chaise-longue* in the Gothic Revival style, made in oak. Although the carved ornament seems extravagant, it was outshone by the excesses of the same style a few years later. c1828.

FIG 249: Regency style mahogany settee with scrolled head and foot; the sabre legs are fitted with brass paw castors; the decoration consists of brass mounts. c1810.

FIG 250: sofa with scrolled ends in the Regency style; the sabre legs are fitted with brass paw castors. The frame is painted white, with brass paterae on the volutes of the scrolls; the upholstery cover is damask, and two bolsters accompany the loose cushion. c1810.

FIG 251: saddle-cheek easy chair similar to a design in Hepplewhite's *Guide*, 1788. The name, of course, derives from the shape of the wings, which resemble saddles. Later examples towards the end of the century tended to have no underframing, and the backs were sometimes fluted. c1780.

245

246

247

249

248

250

251

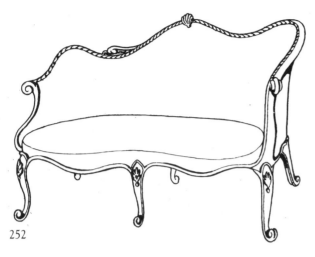

FIG 252: mahogany settee in the French style favoured by Thomas Chippendale, and Ince and Mayhew. The frame is carved with gadrooning, and the cabriole legs end in volutes. c1760.

FIG 253: a *bergère* armchair in mahogany, with caned seats, backs, and arms. They were also called birjair, burjair or (in the 20th century chair trade), berjers; the original designs were French upholstered armchairs. They were fitted with a loose stuffed seat cushion, and often with one for the back as well. It was a remarkably long lived design as the first ones were introduced in the mid 18th century, were revived in the 1890s and 1900s, and again in the 1930s. c1750.

FIG 254: a simple design of French chair in the Chippendale style. He illustrated several more ornate examples in his *Director* which were to be upholstered in leather and damask. This example has flutes worked on the arm stumps and the front legs, and a serpentine-shaped front to the seat; it is sometimes referred to as a Gainsborough chair today. c1750.

252

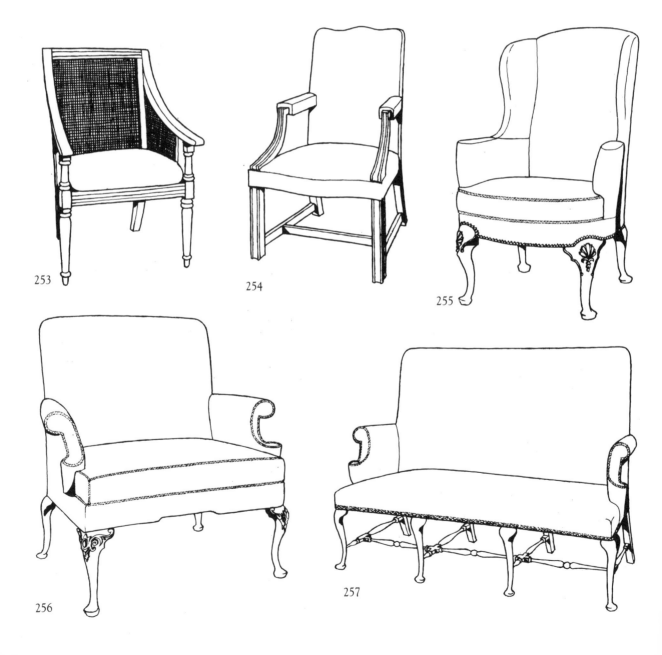

253

254

255

256

257

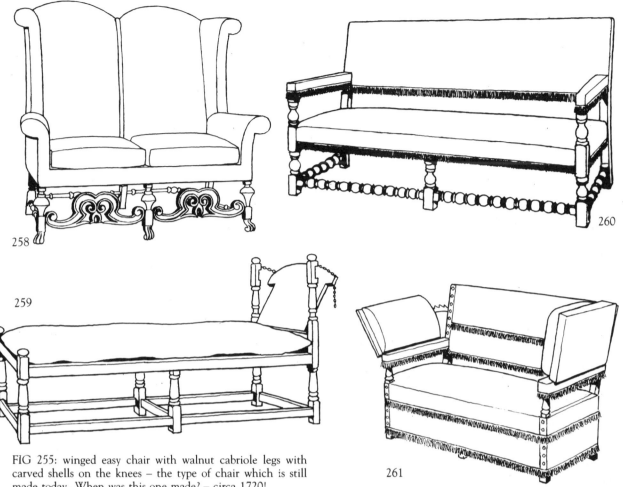

258

259

260

261

FIG 255: winged easy chair with walnut cabriole legs with carved shells on the knees – the type of chair which is still made today. When was this one made? – circa 1720!

FIG 256: a typical Love seat in walnut, with cabriole legs and curved scroll arms. Although the chair is intended to seat two, there is no underframe and only four legs – distinguishing characteristics of the true love seat. Sometimes called a courting chair, both names being contemporary. c1715.

FIG 257: walnut settee with a straight back and double scroll arms; the cabriole legs are joined by turned stretchers. As is common with 16th and 17th century pieces, the upholstery cover is needlework. c1710.

FIG 258: settee in walnut with S-scroll stretchers at the front, the remainder being turned; the faceted legs have Braganza feet. The piece has two features that were introduced around the end of the 17th century; namely, the division of the back, and the addition of wings. c1690.

FIG 259: an oak day bed with turned baluster legs. The headboard can be adjusted to a comfortable angle by means of the chains: the seat boards are sunk to take a squab mattress or palliasse. c1680.

FIG 260: walnut settee with velvet upholstery, trimmed with fringes. The stretchers are ball and ring turning, while the legs and arm stumps are turned balusters. c1660.

FIG 261: an early 17th century sofa with adjustable drop-ends, the movement of which was controlled by a metal ratchet in the case of the Knole Park design illustrated – others had a twisted silk cord that fulfilled the same function when twisted round a knob projecting from the end. The upholstery filling was composed of down or feathers, and the covers were often luxurious damasks or velvets. c1600.

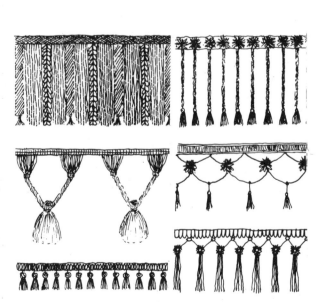

FIG 262: Fringes were frequently employed to trim the edges of upholstered furniture until the beginning of the 18th century, and their styles form a fascinating study on their own.

CHAPTER 10

Windsor chairs

The Windsor chair is one of the most popular of all chair designs. The illustrations cover the very wide range of designs, and the historical notes trace the way in which the primitive designs have developed into the chairs that are appreciated today much as ever they were.

HISTORY AND CONSTRUCTIONAL DETAILS

A Windsor chair is one in which the back legs (called back upstands) do not continue from the floor to the top in one piece but are separated by the seat. Thus there are two component structures; (a) the arm and back framing; and (b) the stool, which comprises the seat, legs, and stretchers. Usually the seat is solid and bottomed out with an adze to form a saddle seat, and this is almost always made of elm with the grain running from front to back. With very wide seats, however, the grain sometimes ran from side to side, which made adzing more difficult but reduced the likelihood of the wood splitting. The legs and stretchers made by the bodgers (see below) were always turned from triangular shaped billets, (usually of beech), which had been cleft with a hatchet and not sawn as in the factory-made chairs from about 1850 onwards. The cleavage always went with the grain and so, in a cleft leg or stretcher, you can always trace the grain along its full length. A saw, however, cut through the wood indiscriminately and the pattern would run out of the timber: fig 288 shows two examples side by side.

The bodgers were wood turners who supplied the turned parts for the chairs; the actual assembly of the chairs took place in the factories in and around High Wycombe in Buckinghamshire. The bodgers built themselves brushwood shelters (which they called hovels) in the Chiltern beech woods, and lived and worked there. They either felled suitable beech trees themselves or bought them ready-felled. The logs were then riven or cleft as already described, and the billets were dressed with a side axe ready for turning; this operation was carried out on a primitive pole lathe. The last bodger retired during the 1930s, and some people in the area still remember them. The Chair Museum at High Wycombe contains many relics of their life and work styles and is well worth a visit if you are interested in the subject.

Elm is a notoriously difficult timber both to season and to work but it is one of the only trees that gives planks wide enough for the seats to be cut in one piece. There are, of course, exceptions where the maker has had a suitable piece of another timber, but they are not usual. The alternative method of treating the seat was to use rush work as the William Morris Sussex chairs. Some of the later (early twentieth-century) versions of the captain's chair had plywood seats, perforated with a pattern of holes. American Windsors usually have plank seats which are cut from one piece of wood but have little or no bottoming, and have the front edge rounded off.

263

FIG 263: farmhouse or Wycombe lath-back Windsor arm chair. The arms are heavy with scrolled ends; the seat is almost square; the double-H underframing has swelled side stretchers with the cross stretchers entering the thickest parts of the swell; the legs have tulip feet and are baluster turned. The comb, or top, to the chair back is called a pear top. c1890.

264

265

266

267

268

269

FIG 264: officers' mess chair. The left arm was deliberately omitted to accommodate the scabbard of an officer's dress sword so that he could stand up to drink a toast without the sword becoming jammed in the chair. c1890.

FIG 265: Roman spindle Windsor small chair, so called because of the ornamental turned spindles in the back; it has a pear top similar to fig 263. The three turned rings in the leg usually denote that it was made in High Wycombe where the style was adopted about 1880. c1890.

FIG 266: captain's chair. Originally an American design and supposedly based on those used by the captains of Mississippi steam boats. Note the metal rods tying the seat to the double box underframing. English versions often had a serpentine front to the seat. c1870.

FIG 267: a William Morris Sussex chair, designed by Philip

Webb, co-founder of Morris's firm and said to be based on a chair design found in the county. The extension of the arm stump into the underframing, and the robust double box underframing are features of these chairs (see also fig 268). Made with a rushed seat. Originally these chairs were stained a dark green to a colour originated by Ford Madox Brown (the artist). The chairs were marketed by Morris, Marshall, Faulkner & Co, established in 1861, which eventually became Morris & Co. c1865 to 1895.

FIG 268: another Morris chair, again with the extended arm stump. c1865 to 1895.

FIG 269: Windsor smoker's chair. The bow, which is sometimes called the yoke, is deeply curved and has a tablet with scrolled ends set centrally on it. This feature appears to derive from similar tablets on 18th century corner and writing chairs. c1850.

How the chairs came to be known as Windsors is a mystery. The popular story is that George III noticed some of the chairs while sheltering from a storm in a cottage near Windsor and ordered some for his own use, hence the name; however, he was not born until 1738 and the name has been traced back to 1724. Probably the chairs were made in the neighbourhood of Windsor and were sent to London by river; it seems feasible that Londoners would call them Windsors.

From a letter dated 1724 we find that Lady Percival was carried around the grounds of Hall Barn in Beaconsfield, Bucks, in a Windsor chair like those at Versailles. During the eighteenth century they were regarded as suitable for outdoor garden chairs, for which purpose they were painted, usually dark green; they are still used in this way at West Wycombe House, Bucks. At the same time, they were also introduced to the great houses and in 1729 a chair maker named Henry Williams supplied some richly carved mahogany Windsor chairs to St James's Palace; Windsor chairs are nothing if not versatile!

Until about 1830 Windsor chairs were being made in several different areas of England. After that date the industry tended to be concentrated around High Wycombe in Buckinghamshire because of the large tracts of beech woods in the locality. Beech is an ideal wood for turning, being straightgrained, free from knots, and capable of being stained and polished readily, and it supplied the raw material for the legs, stretchers, and sticks – the bows were normally ash, which is noted for the ease with which it can be steam-bent. By the late 1800s the town was turning out thousands of them every year, and still continues to do so.

Many of the basic designs are still made today and it is almost impossible to differentiate between, say, a Windsor wheelback chair made in 1920 (which gives sufficient time for it to have acquired its own authentic patina and appearance of age), and one made a hundred years previously, particularly if both chairs were given the same type of finish.

There are a few points that may indicate genuine age, as follows: (a) the bows on older chairs were of a pronounced D-section and had the rounded part at the back and often a scratched groove around the flat front face of the bow; (b) the underside of the seat was adzed and not sawn and it may be possible to see or feel the adze marks; (c) the bottoming of the seats tended to be deeper and more exaggerated than those on later models which were probably machine-adzed; (d) the edges under the seat were almost always heavily bevelled; (e) some parts, such as the back legs, appeared to be turned but were, in fact, shaved with a drawknife similar to a spokeshave; (f) in older chairs, there may well be small discrepancies in the angles at which the legs or back sticks were set.

FIG 270: Windsor *bergère* bow arm chair. The seat and underframe are conventional and the chair relies for its appeal on the depth and curvature of the *bergère* bow. It was made in large numbers for use in offices. c1850 to 1870.

FIG 271: firehouse Windsor chair. An American design; the name is derived from its use in volunteer fire departments. It is lighter in construction than the one shown in fig 272 and lacks the metal tie rods. Note the vestigial tablet at the centre of the bow and the flat plank seat (no bottoming) with a rolled-over front edge. c1850 to 1870.

FIG 272: another firehouse Windsor chair, but of stronger construction than fig 271. The bow or yoke is very similar to the smoker's bow and there is a curved tablet back mounted on four small spindles. Note the metal tie rods, the box underframing, and the flat plank seat. c1850 to 1870.

FIG 273: Windsor scroll back Gothic chair. The back upstands have plain scrolls on the upper ends and the back is arcaded with turned baluster spindles – a feature earning the description Gothic. c1850 to 1914.

FIG 274: Swiss-style Windsor armchair. Apart from the fact that twisted canes replaced the usual laths, this was a conventional design and one which used the motif in several ways to create different models. c1845 to 1860.

FIG 275: scroll-back Windsor chair with spirally turned back stay. The back upstands end in scrolls; the back stay is slightly curved, which means that four centres were needed to turn the spiral in the lathe. It is supposed to represent a rope and is therefore a nautical emblem that commemorates the death of Nelson. Similar features are found on some Regency chairs. c1845 to 1860.

FIG 276: Mendlesham chair. So called after the Suffolk village where Daniel Day (the local wheelwright) and his son made them. An elegant chair with echoes of the Regency style in the splat and the splayed spindles flanking it. In the example shown these spindles are turned to a double arrowhead pattern found on earlier chairs in the 18th century: the turned balls and curved stay are identifying characteristics – indeed, the inclusion of turned balls seems to be a custom in chairs from the eastern counties. Mendlesham chairs were made either in yew or a fruitwood (apple, cherry, or pear) and had elm seats. c1820.

FIG 277: wheelback Windsor chair. The wheel motif dates back to about 1780, but the chairs were not made in any quantity until about 1820 and are still made today. Early specimens had a D-section bow with the flat facing forwards; the seat was heavily bottomed and its edge was bevelled to make it appear thinner. Note the form of the centre stretcher where the sharpness of the earlier arrowhead motif was gradually being smoothed away so that it eventually became a swell. These chairs were also made with two bracing sticks (see fig 278) which entered a tail on the seat – hence the expression 'tail-seat Windsor'.

270

271

272

273

274

275

276

277

278

279

280

281

282

283

FIG 278: a Windsor small chair with a Prince of Wales' feathers motif cut in the splat. A very similar design to fig 277, but it has bracing sticks which enter a tail on the seat. Note that the sticks are very slightly tapered at their ends, while those on the Windsor wheelback are often parallel throughout. c1820.

FIG 279: balloon-back Windsor arm chair. The comb is narrower than the seat and so forces the back sticks inwards to give a balloon effect. Note the absence of underframing and also that the seat is flat without bottoming. It is low in height so that some form of cushion can be used. The shape of the comb and the curved arm stumps, which are attached at their lower ends to the foremost sticks, are unusual features. c1780.

FIG 280: Windsor shawl-back arm chair. This has a higher back than normal, and the comb is deepsawn from a block of wood instead of being steam-bent. It was designed so that a shawl or something similar could be thrown over it to prevent draughts. c1770 to 1790.

FIG 281: Windsor arm chair with elm seat, the remainder in yew and ash. With cabriole front legs and a crinoline (also called a cow-horn) centre stretcher.

FIG 282: Gothic Windsor arm chair with the back shaped as a lancet arch. The splats are pierced with Gothic motifs; the seat shape is re-entrant, which means that there is a pronounced inward curve behind the front legs. The cabriole legs have pierced ear blocks and a low relief carved strapping on the knees; the turned reel on the toes is unusual. Note the crinoline stretcher – always a good sales point. c1760 to 1770.

FIG 283: another Gothic Windsor arm chair with plain splat and arm bow. Note the arrowhead turning on the stretchers, and how the legs are left full at the joints with the stretcher rails; also the cow-horn stretcher. c1760.

284

285

286

287

FIG 284: a Windsor comb-back arm chair with Cupid's bow comb. Note the perfectly plain back splat, sticks, and arm bow; the seat is bottomed out but not shaped as a saddle. The arrowhead style of turning is here shown clearly on the underframe. c1760.

FIG 285: a comb-back Goldsmith Windsor arm chair. So called because a similar chair was bequeathed by Oliver Goldsmith (the playwright) to a friend in 1774; the original is now in the V & A Museum. This design has a shield-shaped seat with a tail and bracing sticks, and the arm bow is all in one piece, unlike some copies where it is in three parts. These copies usually have the conventional shape of seat, and the arms do not reach so far forward as in the original. In common with many other Windsors of the period, this one was painted black. Note the crisp shaping of the scrolled ears on the comb and also the slight fanning of the sticks in the back. c1750.

FIG 286: an elegant comb-back Windsor arm chair with the classical fiddle-shaped splat, and carved scrolled ears at the ends of the comb. Both the front and back legs are cabriole, the front ones having carved shells on the knees and a raised edging carved on the ear blocks. Unless designed and made carefully the cabriole legs at the back could give the whole chair an ungainly appearance: this piece avoids it, which is more than can be said for some examples. c1750.

FIG 287: a Windsor style library chair in mahogany. It has several interesting features such as: (a) the baluster spindles in the back; (b) the carved and curved tablet at the centre of the arm bow; (c) the finely carved acanthus leaf motifs on the cabriole front legs. Obviously this was one of the ancestors of the smoker's bow (fig 269). c1730.

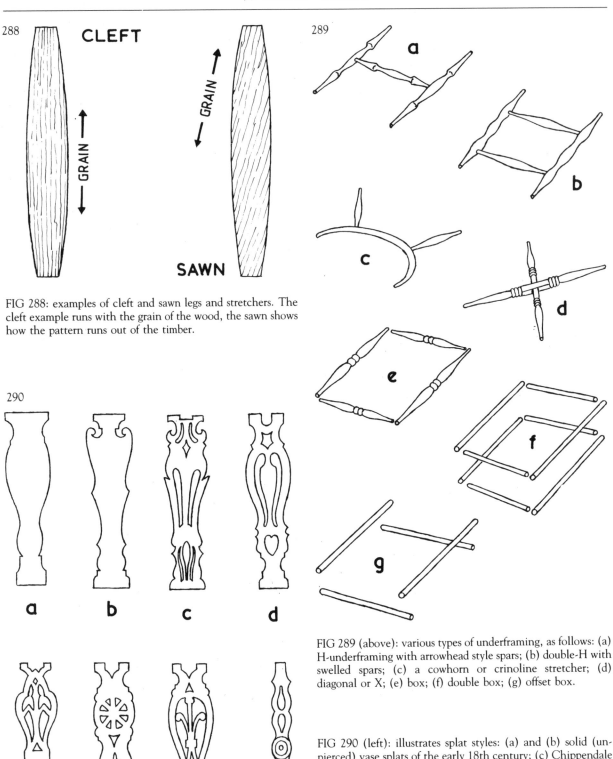

FIG 288: examples of cleft and sawn legs and stretchers. The cleft example runs with the grain of the wood, the sawn shows how the pattern runs out of the timber.

FIG 289 (above): various types of underframing, as follows: (a) H-underframing with arrowhead style spars; (b) double-H with swelled spars; (c) a cowhorn or crinoline stretcher; (d) diagonal or X; (e) box; (f) double box; (g) offset box.

FIG 290 (left): illustrates splat styles: (a) and (b) solid (unpierced) vase splats of the early 18th century; (c) Chippendale style splat, c1770; (d) vase or urn-shaped splat in the classical style, c1770 to 1820; (e) typical Gothic splat, 1750 to 1770; (f) wheelback splat, from about 1800 to 1820 until the present day; (g) Prince of Wales' feathers splat from about 1790 to 1830, which is approximately the Regency period; (h) patera, disc, or blind wheel splat – there were usually three per chair. Blind in trade parlance means not pierced right through. From 1820 to 1830.

CHAPTER 11

Benches

Stools, settles, and benches were some of the earliest kinds of furniture and have a nostalgic charm of their own. William Morris and his followers in particular, with their love for all things medieval, created some romantically sumptuous designs of settles. Even today the original designs are copied more or less faithfully for modern reproductions, and there is no sign of their popularity decreasing.

In early times the terms 'bench' and 'settle' were interchangeable, but by the beginning of the seventeeth century the description 'settle' was reserved for a bench with a back and arms, but not necessarily having a locker under the seat: the latter is more correctly called a box-seat settle. The two kinds probably had different origins, the box-seat settle evolving from the use of a chest placed against a wall as a seat, the other type being a natural refinement of the ordinary bench.

Early Elizabethan and Jacobean settles were made to be moved – after being used as seating at the dining table, a settle would often be moved to a place near the fire and at right angles to the wall, thus creating a cosy and (hopefully) draught-free corner. In some parts of the country, mainly in Wales and the northern counties, settles were actually built into the walls as fixtures but such specimens are comparatively rare. The much sought after bacon-settle had a tall cupboard acting as a back, with a door through which one could get at the bacon, hams, and other victuals stored there.

Fig 291: a bacon-settle in oak; so called because the back is a tall, shallow cupboard in which bacon and hams were hung. The seat contains four drawers (although two is more common) and there are no legs – in most designs the stiles of the cupboard and the back posts are extended to act as feet, or have sledge feet attached to them as in fig 292. Such pieces were widely used in Wales. c1800.

FIG 292: an elm bacon-settle; an imposing example from Wales, made in elm. As these pieces were almost always country-made, readily available timbers such as home-grown ash, elm, oak, or pine were used. Note the sledge feet. c1800.

BACON-SETTLES

291

292

Settle-tables were designs in which the top swung over to rest on the arms and thus formed a table; these are often called monk's benches or monk's seats. It is highly unlikely that they were ever used by monks as by 1540 Henry VIII had closed most of the monasteries, and settle-tables generally belong to a later period.

Stools have a long history, having been used as seating since time immemorial. Chairs were reserved for the highest ranks of royalty and nobility and the 'other ranks' sat on stools or benches. This led to the *tabouret* etiquette, which was strictly observed from the time of Charles II until well into the 1700s, and determined what kind of stool was suited to a person's rank, and where he or she should sit in the hall. Generally speaking, stool designs matched those of the accompanying chairs, but in the first half of the eighteenth century they began to be made as pieces in their own right according to the prevailing fashion, rather than as merely adjuncts to the chairs.

Different types of stool have several names. The joint stool, also called joined or joyned, is often known today as a coffin stool – the name probably being derived from Pepys' mention in his *Diary* (1661) of his uncle's coffin standing on joynt-stools. Window stools of the kind shown in fig 307 have always been popular, as have foot stools, although none have been illustrated as they are almost always smaller versions of a larger stool.

Banquette was the name sometimes given in the early eighteenth century to what is generally known as a double stool.

By Elizabeth I's reign stools were widely used, and Sir John Harington (mentioned elsewhere) wrote in 1596 that every merchant's hall contained 'easy quilted and lined forms and stools'. Apparently Elizabeth did not encourage such soft luxury on the stools at court, as he complained that, 'since great breeches were laid aside, men can scant endure to sit on them.'

BENCH

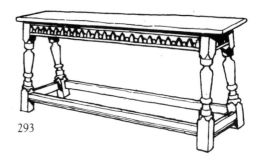

293

CHAIR-TABLES

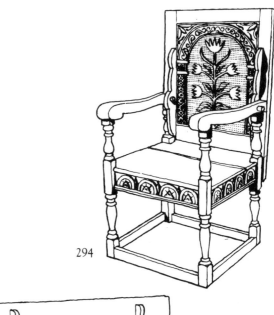

294

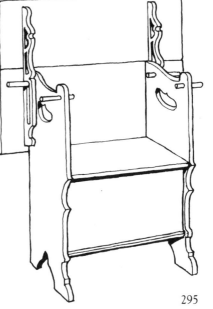

FIG 293: an oak joined bench with splayed legs, which have vase-shaped turning. c1650.

FIG 294: oak chair-table with a beautifully carved back, and baluster turnings. The back pivots on pegs and swings over to rest on the arms. c1650.

FIG 295: oak chair-table with shaped ends and pierced rails on the underside of the top. The top itself is pivoted on pegs at the back and, when swung over to rest on the arms, is secured by two more pegs at the front. c1550.

295

SETTLES

FIG 296: a hall seat in oak in the Quaint style; based on a design made up by the Shoreditch Technical Institute. c1905.

FIG 297: an oak settle, or hall seat, in the restrained English Art Nouveau genre. The top back rail, the back panel, and the panels on the front all contain *repoussé* copper ornament. The ubiquitous heart-shaped piercings in the back splats and the stylised tulip motif are characteristic. There is a hinged, lift-up panel in the seat. c1900.

FIG 298: a coved settle designed by Philip Webb with a wealth of painted decoration. Made by Morris & Co. c1890.

FIG 299: a plain utilitarian box-seat settle in oak with a lift-up panel in the seat. About as typical a piece of sturdy country-made furniture as one can find. c1750.

FIG 300: bench settle in mahogany with cabriole front legs – a country design which was popular over a long period. c1760 to 1810.

296

298

297

299

300

SETTLE-TABLE

301

STOOLS

302

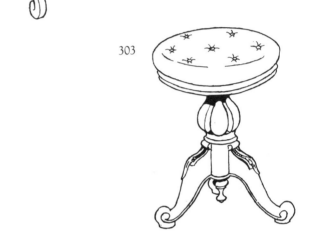

303

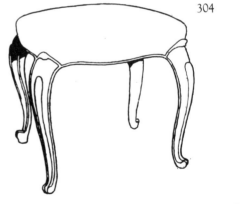

304

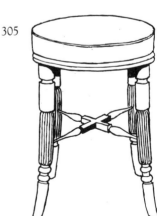

305

FIG 301: a settle-table in oak with the rails carved in characteristic lunette patterns; there is a locker under the seat, and the top swings over to rest on the arms. The piece is supported on sledge feet. c1625.

FIG 302: rosewood stool with vaguely Rococo scrolls; covered with woolwork. c1880.

FIG 303: the Victorian piano stool, which older readers will recognise as an old friend. Again, French influence is evident in the shape of the legs: the top revolves and rises, of course. c1850 to 1880.

FIG 304: a walnut stool, the design of which has obviously been based on contemporary French chairs. The seat is upholstered in plush (a coarser type of velvet made from mohair) with a gimp border. c1850.

FIG 305: music stool in mahogany. The turned and reeded legs splay outwards at the bottom – a typically Regency motif. c1835.

FIG 306: a painted X-frame stool, probably made in beech. The leopards' head are gilt; the feet are (presumably) also leopards', and the whole piece is typical of the Egyptian style fashionable at the time. c1800.

FIG 307: window stool in mahogany and upholstered in leather. The seat rail is fluted and there is a double-H underframing. c1760.

FIG 308: walnut stool on hocked cabriole legs with pad feet. Made at the end of the Walnut period, which dated from about 1660 to 1735. c1730.

FIG 309: mahogany saddle stool with three legs that end in ball feet; turned stretchers. This one was formerly at the Red Lion Inn, Colchester. c1735.

FIG 310: oval stool in walnut with cabriole legs; shells carved on the hipped knees, claw and ball feet. It has a loose drop-in seat. c1720.

FIG 311: walnut *banquette* or double stool with serpentine stretchers and faceted turning on the legs, and scrolled feet. c1700.

FIG 312: walnut stool with carved S-scrolls between the legs, which are themselves reverse-scrolled. Obviously a Restoration design. c1690.

FIG 313: an oak joint (or joyned) stool. The top has a pierced finger-hole so that it can be picked up easily, and the legs are slightly splayed – true to the style of the period. c1680.

FIG 314: oak joint stool with the seat rails carved with strapwork, and the legs turned and fluted. c1620.

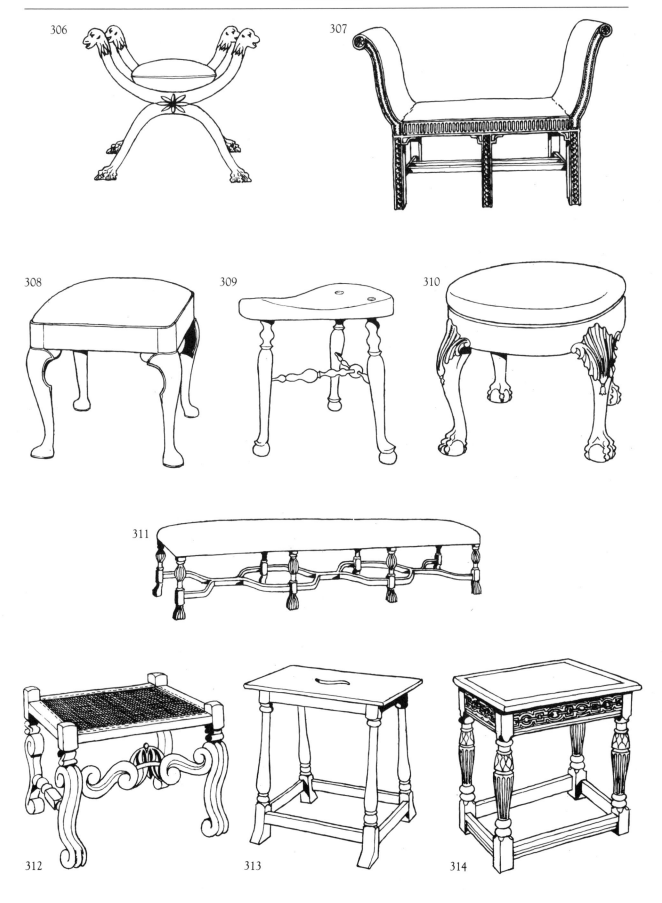

306

307

308

309

310

311

312

313

314

CHAPTER 12

Bookcases

The eighteenth and nineteenth centuries were remarkable for the number of special purpose designs that were introduced and developed. Here you will find examples of bookcases, bureaux, bureau-bookcases, davenports, desks, secretaires, and writing desks. The terms bureau and bureau-bookcase include several variations on the theme of providing a piece of furniture that could be used both for writing and storing documents and articles of value. For clarity, the following are the names of the various designs:

BUREAU

A cabinet fitted with interior drawers and/or pigeon holes; it can be either supported on a stand, as in the case of pieces from 1690 to 1720; or in later examples, it is the upper stage on a set of drawers.

The first designs from 1690 to 1700 frequently had the bureau section overlapping the stand (see fig 321) but from the latter date onwards the bureau part was invariably flush with, or slightly set in from, the lower stage.

The fall front of a bureau is always sloped at an angle (unlike a secretaire), and when open the front can be supported in one of three ways, namely: on lopers; on the partly open top drawer (see fig 145); or on gate-legs as in fig 323.

Instead of a fall front, the bureau section can be enclosed either by a cylinder top, or a roll-top (figs 326 and 327 respectively). The cylinder top consists of a curved front having the profile of a quadrant and this is attached to a metal movement so that the front can swing up or down. The roll-top is formed of tambours, which are thin strips of wood glued to a canvas backing: the opposite ends of each strip are relieved so that they can run in grooves cut in the ends of the carcase. Further, the edges of the strips are profiled so that each slides under its fellow as it follows the curve, thus hiding the backing.

During the eighteenth century the word bureau was commonly spelt buro or buroe. Incidentally, in the USA a bureau is a kind of dressing table and a piece of bedroom furniture – what we call a bureau, Americans describe as a secretary.

DAVENPORT

See figs 326 and 327, where the design is described more fully.

DESKS

The precursors of all types of writing furniture, and until the late seventeenth century the most widely used. They invariably had sloping writing surfaces, and often the framework supporting this contained tills, drawers, and pigeon holes.

DESK AND BOOKCASE

An eighteenth-century term for a bureau-bookcase or a secretaire-bookcase; used by Chippendale, and Ince and Mayhew, among others.

ESCRITOIRE

Although a term generally applied to any piece of furniture designed for writing purposes, it was specifically a drawer fitted with writing accessories and a hinged front which lay flat when the drawer was opened, thus forming a writing surface. When closed the drawer resembled its fellows.

SECRETAIRE, SECRETARY

An eighteenth-century term for a writing desk. Today it refers to what would otherwise be called a bureau or bureau-bookcase except that the fall front is vertical when closed and not sloping as with a bureau. Strictly speaking, the writing and bureau section should be in the form of the escritoire described above.

SCRIPTOIRE, SCRUTOIRE

Obsolete seventeenth- and eighteenth-century terms describing any piece in which the fall front was vertical when closed, not sloping as with a bureau. Usually the fall front was disguised as a drawer as, for example, in an escritoire.

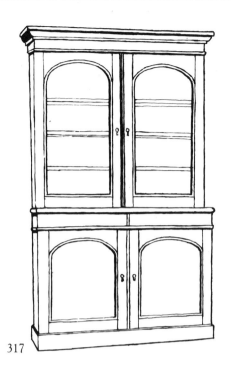

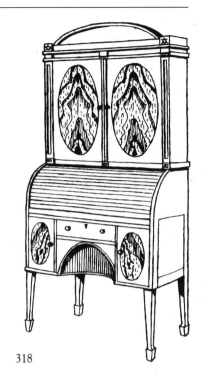

315   317   318

BOOKCASES

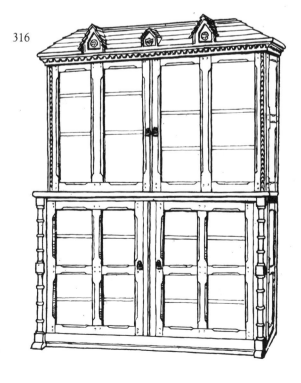

316

FIG 315: an Edwardian-Sheraton design (cf figs 145 and 147) of a bookcase in mahogany set back on a small table containing two drawers. The hump-backed pediment has a marquetry floral motif in the centre, with a vertically striped banding underneath; the drawer fronts have similar marquetry, and the drop ornaments use the husk motif common in the second half of the 18th century. The legs are the spade toe Marlborough type. c1900.

FIG 316: bookcase in the Gothic Revival style, with a gabled and simulated tile roof – a decorative feature much favoured by designers of the period, particularly William Burges, who published *Art Applied to Industry* in 1865. It is in oak, and bears many of the hallmarks of the pseudo-Gothic, namely the pegged joints, heavy chamfering, and applied turned columns. c1860.

FIG 317: a pleasant and unpretentious bookcase with cupboards in the lower section; made in mahogany. A design that was popular for many years. c1840 to 1880.

BUREAUX

FIG 318: a fine bureau cabinet in the Regency style, made in harewood (sycamore treated with sulphate of iron to give it a grey colour), with the oval panels in curl mahogany veneer. The curved fall or roll-top for the secretaire section consists of horizontal tambours, while the cupboards at the back of the kneehole are enclosed by vertical tambour doors. There is the usual arrangement of nests of drawers and pigeon holes in the bureau interior, while the upper doors enclose further drawers and shelves. c1810.

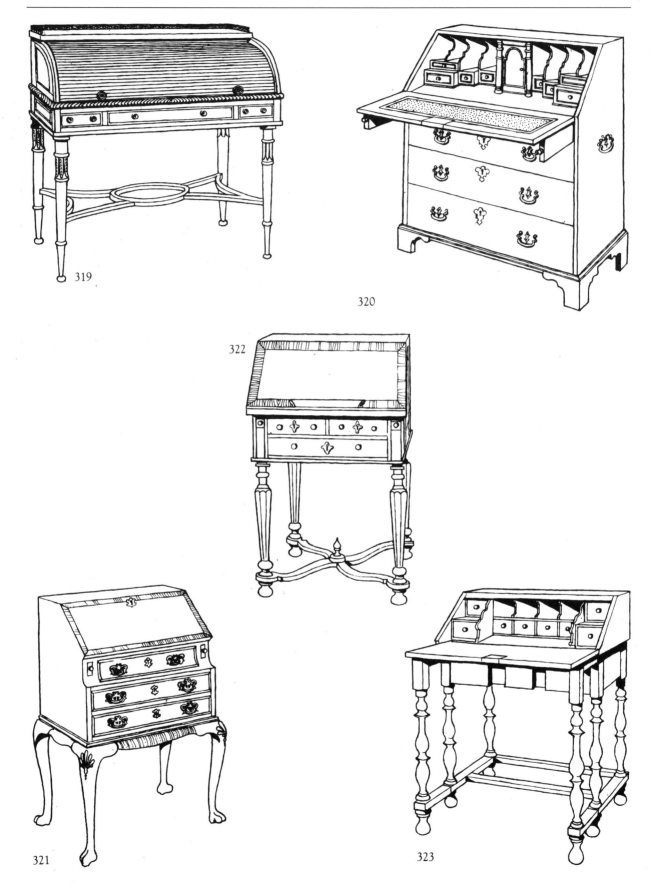

319

320

322

321

323

BUREAU-BOOKCASES AND WRITING DESKS

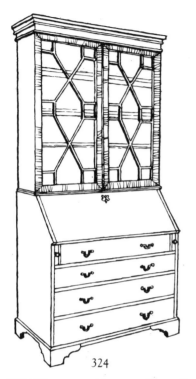

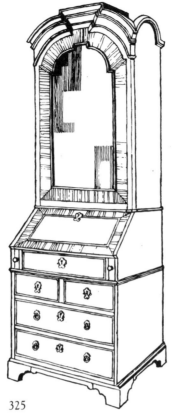

324   325   326

FIG 319: rosewood bureau with a roll-top tambour front. The gallery around the top is brass, while the embellishment on the legs is ormolu (gilt bronze), and incorporates the then fashionable anthemion motif. The whole effect is one of restrained Neo-Classicism. c1800.

FIG 320: an unpretentious but nevertheless handsome bureau in yew, with inlaid holly stringing. The central cupboard in the interior is flanked by split-turned pilasters – almost certainly these either pull out or can be manipulated in some way to disclose a secret compartment, as it was a favourite device of secret drawer enthusiasts (amongst whom, Louis XVI of France was probably the most aristocratic!). Note the carrying handles; also the lopers which support the fall. c1750.

FIG 321: a walnut-veneered bureau of Queen Anne style. Her reign was from 1702 to 1714 but her name was applied to furniture made many years after her death. It was common for 'case furniture' (that is, furniture having a carcase such as chests, wardrobes etc as opposed to chairs and tables) of the period to be veneered all over, even to the extent of covering carcase ends and shaped mouldings (where there was a real risk of the veneer lifting or being chipped). Here, the curved drawer front below the fall front is veneered, as are the carcase ends; the shaped apron between the front legs is also veneered with crossgrain, and all of these features push veneering to its limits. The carved shells on the knees and the trefoil feet are characteristic.

This particular bureau has the interior drawers and pigeon holes made in sycamore arranged in a chequered pattern. This is unusual, as most walnut or oak bureaux of the time had oak or pine interiors, and it was not until mahogany became the

favoured timber from about 1730 onwards that they were made in any other wood. c1715.

FIG 322: walnut bureau in the William & Mary style, the fall front being fitted with a book rest. The legs are faceted and are sometimes called trumpet pattern. Note the small finial at the centre of the underframe; such underframes frequently carried a similar ornament, or decorative patera. c1690.

FIG 323: an unusual oak bureau with the fall front supported by a pair of gate-legs; the legs are the turned baluster pattern with ball feet. c1690.

FIG 324: what one might call a basic late Georgian mahogany bureau-bookcase with very little decoration apart from the crossbanded veneers around the doors. c1780.

FIG 325: a small bureau-bookcase veneered in walnut, with a mirror in the door. The mirror surround is crossbanded, and the drawers are fitted with an early example of cock beading. The most notable feature is the coved top, which is returned; that is, a moulding which matches that at the front is also planted on the ends, and the whole top is boxed in. A piece of really fine cabinet making. c1700.

FIG 326: a lady's cylinder-fall writing desk in mahogany. The pull-out drawer includes a lift-up writing panel with a well underneath and a trough for pens, pencils, inks, etc. The front pillars have spiral reeding at the top and fluting at the bottom; this feature, plus the brass gallery around the top and the turned, tapered feet give the piece a definite Neo-Classical appearance. c1820.

DAVENPORTS AND SECRETAIRES

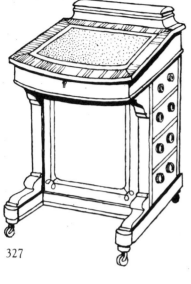

327

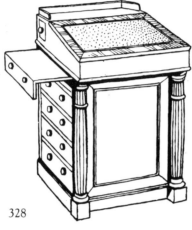

328

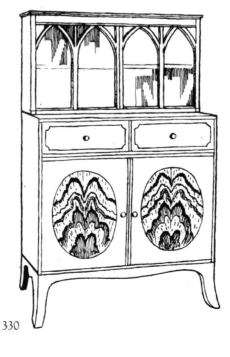

329

330

FIG 327: a davenport desk veneered in figured walnut, with a leather-lined top; four drawers on the right hand side are matched by four dummy drawers on the left hand. The top lifts to reveal a fitted interior, and the small box at the back of the top contains inkwells, etc.

Davenports were so called after a Capt Davenport who first ordered one from Gillow & Co in the late 18th century. The design always incorporates a desk-like top with a sloping lid, and the drawers are invariably set in one, or both, sides of the pedestal support and rarely in the front; often the top carries a small gallery. The Victorians were greatly taken with the design and many variations of the basic style were produced, becoming more and more florid in appearance; however, by about 1880 the design had had its day. The example shown is a comparatively plain one. c1850.

FIG 328: another davenport desk, this time taken from an illustration in J. C. Loudon's *Encyclopaedia* (1833). Incidentally, he refers to the design as a devonport. c1833.

FIG 329: a secretaire bookcase set on a plinth; with carving on the doors, the fronts of the ends, the secretaire fall front, and the centre of the swan necked broken pediment. It is in fumed oak; that is, oak which has been exposed to ammonia fumes to darken its colour. The style seems to be eclectic – that is, the manufacturers (Norman and Stacey) have chosen bits from various periods and amalgamated them into quite an acceptable design. This practice was certainly not confined to them but was, and still is, prevalent amongst furniture manufacturers. Such pieces were also made in walnut or mahogany. c1900.

FIG 330: a secretaire in satinwood with mahogany-veneered oval panels; the upper section is glazed and has the bars in the shape of lancet arches. Note the slightly splayed and curved Hepplewhite design of the feet – this motif reappeared in the 1900s although it was then more exaggerated in shape. c1790.

CHAPTER 13

Chiffoniers

What is known as 'case furniture' is the subject of this chapter – that is, furniture in which cupboards, shelves, and other forms of storage space are incorporated. Examples are: aumbries, chiffoniers, corner cupboards, court cupboards, credenzas, display cabinets, hall cupboards, livery cupboards, presses, sideboards, and wardrobes.

CABINETS

The very earliest cabinets appeared in France early in the sixteenth century and one was described in 1590 as 'a small piece of furniture more or less portable, with or without feet, sometimes placed on a buffet or chair, or a table, but always square in shape and containing many neat, small drawers.'

By the time of the Restoration (1660) the 'small piece of furniture' had become a large cabinet, enclosed by doors, and mounted on a stand (fig 340); it was the kind of design that called out for decoration and the craftsmen of the time took full advantage. Some examples were covered with seaweed or arabesque marquetry, some were lavishly carved and gilded, and others were beautifully lacquered. All contained nests of drawers and/or pigeon holes for the accommodation of trinkets, curios, or more important items such as cash or valuable documents.

In many cases the cabinet could be lifted off its stand to accompany the owner on his or her travels – the same idea was applied to some bureaux, in which the whole assembly of pigeon holes, etc, could be withdrawn completely.

331

FIG 331: a typical Edwardian-Sheraton style display cabinet, in mahogany with satinwood inlays and banding, and a broken pediment. Glass shelves in the interior. c1900.

FIG 332: mahogany side cabinet, again with satinwood inlays and bandings. The upper stage contains mirrors and carries a swan neck pediment. In a class of its own as regards style, which can only be called late Victorian – nevertheless, many similar pieces were still being sold as fashionable in the Edwardian period. c1900.

332

China cabinets with glazed doors became fashionable in the middle of the eighteenth century, when china and porcelain were being imported in enormous quantities. By the middle of the nineteenth century they had become display cabinets for showing off the vast arrays of bric-à-brac loved by the Victorians, and as such they were made in whatever new style the caprice of fashion dictated.

FIG 333: a side cabinet in mahogany with English Art Nouveau motifs; namely, the block feet, the capped uprights, the stained-glass pattern in the upper parts of the doors, and the shaped apron. c1900.

FIG 334: English Art Nouveau at its most typical; a mahogany display cabinet probably sold by Liberty's of Regent Street, London, who were well known for their patronage of avant-garde fashions. c1900.

FIG 335: a commercialised version of the Japanese art furniture style developed by William Godwin (1833 to 1886); this display cabinet is in ebonised mahogany with sycamore bandings. c1890.

FIG 336: a perfect example of a side cabinet executed in the manner of the Aesthetic Movement. The central panel of the lower section contains a mirror, and so do the three panels on the upper stage. The spindled galleries, simulated bamboo turnings on the legs, and the floral inlays are typical. It is made in ebonised baywood (Honduras mahogany). Liberty's were renowned for their encouragement of the style. c1880.

FIG 337: hanging display cabinet in mahogany, inlaid with brass; the glazing bars are brass and wood combined. c1790.

FIG 338: mahogany china cabinet with the finials and oval panels in satinwood; the door frames are crossbanded. c1790.

FIG 339: china cabinet in Cuban mahogany with a broken pediment and bracket feet – both typical of the period. The shaped door framing, on the other hand, is very uncharacteristic, being similar to the French provincial styles during the reign of Louis XV (1715 to 1774). Possibly the piece was made by a Huguenot immigrant. c1720.

FIG 340: a cabinet in figured walnut with oyster veneering on the drawer fronts; twist pillar supports which have faceted balusters below the twist sections. The interior is fitted with a multiplicity of drawers, also in walnut. c1685.

334

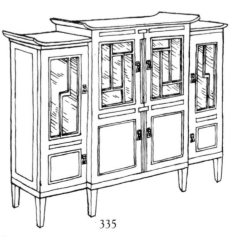

335

336

337

338

339

340

CHIFFONIERS

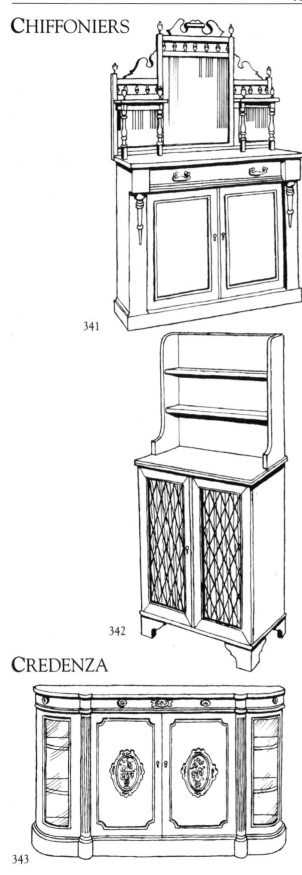

341

342

CREDENZA

343

FIG 341: a Victorian chiffonier can be regarded as archetypal. A chiffonier (or *cheffonier*) was defined in France as 'a piece of furniture with drawers in which women put away their needlework'. Chippendale refers in one of his bills to 'a neat shiffener writing table . . .', but by the early 19th century they were described as low shelved cupboards 'useful chiefly for such books as are in constant use, and not of sufficient consequence for the library.' The Victorians soon altered that, however, and by 1840 chiffoniers were being equipped as sideboards, complete with shelves and cutlery drawers – hence their inclusion in this section. Our example is c1900.

FIG 342: chiffonier in mahogany with the doors fitted with brass lattice work, backed with a pleated silk lining. They enclose a cupboard containing bookshelves. c1810.

FIG 343: a *credenza*, based on an Italian sideboard design and called a side cabinet in England. This one is in walnut with porcelain oval panels – a very popular motif from 1860 to 1880. The two end cupboards are, of course, glazed. c1860.

SIDEBOARDS

'Sideboard' was one of the names (cupboard or buffet were the others) given to a series of platforms arranged like steps upon which gold and silver plate was displayed when the owner was entertaining during the Middle Ages. The higher your status, the more platforms or tiers you were allowed; thus Henry VII had ten; the Queen of France, five; countesses, three; and so on. During Tudor times sideboards developed first into buffets and then into court cupboards and dressers; by the early eighteenth century sideboard tables appeared – these were more ostentatious than dressers and the latter were relegated to the kitchen.

From about 1730 onwards, furniture for dining purposes began to receive a lot of attention from designers, and in particular from Robert Adam (1728 to 1792). He was determined to invest dining room furniture with all the elegance and ornamentation he was capable of (and this was considerable); besides, he observed that the English were accustomed by habit, or induced by the nature of our climate, to indulge in the joys of the grape more than the French, and also to conduct business at dinner!

As a result, sideboard tables and sideboards were built to epic proportions, often consisting of a long sideboard table flanked by a pair of urn pedestals, the whole thing being decorated with classical motifs. Later in the eighteenth century, and certainly by the early nineteenth, sideboard tables became less popular, being replaced by sideboards and chiffoniers; (see fig 341).

344

345

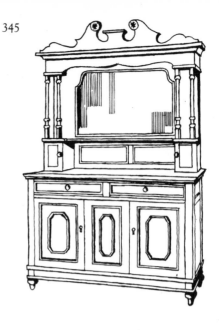

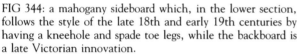

346

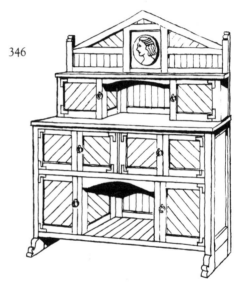

347

FIG 344: a mahogany sideboard which, in the lower section, follows the style of the late 18th and early 19th centuries by having a kneehole and spade toe legs, while the backboard is a late Victorian innovation.

The satinwood inlays are, of course, in the English Art Nouveau manner. Many Victorian sideboards, like this one, had mirrors set in the backboard, probably to provide better vision by reflecting the light. Again, this is the type of design favoured by Liberty's. c1900.

FIG 345: typical late Victorian sideboard: a hybrid of styles with possibly a vague Jacobethan look being dominant. There were hundreds of variations on the theme, all with several characteristics in common, notably the large mirror in the backboard, an imposing pediment, turned pillars flanking the mirror, and the door panels embellished with either applied mouldings or by fielding. This design is in oak, but many were made in walnut. c1900.

This is the kind of furniture that the members of the Arts and Crafts and the Aesthetic movements inveighed against; to them it was ugly, ostentatious, and representative of money-grabbing materialism. The Victorian middle classes ignored them and continued to buy it on a 'I may not be an aesthete, but I know what I like' basis, which emphasises the fact that all the Victorian and Edwardian avant-garde movements appealed to a very limited stratum of the public.

FIG 346: an oak sideboard in the Eastlake manner; the diagonally tongued and grooved panels and the L-shaped hinges are typical motifs. Note the dog kennel between the bottom cupboards. Compare this design with those in fig 416. c1870.

FIG 347: known as a chiffonier-sideboard but more correctly it should be called a sideboard: it seems that, to some collectors, any sideboard fitted with a backboard automatically qualifies as a chiffonier.

This particular model was popular from about 1840 to 1870 and was made in mahogany. The identifying characteristics are: the acanthus leaf carving on the backboard, the carved brackets (sometimes called consoles) on the corner posts, the ogee-shaped drawer fronts, and the flattened arch panels on the doors. c1840 to 1870.

FIG 348: a mahogany kneehole sideboard with satinwood stringing. The general style is Neo-Classical; the lion masks and bear paw feet are motifs often used by Thomas Hope. c1830.

FIG 349: an elegant bow-fronted sideboard in mahogany, with turned and reeded legs which have carved lotus leaves at the tops. The latter is an Egyptian motif, as is the beading, in the form of rectangles with re-entrant corners, which appears on the drawer fronts. The railing along the back of the top is in brass. c1820.

FIG 350: a mahogany sideboard with a break front. The apron is reeded, and the spade toe tapered legs have carved husk drop ornaments at their tops. c1785.

FIG 351: mahogany sideboard table, with a curved breakfront: on tapered legs with block feet; the legs carry carved husk ornaments. The frieze rail is fluted and has carved paterae in the leg squares. c1780.

FIG 352: an early sideboard table in walnut with a marble top. The legs are the most outstanding feature, as they are primitive-cabriole in shape with Spanish scroll feet; this type of foot is also called a Braganza foot, after Catherine of Braganza, the Portuguese wife of Charles II.

Note the serpentine-shaped stretchers, and also the straight turned back legs which indicate that the table was intended to stand against a wall. The marble top was not only something of a status symbol, but could easily be wiped clean if food was spilt on it. c1710.

FIG 353: a cupboard in oak, probably country-made as the decoration is rather gauche: it is unusual in that the top section is an aumbry – in other words, a compartment ventilated for food storage. c1760.

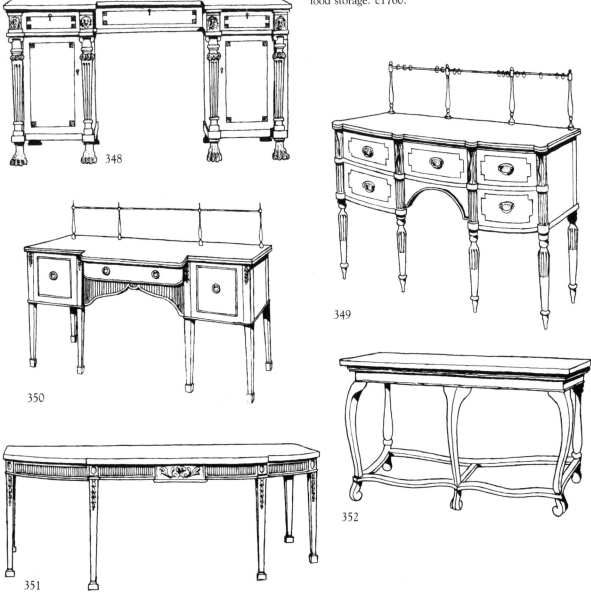

348

349

350

351

352

353

354

FIG 354: a food cupboard, or aumbry, in walnut; the doors are filled with slender baluster turnings which allow ventilation but keep out domestic pets and vermin. c1680.

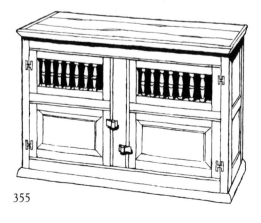

355

AUMBRIES

Aumbries (also called ambrys, almerys, or armories) were originally recesses in church, monastery, or castle walls, and were enclosed by doors. They were used for the general storage of goods such as holy relics, vestments, church ornaments, documents, clothes, and (when the doors were pierced for ventilation) for food. During the second half of the fifteenth century they had evolved into free-standing cupboards used mainly to contain food, and also into small cupboards built into larger pieces of furniture.

CORNER CUPBOARDS

Corner cupboards came into general use at the end of the seventeenth century, when they were usually the hanging type and employed to house china and porcelain. By the middle of the next century standing corner cupboards became popular. In addition to the freestanding examples of these, many were built into wall panelling and were finished to match it, often being made of pine. The compactness of corner cupboards made them favourites with prosperous farming communities, and many pieces were made by country craftsmen. Most of these had H-hinges on the doors instead of the butt hinges used on better class work (the latter were more time-consuming to fit), and the interiors were painted dull red or green. Although both hanging and free-standing corner cupboards continued to be fashionable throughout the eighteenth century, the basic design was not developed by the Victorians to any degree, although some were still being made in the provinces.

An *encoignure* is a small cupboard, standing on feet or a plinth, with a set of open shelves above. The design was introduced from France in the second half of the eighteenth century, and was known at the time in England either as an ecoinear or a coin. Ince and Mayhew included two designs in their book *The Universal System of Household Furniture* (1759 to 1762); both have bow-fronted cupboards surmounted by sets of quadrant shaped shelves diminishing in size upwards; in one example there were three shelves, and in the other, four. Such designs greatly appealed to the Victorians, who replaced the cupboards with extra shelves or used them to make corner what-nots.

FIG 355: an oak aumbry or food cupboard. The upper halves of the doors are filled with turned spindles, and the doors themselves are secured by turn buttons. Note the fielded panels and H-hinges – both typical of country-made furniture of the late 17th century. c1675.

FIG 356: a hanging corner cupboard in mahogany with satinwood inlays and reeding on the front corners. c1880.

FIG 357: satinwood corner cupboard with marquetry decoration. The design is a more or less faithful copy of a type popular in the 18th century. It does, however, illustrate the fact that the Victorians could not resist adding their 'improvements' – in this case, making the piece in satinwood instead of mahogany and employing a mixed bag of marquetry as 'decoration'. c1870.

FIG 358: mahogany bow-fronted hanging corner cupboard with reeded pilasters. Although there are two escutcheons, only one is fitted with a lock, the other being a dummy. c1800.

FIG 359: a mahogany corner cupboard of elegant proportions. The most striking feature is the beautifully matched feather veneer on the door panels. c1800.

FIG 360: an oak hanging corner cupboard of the kind likely to have been made by a provincial cabinet maker. Note the two drawers below the door – always an improvement. c1800.

FIG 361: a mahogany and satinwood hanging corner cupboard. The fluted pilasters and the frieze rails are in satinwood, with inlaid decoration; the doors have fielded panels. c1785.

FIG 362: An *encoignure* (called a coin in England) with a cupboard below and open shelves above. As the original name implies, the design was introduced from France; Ince and Mayhew illustrate two examples in their book *The Universal System of Household Furniture* (1759 to 1762) in which they refer to them as ecoinears or corner shelves. c1770.

COURT CUPBOARDS

363

From the twelfth or thirteenth century until the sixteenth, cupboards, like sideboards, were sets of platforms arranged as steps on which gold and silver plate and other valuables were displayed – in fact, in 1603 Sir Thomas Kyton graphically described a cupboard as 'a thing like stayres to set plate on'. Obviously, it was a status symbol and the larger the number of tiers, the greater the status of the owner.

The platforms, or desks as they were called, were always draped with fabrics or carpets when in use, and this practice continued when the original cupboards developed into buffets, a piece of furniture in which the desks were arranged above each other instead of being stepped. Status was still very much involved, and in the sixteenth century Cardinal Wolsey had a 'cup-board . . . of six desks high full of gilt plate, very sumptious [sumptuous]'.

By about 1550 the first court cupboards of the type we know today began to appear. The modern use of the term for what is a hall or press cupboard (fig 363) is wrong. The idea that the description court has royal connotations is almost certainly wrong, too – the word is, of course, French for short and refers to the low height of a true court cupboard which is usually under 1.25m (4ft).

364

FIG 363: oak splay-fronted court cupboard – the small cupboard under the canopy is sometimes called an aumbry although, as it is not pierced for ventilation, it does not really qualify for the general use of the term. The legs are gunbarrel turned, and the carved ornament consists mainly of faceted lozenge shapes – a motif popular in Cromwellian times. Note the plain back legs – this was a characteristic even on pieces that were otherwise extremely ornate. c1670.

FIG 364: oak court cupboard with an arched frieze rail: there is a drawer fitted in the middle section – its convex front is called pulvenated or cushion. The turned supports in the upper stage are gunbarrel and bulb, while those on the lower are plain cup and cover. c1640.

365

FIG 365: the court cupboard in all its glory. In oak, it bears all the characteristics of a superb piece of craftsmanship. Starting from the top, the edges are carved with egg and tongue mouldings; beneath it is a frieze rail inlaid with a chequer pattern of ebony and holly; all the bulbous supports have Ionic capitals, with cup and cover (or melon) bulbs; the covers are gadrooned (also called nulling) and the cups are carved with acanthus leaves. Continuing, the middle shelf is pulvenated and carved with strapwork; the bottom rails are inlaid with a contrasting herringbone pattern; and the back posts are carved in a chevron pattern. Both the frieze and the middle rails contain drawers which run on side grooves – typical of the period. c1590.

HALL CUPBOARD

The largest of the cupboards was the hall cupboard, a term which also includes parlour cupboards and press cupboards: as previously mentioned, it is also what is called today a court cupboard. Such cupboards were introduced during the second half of the sixteenth century and continued to be made during the whole of the seventeenth – indeed, some were being made later than 1700 in country districts. From contemporary records it appears that they were intended for use in dining halls, living rooms, and parlours rather than bedrooms or kitchens. From about 1650 onwards the bulbous pillar supports tended to be replaced by turned pendant finials, and in some examples the length was increased to more than the height to provide more storage space. Thus where a normal hall cupboard was about 1.37m (4ft 6in) wide by 1.67m (5ft 6in) high, the larger ones were the same height but up to 2.13 or 2.44m (7 or 8ft) wide. At about the same date, the splay-fronted aumbry under the canopy was replaced by a set of three flat-fronted cupboards: the pilasters that flanked the central one were considered ideal for providing a secret compartment, or masking a secret keyhole. The Cromwellian style of projecting mitred panels continued to be used; but whereas each cupboard door in the main section was formerly often sub-divided into four panels, it now became fashionable to introduce a central muntin so that each door was divided into three panels.

Livery cupboards were part of the furniture for a bedroom, and held the *livre* or livery. This was an allowance of candles, food and drink (probably spiced wine or beer, and bread) given to all the family, guests, and retainers for sustenance during the night. There seems to have been no definite basic design and probably our modern bedside cupboards could easily become livery cupboards!

In Chaucer's time, a wardrobe was a privy: the term *garde-robe* was also used for a small room in which clothes were kept. This was often situated above the privy so that the ammonia fumes would keep the moths at bay! To trace the modern form of wardrobe we have to go back to the fourteenth- and fifteenth-century *armoire* (or its English equivalent, the press). Early ones were plain cupboards enclosed by doors and sometimes had shelves, sometimes not. By 1600 these had evolved into the more elaborate kind of press, with sliding drawers or trays in the upper part, and a set of long drawers in the lower section. Provision of space for hanging clothes as opposed to

laying them flat was introduced in the eighteenth century; until then, hanging space was often provided in cupboards and recesses built into the panelled walls of a bedroom.

In the middle of the eighteenth century the breakfront design of press appeared, which provided hanging space in the wing sections, and shelves and/or trays and drawers in the central compartment. On some examples the full length doors on the wings were provided with dummy drawer fronts to match those on the centre.

Wardrobes as we know them today had replaced the old presses by about 1820, and mirrors were added about 1860 – however, the old name of clothes press was not completely replaced by the term wardrobe until well into the nineteenth century.

FIG 366: oak hall cupboard; the canopy is supported by reversed baluster turnings. The centre door of the upper cupboard has a coat of arms carved upon it, and this means that the piece was probably made as a wedding present; the flanking panels have a stylised flower carved on each. Rope carving forms the remainder of the decoration. c1675.

LIVERY CUPBOARD

FIG 367: a livery cupboard in oak; the cupboard is splay fronted, and the supports are baluster-turned. c1600.

PRESSES

FIG 368: mahogany clothes press with veneered doors and drawer fronts; the doors carry ogee-shaped Gothic panels edged with a beaded moulding. The drawer fronts are faced with quartered veneer and are edged with cockbeading. c1800.

FIG 369: mahogany clothes press; the doors have moulding around the panels with paterae set in corners. As with most clothes presses, the bottom section is fitted with drawers, although a few had cupboards instead. c1770.

WARDROBES

FIG 370: a wardrobe in oak; the interior fitted for hanging clothes, with drawers for ties, handkerchieves, cuff links etc, while the long drawers in the bottom section contained trouser presses. c1890.

FIG 371: an oak wardrobe in the manner of Charles Locke Eastlake; exemplified by the diagonal tongued and grooved panelling, the use of chamfering on the framing and the corner posts, strap hinges, trefoil arch headings, and inlays – his favourite decorative devices. c1870.

366

367

368

369

370

371

CHAPTER 14

Chests

This chapter includes illustrations of chests and coffers, plus chests of drawers, bachelors' chests, chests on stands, and tallboys.

Chests were the earliest kinds of receptacles used for storing clothes, linen, valuables, documents, or household utensils, and as such date back to Ancient Egypt, where the craft of making chests was highly developed.

Their techniques did not reach Western Europe, however, where the first chests were simply logs with a storage recess hacked and burned out; these are known as dug-out or monoxylon chests. The next stage in their evolution was the making of boarded (or borded) chests which, as their name implies, were made of boards or planks nailed together to form what were basically boxes with lids (figs 375 and 378).

Note the three locks on the chest shown in fig 378. This was an early security measure as each lock had a different key; a key was given to each one of three local worthies and unless they were all present, the chest could not be opened. The strap hinges, hasps, and staples were all of massive construction in wrought iron, although early examples in the twelfth and thirteenth centuries sometimes had wooden pin-hinges.

By the end of the fifteenth century, joined construction (then called joyned) was introduced from the Netherlands, and this consisted of panels grooved into a framework – figs 374 and 380 are good examples – and this type of framed construction continued until well into the eighteenth century. Often a small, lidded box was fastened across one end of the chest and held sweet-smelling herbs.

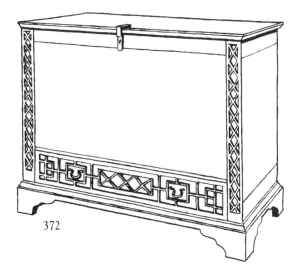

372

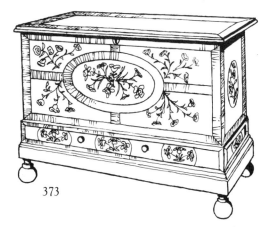

373

374

FIG 372: mahogany chest with a drawer in the base; the trellis work carving is in light relief and is a half hearted attempt at Chinoiserie. Many domestic chests from the earliest examples until the end of the 18th century were fitted with carrying handles, although this one is not. c1760.
FIG 373: a pretty chest in walnut, the panels containing marquetry in various woods on ebony backgrounds; the top is crossbanded but has no other decoration. c1675.
FIG 374: an oak chest decorated with split turnings and faceted lozenges etc. The top consists of framed panels, a normal feature for 16th and 17th century pieces. c1660.

Before discussing the various kinds of chests, it would be as well to differentiate between a chest and a coffer.

In medieval times the terms were interchangeable, although one school of thought at the time referred to small chests as coffers; another, that the term chests should be confined to those of joined construction and that coffers should be used to describe those of boarded construction. Yet another authority, Randle Holme in his *Academy of Armoury* (1649), wrote that the shape of the lid determined the name – if flat, it was a chest; if curved, a coffer – and this is still accepted as the distinction today.

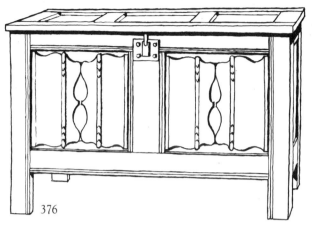

376

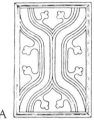

376A

375

377

FIG 375: an oak borded (boarded) chest, the front carved with a crude representation of a rose, with buds and leaves, on each panel. c1620.

FIG 376: a small oak chest with linenfold carving in the panels; this linenfold is interesting as it is a variation of *purchemin* (see fig 376A). Note the framed and panelled top, c1590.

FIG 377: oak framed chest with carved Romayne heads in the outer panels and the inscription 'Fere God: Love God' incised on the frieze rail. Note the iron bandings that reinforce the corners – typical of the period. c1535.

FIG 378: a good example of an early oak boarded chest, complete with chipcarved Gothic decoration, and three locks for security. This kind of ornament is called a roundel. c1300.

COFFER

379

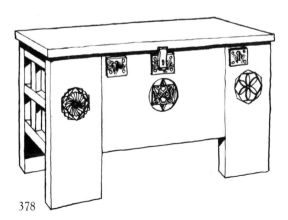

378

FIG 379: an oak coffer in the Gothic Revival style exhibiting some characteristics in the carved zig-zag mouldings and the ecclesiastical-looking columns. The coved top gives it the modern designation of coffer. c1870.

380

FIG 380: a dower chest in oak, with drawers in the frieze under the top. The drawer fronts carry the initials of the young lady whose dowry formed the contents: the tulips and carnations in the vases were painted on the panels in reds and greens. c1650.

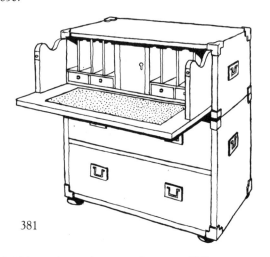

381

FIG 381: a military chest in mahogany. c1870.

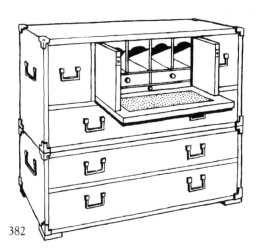

382

FIG 382: military chest in pine; probably for a junior officer as chests for senior ranks were made in more expensive woods such as cedar or mahogany. The writing flap folds up so that the secretaire front can be closed. c1820.

DOWER CHEST

Dower chests were large oak chests that, during the sixteenth and seventeenth centuries, were used to store the linen, curtains, clothes, etc, which were part of a bride's dowry – the modern bottom drawer, in fact. Almost always they contained the herb box already mentioned, and often the young lady's name or initials were incised on the frieze rail.

MILITARY CHESTS

Military chests were introduced in the late eighteenth century and continued to be made during the nineteenth; they were used to transport the officer's personal accoutrements, for which he had to pay. The distinguishing features of such a chest were that it comprised two sections, each of which was fitted with stout carrying handles, and that the corners were reinforced with metal mounts, usually of brass. The top drawer of the upper section was often either a secretaire drawer throughout its length, or could have a secretaire unit fitted in the middle.

MULE CHESTS

A mule chest is so called because, like a mule, it is a hybrid, being part chest and part drawers. Many chests had a long drawer fitted into the base, but the term is more properly applied to those with at least two, and preferably three, drawers.

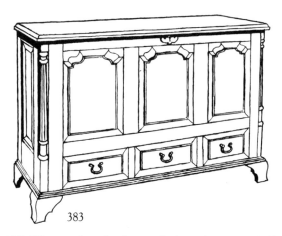

383

FIG 383: an oak mule chest with three drawers in the base. The features that date it are the ogee-shaped bracket feet, the shaped heads to the fielded panels, and the quarter-round reeded pillars in the corner stiles at the front. c1770.

SPECIMEN CHESTS/CABINETS

Specimen chests were made for those indefatigable collectors, the Victorians, to house their collections of coins, flora and fauna, and similar small articles. A typical specimen chest would contain from six to twelve drawers and if there were more than eight, they would be quite shallow; the chest itself would be between 460 to 610mm (18 to 24in) wide.

The Wellington chest was similar, but had drawers of equal depth. What distinguished it from an ordinary specimen chest was the provision of a locking stile which was hinged to the right hand front corner. When this was brought round to the front and locked it prevented the drawers from opening as it overlapped their ends; the same device was used on office desks and filing cabinets well into living memory. They were introduced during the lifetime of the first Duke of Wellington and although there is no evidence that he invented them or even used one, it was quite normal at the time to name types of furniture after national heroes or victories – Nelson, Trafalgar, and Waterloo were all thus honoured.

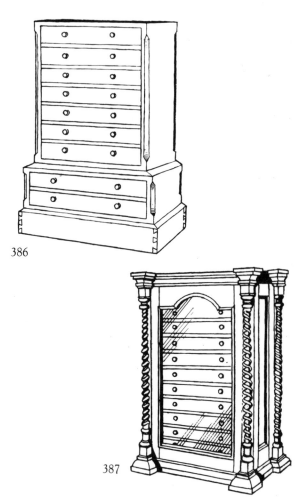

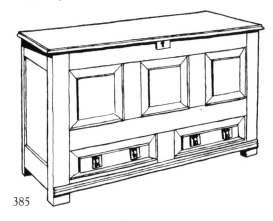

FIG 384: a mule chest in elm, almost certainly of country origin as the appearance lacks elegance – the cabriole legs are badly shaped, the two horns on the apron are ugly, and the top rail of the chest is too wide. c1720.

FIG 385: mule chest in oak with fielded panels on the front, and two drawers at the base which have their fronts fielded. The absence of any decoration makes it likely that is a country piece made more for use than ornament. c1700.

FIG 386: specimen cabinet made in oak. The design is so plain that it is difficult to date; however, the chamfered corners and dovetails showing on the plinth indicate that it is probably a design inspired by the Arts and Crafts Movement. c1900.

FIG 387: another specimen cabinet, this time of comparatively ornate design in mahogany. The spirally turned pillars swell slightly at their centres – a design feature which makes them appear slender; the door front is glazed. The style is vaguely reminiscent of the William and Mary period, but as is common with most Victorian furniture, design motifs of several periods are intermingled. c1860.

WELLINGTON CHEST

FIG 388: a Wellington chest in oak, with carved leaf brackets under the top; the right hand side has a locking stile hinged on the front of the end which has to be unlocked before the drawers can be opened. This is the definitive feature of such chests. c1870.

BACHELOR'S CHEST

FIG 389: bachelor's chest, veneered in walnut. As with all such chests, the top folds over and rests on lopers; a brushing slide is fitted between them. c1740.

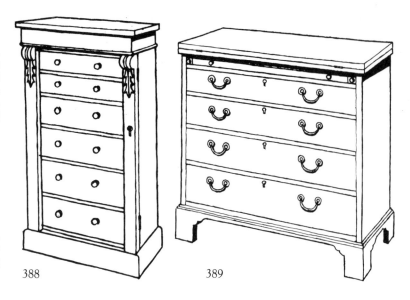

388

389

CHESTS OF DRAWERS

As one would expect, chests of drawers evolved from the chests in which clothes and linen were stored before about 1650. The next development was the mule chest (see figs 383, 384, 385), which was a combination of a chest with drawers under it. Shortly after the Restoration (1660) the first chests of drawers appeared and were usually fitted with three long drawers and two small ones at the top. The drawer fronts should be graduated in depth with the largest at the bottom and the smallest at the top, with about 25mm (1in) difference in each case.

The earliest examples came at the end of the period during which oak had been almost the only cabinet-making wood, and they were often embellished with bevelled, deeply fielded drawer fronts (sometimes called cushion fronts), plus geometrically arranged mouldings. During the latter half of the seventeenth century and the first quarter of the eighteenth century (the Walnut period), the early examples had fronts which were completely veneered with the grain running vertically, even on the fronts of the drawer rails and the bracket feet – a feature sometimes known as waterfall veneering in the trade. Later examples were veneered with highly figured or burr walnut veneers; and the drawer fronts, the carcase ends, and the tops frequently carried panels of floral or arabesque marquetry.

The advent of mahogany from about 1730 onwards brought about the replacement of marquetry with carved ornament, and drawer fronts were often cockbeaded. Serpentine and bow fronts were also introduced about 1750, and such pieces were then called dressing chests or commode chests, and frequently included a pull-out slide (called a brushing slide). Dressing chests were distinguished by having the top drawer subdivided into compartments to hold toilet articles. During the Victorian period chests of drawers were regarded as purely functional pieces of bedroom furniture, and the emphasis was on making them as commodious as possible and only meagre attention was paid to decoration.

390

FIG 390: a mahogany chest of drawers with the edges of the drawer fronts bevelled – apart from the brass handles, this is the only decoration. The arrangement of the upper drawers is similar to that used on some 18th century presses; the deep central drawer was used for hats. Sometimes the design is called a Scotch chest. c1900.

391

392

393

395

394

FIG 391: a typical good class Victorian chest of drawers in mahogany, of which thousands must have been made. It is slightly bow fronted, with turned wooden knob handles and turned onion feet, and dustboards are fitted between the drawers. c1870.

FIG 392: bow-fronted chest of drawers with walnut veneer. The shaped apron between the turned front legs gives it an awkward appearance, but it was a feature used on several similar designs and sometimes contained a drawer. c1870.

FIG 393: a chest of drawers in mahogany, the design being reminiscent of the French Empire style – very much simplified, of course. The gradation of the drawer fronts is poor as the two central ones are more or less the same depth. As with almost all Victorian chests of drawers the handles are turned wooden knobs although a piece of this character would look better if fitted with brass handles. c1850.

FIG 394: mahogany chest of drawers, bow fronted, with spiral twist columns and brass lion-mask handles. c1810.

FIG 395: chest of drawers showing the influence of the Egyptian style beloved of Thomas Hope in the treatment of the front corners. Note, too, the reeded edge around the top – this is typical of the period. c1810.

396

397

398

399

400

401

CHESTS ON CHESTS

The chest on chest (also called a double chest or tallboy) was developed from the chest on stand (see below) and was introduced early in the eighteenth century, becoming popular from about 1750 until the early nineteenth century – George Smith in *Household Furniture* (1808) wrote that the double chest of drawers was an article of such general use that it needed no description. The design incorporates two sections, namely a bottom chest of three drawers upon which stands another case containing three long drawers, and two or three small drawers at the top. As they were frequently 2m (6ft) tall, they were always massive pieces of furniture and often carried imposing cornices and pediments.

The chest on stand was the forerunner of the chest on chest, and made its appearance at the same time as the chest of drawers. It is often called a tallboy, but as the overall height rarely exceeded 1.52m (5ft) it is better to restrict the use of the term to the chest on chest. In general, their decoration is similar to the contemporary styles of chests of drawers, except that the tops are usually plain and not veneered – presumably our ancestors were shorter than we are and considered that as the tops were at or slightly below their eye level, any decoration would be wasted!

402   403   404

FIG 396: mahogany chest of drawers, the drawers being crossbanded with satinwood veneer contained between stringing lines. Fitted with a brushing slide. c1795.

FIG 397: a chest of drawers veneered in walnut, made when mahogany was becoming the fashionable cabinet-making wood. The drawer fronts have their edges crossbanded – this not only added to the decorative effect but also meant that the vertically grained veneer would not be chipped in use. The bracket feet are the ogee shape of the period. c1740.

FIG 398: walnut chest of drawers; the drawer fronts lap over the framing and carry stringing. There is a brushing slide: note the ovolo moulding which forms a flush edge to the top – this feature was quite common at the time. c1730.

FIG 399: small chest of drawers, with the drawer fronts veneered with walnut oysters; the legs are ring and bobbin turnings. c1685.

FIG 400: oak chest of drawers with fielded and veneered drawer fronts in partridge wood (also known as brown ebony

– it is a hard, straightgrained wood with dark red and brown streaks). c1685.

FIG 401: walnut chest of drawers decorated with marquetry panels of floral patterns on the drawer fronts, ends, and top. There are also herringbone bandings in ebony and holly. A perfect specimen of the post-Restoration period. c1680.

FIG 402: bow-fronted chest on chest (or tallboy) in mahogany on Hepplewhite style serpentine-shaped apron and splayed feet. The pediment carries black stringing decoration with a patera at each corner. c1820.

FIG 403: mahogany chest on chest with swan-necked pediment and dentil moulding on the cornice under it: Corinthian columns on upper section. All drawer fronts are cockbeaded. c1780.

FIG 404: a mahogany chest on chest with ebony boxwood banding around the drawer fronts: the corner posts of the upper section are canted and reeded. c1770.

CHESTS ON STANDS

405   406   407

FIG 405: an oak chest on a stand fitted with a secretaire drawer. The cabriole legs have club feet; note the shaped apron and the fact that the drawer fronts lap over the framing slightly, which was often done at this time. c1740.

FIG 406: oak chest on a stand with a chest surmounting two drawers; the inlays are in sycamore. The shaping of the front stretcher and the bulbous turned legs are based on 17th century designs, and the piece was probably made by a country craftsman wanting to imitate the ornate styles of the preceding century. c1730.

FIG 407: a walnut chest on a stand having a shaped apron carrying a carved shell motif; there are similar shells on the knees of the cabriole legs, which have claw and ball feet. The top, and the panels of the chest, are all crossbanded. c1720.

408

409

FIG 408: chest on a stand, veneered in burr walnut. The drawer fronts are lipped with a convex beading that laps over the framing. Note that the upper surfaces of the stretchers are veneered to match the rest of the piece: the legs are faceted (what is called in the trade, square-turned) and are the vase shape popular at the time, as were the ogee curves of the apron. c1690.

FIG 409: an oak chest on a stand with the geometrically shaped and moulded drawer fronts characteristic of the period. The shaped end panels and stretchers make it a particularly good example. The legs are baluster turned with turnip feet. c1680.

CHAPTER 15

Dressers

The Welsh dresser is one of the most sought-after antiques today. Not that all dressers are of Welsh origin; the illustrations and notes in this chapter will help you to identify the various types.

In medieval times dressers were sets of open shelves, sometimes having an enclosed locker (or aumbry) between two of the shelves; they were used to display plate, flagons, goblets, etc, and the higher the rank of the owner, the greater the number of shelves. They were, literally, cup-boards, and later developments included court and press cupboards and sideboards, as well as dressers. The word dresser is probably derived from the Norman-French *dressoire*, which was a side table on which food was dressed for a meal and from which it was served.

Today, dressers have largely been replaced by kitchen cabinets; with one or two exceptions, the Victorians relegated them to the kitchen and considered them unworthy of any special treatment. However, some were designed in the late nineteenth century by members of the Arts and Crafts movement and similar societies but they were usually commissioned by private buyers and proved much too expensive for the general market; see figs 411 and 412. In 1833, J. C. Loudon included a simple and basic design (fig 414) in his *Encyclopaedia*, although many of his other furniture designs were, contrastingly, revivals of Roman and Greek styles.

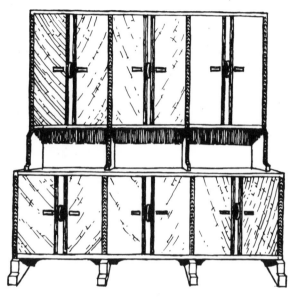

410

FIG 410: an oak dresser by Ernest Gimson. A good example of his style as such decoration as there is, is integral with the piece and not applied. Note the chamfers, the handles, and the shaped sledge feet which, with the natural colour and grain of the wood, make up the only decoration needed. c1900.

FIG 411: made in pine, this design could function as a dresser with the upper part being used as a display case, as it is enclosed by glazed doors, or as a cupboard/bookcase. The diagonally grooved strips in the panels on the cupboard doors, plus the heavily faceted corner posts, are simplified expressions of the sentiments in Charles Locke Eastlake's book, *Hints on Household Taste* (first published in 1868) and Bruce Talbert's *Gothic Forms Applied to Furniture* (published 1867). Both men advocated a return to a romantic simplicity of style in the medieval manner. c1880.

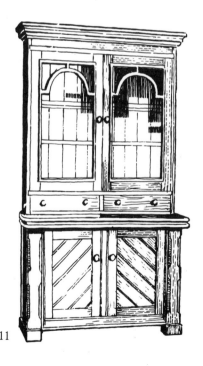

411

412

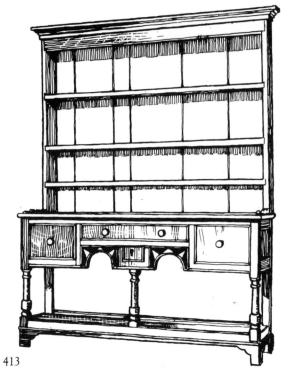

413

FIG 412: as with the example in fig 411 this design has revived Gothic medieval motifs such as the diagonal strips on the doors and the chamfered edges of the central muntin in the dresser back, and on the door framing. c1880.

FIG 413: 'pot-boarded' dressers such as this are usually associated with South Wales. All the drawers have cockbeading around their edges, as do the lower edges of the cupboard section and the semicircular arcaded apron. The small central drawer above the central leg is often a dummy so that the leg may extend right through the carcase and provide extra strength – in this case, however, it is an actual drawer. Note the simple decoration in mahogany on the arcading – the remainder of the piece is in oak. With random-width back boards. c1850.

The eighteenth century and the first years of the next were the age of elegance, and the humble dresser received its share of attention. During this period it was still consigned to the kitchen in the great houses, but farmers and prosperous country folk liked to have them in their dining rooms and parlours so that the family china, pewter, and ornaments could be displayed to advantage.

Dressers of this period, (figs 417 and 418), were often made in mahogany and had cabriole legs at the front with plain posts at the back, or shaped bracket feet after the style of Chippendale. Classical dentil or Grecian key ornaments and inlays were employed as decoration; drawers and door panels were surrounded with cockbeading, and finely cut dovetails appeared on the drawer fronts instead of the cruder ones found

on earlier examples. Sometimes the drawers carried brass bail handles; when turned knobs were fitted they often had ivory or mother of pearl inserts. Lock escutcheons, too, were frequently made of the same materials. A distinguishing feature was that the backs of the upper parts were built up from boards of equal width that were properly tongued together, and not merely planks of random widths butted side by side as in earlier and less sophisticated pieces.

These were the years of the development of regional styles of dressers, such as Welsh dressers; there were other less well known designs of equal merit from other parts of the country, notably Lancashire, Suffolk, and Yorkshire. There were two more local designs, which are not illustrated as in most respects they resemble other dressers. One was the Bridgwater dresser, on which the dresser ends extended from the floor to the top of the back so that the superstructure of shelves was integral with the cupboard section; the other was the Devon dresser on which the shelves were enclosed by panelled doors.

The history of authentic Welsh dressers is a law unto itself, posssibly because Wales was distant from any of the large centres of fashion and tended to go its own way; so we find that as late as 1840 and 1850 they were still being made and as popular as ever. As examples, the North Wales dresser (fig 415) was made in 1850, as was the South Wales design (fig 413).

Several distinguishing types of construction were variations of the main design. Thus, the super-structures of shelves could be open and without any back boards; if they had backs, the component boards in early examples were usually of random widths and butted against each other with open joints between them. Most superstructures were constructed as separate units and were fixed to the lower cupboard section (except in the case of the Bridgwater dresser already mentioned). The Yorkshire design (fig 419) had a clock built into the centre of the shelves; the Lancashire dresser was very similar in style but had no clock. It was also quite common to find small spice cupboards set in the shelves, either centrally, or one at each end (see fig 418).

The lower cupboard sections often displayed local differences. For instance, the South Wales or Glamorgan design (fig 413) had the usual shelf superstructure but the lower section consisted of a row of drawers supported on pillars which were joined at their bases by a 'pot-board'. The West Wales dresser had a row of drawers underneath the top of the lower section, below which were two cupboards flanking a central kneehole called a 'dog kennel'; (fig 416).

Two other pieces of furniture unique to Wales (although similar designs are found in Brittany) belong to the family of dressers, and they are the *Cwpwrdd Deuddarn* and the *Cwpwrdd Tridarn*. The *deuddarn* had two sections – a high press cupboard surmounted by a smaller cupboard having a heavy canopy with turned pendant knobs or finials at the front corners; it first appeared about the beginning of the sixteenth century. A third section comprising a shelf for the display of pewter or earthenware was added in the middle of the seventeenth century and the piece became known as a *tridarn*.

Dressers of the period 1630 to 1700 were long side tables often up to 2.13m (7ft) long by 610mm (2ft) deep. Typical examples (see figs 425 and 426) had a row of drawers set in the frieze rail under the top, supported by pillars at the front and never more than two plain posts at the back. The pillars were usually baluster turned from about 1650 to 1700, although legs with a graduated spiral twist were introduced circa 1675; flat shaped legs to resemble pillars in silhouette appeared about 1670; see fig 427.

In the 1690s this kind of dresser underwent a change, namely the addition of a low backboard with a shaped top and ends extending the full width of the dresser top. At about the same time it became customary to attach a separate set of open shelves to the wall immediately above the dresser with iron staples or spikes. By 1720 these sets of shelves were being fitted with boards at the back. The earliest examples had narrow rails fixed to the front edges of the shelves to stop articles falling off, but these were soon superseded by the more familiar semicircular grooves.

Most dressers of the seventeenth and eighteenth centuries were made in solid timber, usually oak, but often with a variety of local and readily available woods being used for the less important parts in the interior and inside drawers – ash, elm, chestnut, and fruitwoods such as cherry or pear being the most likely. Any veneers should be of the sawcut variety and at least 2mm (1⁄16in) thick.

The backs of the shelf superstructures were built up from boards of random widths until the advent of the finer pieces of the late eighteenth and early nineteenth centuries. On early examples, the boards would be simply butted against each other as already described. Look for the saw marks left by pit-sawing, particularly on the normally hidden side of the back.

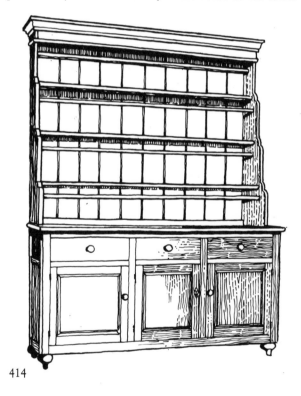

414

FIG 414: in 1833 John C. Loudon wrote his *Encyclopaedia of Cottage, Farm and Villa Architecture and Furniture* in which he described dressers as 'fixtures essential to every kitchen, but more especially to that of the cottager to whom they serve both as dressers and sideboards'. This design, which is similar to a design from that book, can be regarded as the archetype of the dressers to be found in many a Victorian kitchen. c1833.

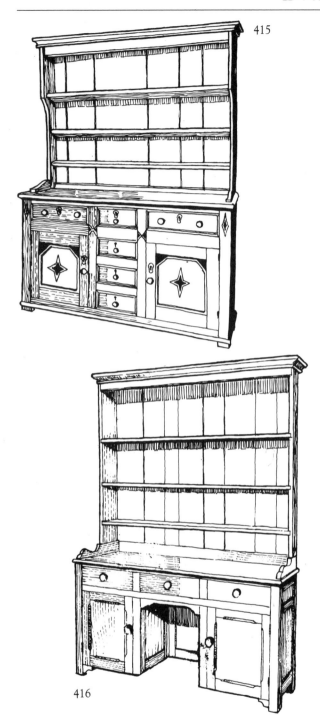

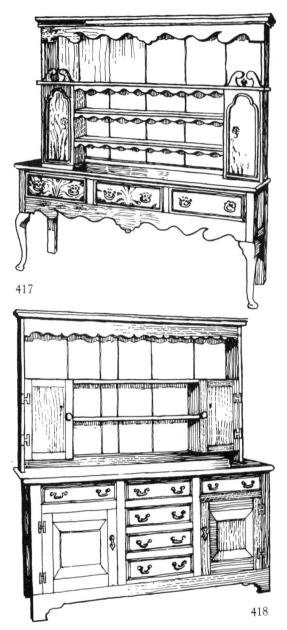

FIG 415: a cupboarded-dresser (also called enclosed) which is considered to be the hallmark of a North Wales design. This one is in oak with inlaid mahogany stars, diamonds and spandrels on the doors; the drawers are all cock beaded. c1850.

FIG 416: made in pine (although they were also constructed in any suitable local woods), this is a 'dog-kennel' Welsh dresser, so called because of the open space under the central drawer. The design probably originated in Pembrokeshire, and examples were usually plain and simple with little or no embellishment. c1830.

FIG 417: an example from the age when dressers received the 'grand treatment'. This one is made in oak with crossbandings around the drawers and with the cupboard doors in mahogany; the swan-neck pediments over the cupboards sometimes had paterae on the scrolls. The front legs are cabriole, while the back legs are merely straight supports – cabriole legs here would prevent the dresser from standing against a wall. Note the elaborately shaped frieze and the unusual scallop-shaped shelf fronts. Sometimes called a Suffolk dresser. c1780.

FIG 418: enclosed dresser, made in oak with cupboards fitted in the shelves. Often called a North Wales dresser, although they were also made in Lancashire and Yorkshire. In the example illustrated, the cupboard doors have fielded panels, while the small cupboard doors in the shelves are solid. Some early designs (c1750) have curved tops to the door panels, while in later ones the tops are ogee shaped. c1780.

FIG 419: a magnificent example of a Yorkshire dresser with a clock built in to the cupboard in the centre of the dresser back; similar designs without the clock are known as Lancashire dressers. Made in oak. c1750.

FIG 420: a pot-boarded South Wales dresser in oak with only two drawers, and an open back. The elaborately shaped plate-rack ends and frieze echo the shaping of the deep apron. c1740.

FIG 421: very much a country carpenter's piece, this dresser lacks any closed storage space. The front supports are shaped

in an effort to simulate turned balusters, and this is a feature often found on earlier dressers such as fig 427. This example was probably constructed of several locally-grown timbers such as ash, chestnut, elm or oak. c1720.

FIG 422: this is a hybrid between a dresser, a *Cwpwrdd tridarn* (fig 428), and a hall cupboard. The cupboard section, and the canopy with turned pendants at the front corners, both derive from the hall cupboard, while the arrangement of the cupboards and shelves in the back are strongly reminiscent of the *Cwpwrdd tridarn*. The door panels and drawer fronts are fielded. In oak. c1700.

419

421

420
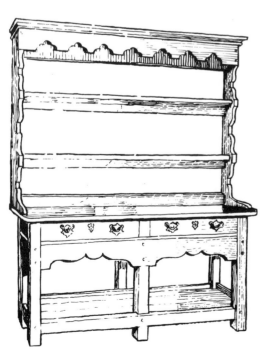

422

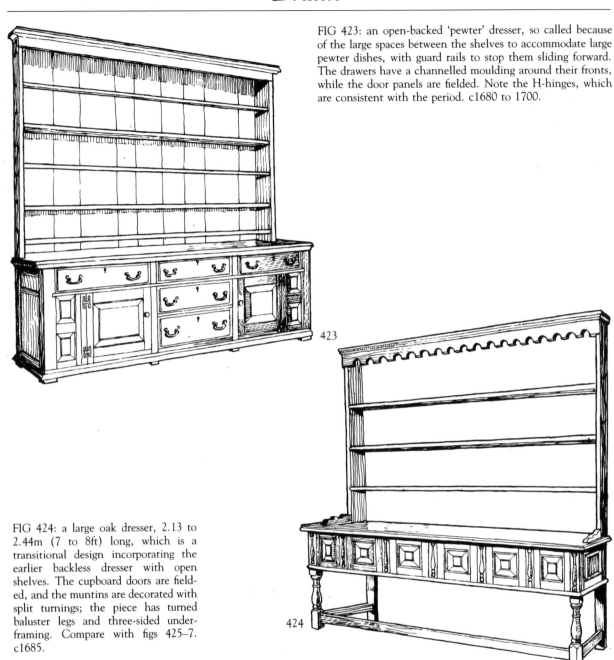

FIG 423: an open-backed 'pewter' dresser, so called because of the large spaces between the shelves to accommodate large pewter dishes, with guard rails to stop them sliding forward. The drawers have a channelled moulding around their fronts, while the door panels are fielded. Note the H-hinges, which are consistent with the period. c1680 to 1700.

423

FIG 424: a large oak dresser, 2.13 to 2.44m (7 to 8ft) long, which is a transitional design incorporating the earlier backless dresser with open shelves. The cupboard doors are fielded, and the muntins are decorated with split turnings; the piece has turned baluster legs and three-sided underframing. Compare with figs 425–7. c1685.

424

425

FIG 425: a backless oak dresser typical of the last examples before dressers with backs became common. The drawer fronts are edged with a heavy 'picture-frame' style moulding; the front legs are spirally twisted, the thickness of the twist diminishes towards top and bottom to give a swelled effect. In common with all dressers of this style it has two back legs (never more) which are quite plain. Only the two right hand drawers can be locked. c1675.

426

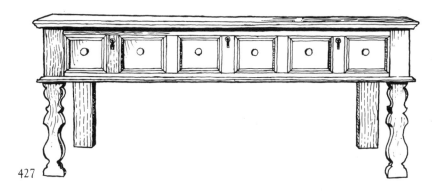

427

428

FIG 426: backless oak dresser with three drawers, the fronts carrying carved geometrical patterns of the period and furnished with turned knobs which are carved on the fronts. The front baluster legs have 'ears' or spandrels, which are also carved, and there are split-turned decorations on the corner posts and muntins. c1670.

FIG 427: although this oak dresser appears to have six drawers, there are in reality only three, as indicated by the number of locks. The 'picture-frame' mouldings around the drawer fronts (and in fig 425) are typically Carolean. The shaping of the front legs is similar to that used on some gate-leg tables of the period. c1670.

FIG 428: a *Cwpwrdd Tridarn* (cupboard with three stages or sections). These were made in Wales and the Welsh Border counties in comparatively large numbers from about 1500 to 1800, when they were superseded by the dresser. An earlier design was the *Cwpwrdd Deuddarn* (cupboard with two stages), which comprised a high press cupboard, about 1.45m (4ft 9in) tall, surmounted by an upper smaller cupboard carrying a heavy canopy with turned knobs or bosses at the front corners. The *tridarn* had a third stage comprising an enclosed shelf for the display of pewter or earthenware. They were often given to a newly-married couple, or commissioned by them, and in many cases the piece bears the couple's initials and the date of their marriage. The one illustrated is dated 1695, and is more elaborate than most.

CHAPTER 16

Designers

When reading through chapters 6 to 15 you will find that the names of many furniture designers are mentioned. As a particular style is often known by the name of its designer, as in the case of a 'Chippendale' chair or a 'Sheraton' table, it is obviously worth knowing about his history and background and the following notes include most of the influential British designers, arranged in alphabetical order.

ADAM, Robert (1728 to 1792)

Born in Kirkcaldy, Fife, he was the son of a well known Scottish architect. In 1758 he returned from Italy where he had lived for several years, and set up an architectural practice in London with his brothers. While in Italy he greatly admired the Palladian style and used classical Grecian and Roman ornaments in his designs for both buildings and furniture. However, he broke new ground by introducing an interpretation of the style which he called Grotesque; he says 'by grotesque is meant that beautiful light style of ornament used by the ancient Romans in the decoration of their palaces, baths, and villas'. This is the basis of the Neo-Classical style of which Adam was the principal British exponent. In 1773, 1779, and 1822 the three volumes of *The Works in Architecture of Robert and James Adam* were published; posthumously in the case of the third volume.

BARNSLEY, Ernest (1863 to 1926)

Architect and furniture designer, and elder brother to Sidney. In 1886 he was working as an architect in London where he met Ernest Gimson; the two brothers and Gimson became involved with the various societies and groups that eventually became the Arts and Crafts Movement; in 1887 he went to Birmingham and set up his own architectural practice.

The year 1894 saw a complete change in his lifestyle as he moved to Pinbury, near Cirencester (Glos) with his family to live in an Elizabethan farmhouse; his brother and Gimson occupied adjacent cottages. Their aim was to become virtually self-supporting by baking their own bread, keeping goats and hens, etc.

In 1901 he entered into partnership with Gimson but in 1905 it was dissolved and he returned to architecture.

BARNSLEY, Sidney (1865 to 1926)

The archetypal artist-designer-craftsman who was one of the few men to make up his own designs with his own hands. As is usual with such craftsmen, he was modest and self-effacing. He was the younger brother of Ernest Barnsley and while an architectural student he was introduced to Ernest Gimson. In 1889–90 he made two trips to Greece to study Byzantine architecture, and between 1890 and 1892 he combined with several colleagues to set up the firm of Kenton & Co. The year 1894 saw the two Barnsley brothers and Gimson living at Pinbury (Glos) where, they thought, the environment would be more conducive to their kind of work, but in 1901 Sidney left to work on his own for the rest of his life.

His designs are uncomplicated and honest, often with the constructional joints showing; almost always they were made in solid wood (usually oak). One of the characteristics of his furniture is the hayrake stretcher, in which each end diverged into two arms like the old fashioned hayrake. A permanent display of his work is at Cheltenham Museum.

CHIPPENDALE, Thomas, senior

Baptised at Otley, Yorkshire, in 1718, he was the son of a joiner on a country estate; some researchers believe, however, that his father was a cabinet maker in London.

The exact date of his arrival in London is not known, but in 1745 he was living at Conduit Court, Long Acre, and married Catherine Redshaw in 1748. He moved to St Martin's Lane in 1753 or 1754 where he set up his workshops. James Rannie, who died in 1766, was his first partner; Chippendale then took Thomas Haig as a partner in 1771 when the firm adopted the name of Chippendale, Haig & Co. Haig outlived Chippendale senior (who died in 1779) and continued the partnership with Thomas Chippendale, junior.

During the first half of the eighteenth century the

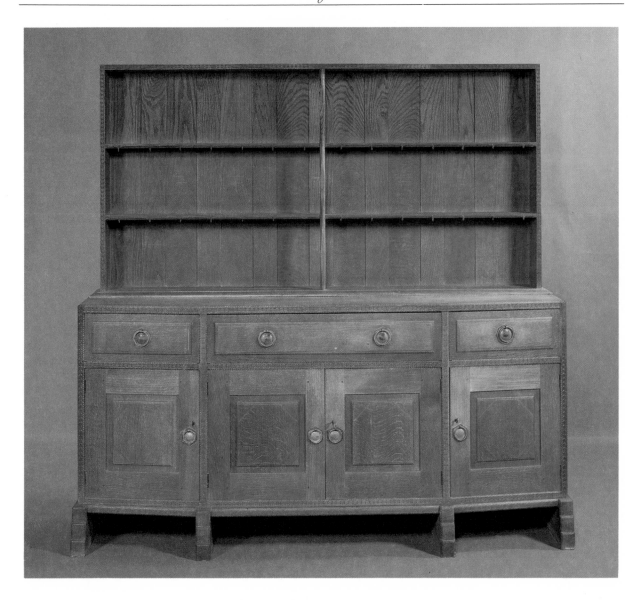

country was swept by a craze for all things Gothic (see Gothic style), which strongly influenced contemporary architects and furniture makers. Chippendale was no exception, and both his Rococo and Chinese periods contained designs with Gothic motifs. Later in his career he worked with Robert Adam and produced furniture to the latter's designs. Chippendale is also remembered for his book *The Gentleman and Cabinet-Maker's Director* which was first published in 1754, with subsequent editions in 1762 and 1775.

CHIPPENDALE, Thomas, junior (1749 to 1822)
He was the eldest son of the eleven children of Thomas Chippendale, senior. He carried on his father's business at St Martin's Lane but was made

Walnut dresser c1903 by Sidney Barnsley. Note the chip carving on the edges of the frame rails – a form of decoration that he often used

bankrupt in 1804. Fortunately he was able to re-establish the business in 1805, largely as a result of furnishing Stourhead (Wiltshire) for the Hoare family of bankers. His furniture designs were strongly influenced by the French Neo-Classical styles but, unlike his father, he was not fond of ornate decoration.

EASTLAKE, Charles Locke (1836 to 1906)
An architect and furniture designer who advocated a return to simple, joined construction and the avoidance of any kind of polished or varnished finish: in his

Writing table c1810 based on a design by Gillows of Lancaster. In rosewood, with brass mounts, it has two drawers on one side and two dummy drawers on the other

own words 'the moment a carved or sculptured surface begins to shine, it loses interest.' His ideas were taken up by both the Aesthetic and the Arts and Crafts Movements but were far more influential in the USA, where they initiated a cult.

GILLOW & COMPANY

The firm was founded in 1695 by Robert Gillow, who was a joiner. Fortunately the company's records, which go back to 1731, have been preserved; further, it was the only English furniture maker of that period who stamped their pieces, and this means that they can be identified. The stamped signature was usually on drawer edges and appeared as 'Gillows', or 'Gillows Lancaster'; the practice was later adopted by

some manufacturers in the nineteenth century.

At first the company was mainly concerned with architectural and building work, but about 1740 Robert Gillow began sending furniture to London, and in 1761 a shop was opened in Oxford Street (then Tyburn Road), London. At first it was known as Gillow and Barton, but soon became Gillow, and (at the present day) Waring and Gillow.

The company's furniture was considered by contemporary critics to be solid, well made, but unadventurous – this last comment seems unkind as Gillows introduced the Davenport desk (figs 326 and 327), and also patented a telescopic extending dining table.

GIMSON, Ernest (1864 to 1919)

Originally articled to an architect in Leicester in 1881, he met William Morris in 1884 at a lecture and was persuaded by him to pursue his architectural studies in London, which he did from 1886. There he met Ernest and Sidney Barnsley, and all three men became involved in the various groups and associations which culminated in the Arts and Crafts Movement.

During 1889 and 1890 he travelled throughout Europe and on his return apprenticed himself to Philip Clisset, a master chair maker in Ledbury, Herefordshire. From 1890 to 1892 he, with four other like-minded architects, set up Kenton & Co. In 1893 he went with Sidney Barnsley in a move to the Cotswolds, where they were eventually joined by Ernest Barnsley. In 1901 the latter united with Gimson in a partnership in Cirencester and hired cabinet makers to make up their designs: Peter van der Waals was the foreman, and Harry Davoll, Ernest Smith, and Percy Burchett were the original team. About 1905 Barnsley left the partnership and Gimson continued on his own; in 1903 he became a partner with Edward Gardiner in a venture to produce turned chairs at Daneway (Glos).

Figs 156, 158, 161A and B show typical examples of his chairs. His cabinet work is distinguished by an elegant simplicity of style with little adornment as he relied upon chamfering and simple gouged decoration; he preferred to leave his pieces in their natural colours, with a waxed finish (see fig 410). He was also a skilled designer in metal work, plaster work, and embroidery.

GODWIN, Edward William (1833 to 1886)

An architect and furniture designer who was a leading member of the Aesthetic Movement. Although he worked in the revived Gothic style he is best remembered for the pieces that reflect his intense interest in Japanese art. These designs were frequently made up in ebonised wood, with embossed leather or woven Japanese fabrics, and were invariably light and graceful in construction.

HEPPLEWHITE, George (Date of birth unknown; died 1786).

Cabinet and chair maker who is believed to have been apprenticed to Gillow & Co. His cabinet-making shop was in Red Cross Street, St Giles, London, and the business was carried on by his widow after his death. His well known book *The Cabinet-Maker and Upholsterer's Guide* was published posthumously in 1788 with subsequent editions in 1789 and 1794. His furniture designs are light and elegant, and are best described as in the Neo-Classical style, with a judicious admixture of French fashion. He was particularly fond of painted furniture,

but is best remembered for his shield-back chairs, (figs 181, 184, and 185); and the Pembroke table (figs 58 to 61). It is ironic that in spite of his fame, not one stick of furniture has ever been found which could be ascribed to him.

HOPE, Thomas (1769 to 1831)

A wealthy dilettante who travelled widely through the Middle East and Spain. He was a fervent collector of classical and Egyptian antiquities and in 1807 published *Household Furniture and Interior Decoration*. His designs were severely classical and employed such motifs as lotus and palm leaves, the anthemion (honeysuckle), monopodia (decorative supports formed from the heads and legs of animals, usually lions or griffins), sphinxes, caryatids, sarcophagi, vases, urns, human masks, etc.

INCE AND MAYHEW

A cabinet-making partnership between William Ince and John Mayhew, who were in business from 1759 to 1803. Between 1759 and 1762 they published *The Universal System of Household Furniture*. Their designs closely resembled those of Thomas Chippendale senior, and there could well have been some mutual plagiarism.

JONES, Inigo (1573 to 1652)

He was the only son of a London cloth worker and little is known of his early life except that he was apprenticed to a joiner in St Paul's Churchyard, and that he visited Italy while still a young man. He began his professional life by designing court masques for James I; in 1611 he was appointed Surveyor to the Prince of Wales, and Surveyor of the King's Works in 1615. From then until the Civil War in 1642 he was engaged in supervising various projects at the Royal palaces.

He was more of an architect than a furniture designer, although it is probable that he did design some pieces; his chief claim to fame is that he clarified the systems of design represented by the classic orders of architecture, and so made it possible for subsequent designers to interpret and adapt them.

KENT, William (c 1686 to 1748)

Born at Bridlington, he seems to have been apprenticed to a coach painter in Hull when a young lad. During his life he embraced several professions such as furniture designer, mural painter, architect, and landscape gardener. He was fortunate enough to have had several influential patrons, chief of whom was the third Earl of Burlington, and Kent became a per-

Satinwood Pembroke table c1790, similar in design to those originally made by Ince and Mayhew (*qv*). Such tables often incorporated panels which opened to reveal chess and/or backgammon (tric-trac) boards. The set of pigeonholes and drawers rises on springs and is the feature which gives the piece its alternative name of a 'Harlequin' table

manent member of the household (which included George Frederick Handel for a short time). Lord Burlington found him many commissions, including the building of Holkham Hall, Norfolk, and painting some of the ceilings at Kensington Palace.

He designed the interior decoration and furniture for several great houses; his style had Baroque characteristics and was lavishly decorated with carved and gilt scrolls, acanthus foliage, shells, and masks. He became so famous that Horace Walpole said that his (Kent's) style 'predominated authoritatively during his life; and his oracle was so much consulted by all who affected taste, that nothing was thought complete without his assistance. He was not only consulted for furniture, as frames of pictures, glasses, tables, chairs etc but for plate, for a barge, for a cradle.'

LETHABY, William Richard (1857 to 1931)

Born in Barnstaple, Devon, he became an architect, a teacher, and a designer. He was the author of numerous articles and essays on the subject of industrial design, and in 1922 published some of them under the title of *Form in Civilisation*. His designs were mainly in the style of those of the Arts and Crafts Movement.

LIBERTY, Arthur Lasenby

A furniture retailer who opened his first shop in Regent Street, London in 1875 (it is still there). He was involved with the avant-garde designers of the period and had close associations with the Aesthetic and the Arts and Crafts Movements; he also advertised and sold furniture and artefacts in Japanese, Moorish, and Arabic styles. His efforts were so successful that they created the Liberty style, which was in great demand amongst those who craved something different from the ordinary run of factory produced furniture.

LOUDON, John Claudius (1783 to 1843)

The son of a Scottish farmer, he became a versatile writer on various subjects such as landscape gardening, architecture, and furniture design. Apart from his well known *Encyclopaedia of Cottage, Farm and Villa Architecture and Furniture* (1833), he founded and edited *The Architectural Magazine and Journal of Improvement in Architecture, Building, and Furnishing and in the various Arts and Trades connected therewith* (1834 to 1838) – surely the longest magazine title in history!

He pioneered the use of metal furniture, and suggested basic designs of mass-produced furniture for the artisan classes who could not afford expensive pieces. The designs themselves ranged from the very functional to early examples of the Victorian Vernacular.

MACKINTOSH, Charles Rennie (1868 to 1928)

A Scottish architect and founder of the Glasgow School of designers. His furniture was highly individual and embodied motifs from both Art Nouveau and the designs of the Arts and Crafts Movements but he added to them his own interpretation of the sculptural quality which he thought furniture should have. The results, although spectacular, were seldom comfortable (see fig 159). He often used a stylised tightly furled rose as a personal symbol.

MACKMURDO, Arthur H. (1851 to 1942)

An architect and furniture designer who was a founder-member of the Century Guild. He believed that a designer's inspiration should come from natural forms such as flowers and foliage, and in fact once said in a lecture that the love of nature that had made the English landscape painters so successful should imbue the whole of a designer's work.

He was particularly fond of panels that were fretcut in the swirling patterns of Art Nouveau (see fig 162). Unfortunately, these often struck a note of incongruity, as the remainder of the design would be comparatively stark and in the simple styles of the Arts and Crafts Movement. In 1889 he and a fellow-designer, Herbert Horne, set up a company to manufacture their designs but it was short lived as they were more interested in teaching and writing about the aesthetics of design than in commercial enterprise.

MORRIS, William (1834 to 1896)

An artist-craftsman and social refomer – he was a founder member of the Socialist League. His aims were to promote a return to a golden age of medieval craftsmanship (which, it must be said, existed mainly in his own imagination), and to avoid the use of machinery 'if it removed from work the pleasure of it', to quote the words of Edward Barnsley.

As far as is known, Morris never designed any furniture but devoted his attention to other crafts, particularly printing, fabrics and book production; furniture design was the province of Philip Webb.

In 1860 Morris, in conjunction with Webb, Burne-Jones, Ford Madox Brown, and Rossetti, formed Morris, Marshall, Faulkner & Co. Its aims were to promote the appreciation of better design standards amongst the middle and artisan classes, and to offer them honestly made domestic artefacts. The theme of most of the early designs derived from Morris's romantic interpretation of the work of the medieval guilds, ignoring the fact that the guilds were most influential in the sixteenth and seventeenth centuries.

As regards furniture, the range of designs eventually came to comprise two categories. On the one hand there were the comparatively simple, plain and utilitarian designs as exemplified by the Sussex chair in fig 267 and the ladderback chair in fig 165; and on the other, pieces which were ornate in the extreme, with elaborate decoration and painted panels of pre-Raphaelite subjects by Burne-Jones, Madox Brown, or Rossetti. Several pieces of the latter style were displayed by the firm at the International Exhibition of 1862, held in London.

The painter, William Holman Hunt, also worked with the firm. In 1857 he had designed and made for himself an oak table, which he stained green: this kind of coloured finish was adopted by the firm and applied to many of the simpler pieces and became a distinguishing feature.

PUGIN, A. W. N. (1812 to 1852)

A strongly religious Roman Catholic, he believed that the original medieval Gothic architecture was essentially the expression of the Christian faith in stone, and that this applied just as forcibly to furniture design. He wrote two books, *Contrasts* in 1836, and *Gothic Furniture in the Style of the Fifteenth Century* in 1835. In *Contrasts* he compared medieval architecture to its equivalent in his day, to the great detriment of the latter. See also Gothic and Gothick styles.

SHERATON, Thomas (1751 to 1806)

Born in Stockton-on-Tees, he settled in London about 1790, at Wardour Street, Soho, and later moved to Golden Square. His journey from Stockton to London seems to have taken several years, during which time he almost certainly earned his living as a peripatetic cabinet maker; however, his trade card describes him as teaching perspective, architecture, and ornaments; also designing for cabinet makers, and selling all kinds of drawing books. He was a Baptist lay-preacher and from his writings appears to have been of rather a pedantic nature.

As is the case with Hepplewhite no furniture actually made by him has ever been found, and his recognition rests on the two books he wrote – *The Cabinet-Maker and Upholsterers' Drawing Book* (1791 to 1794), and *The Cabinet Dictionary* (1803). He was writing an *Encyclopaedia* when he died, but it was only a quarter finished.

His designs were drawn from the same sources as Hepplewhite's and Gillow's and it is often difficult, if not impossible, to differentiate between them. He did, however, delight in incorporating mechanical contrivances in his furniture, and many pieces are dual-purpose or have concealed compartments – the best known is probably his Harlequin table, but there was also a cradle which rocked automatically, a set of library steps cum Pembroke table, and several others.

SMITH, George

A designer and astute business man, Smith was 'Upholsterer and Cabinet-Maker to HRH Prince of Wales' (later to become George IV) and 'Upholsterer and Draughtsman to His Majesty, and Principal of the Drawing Academy'. In 1804/5 he published *Collection of Designs for Household Furniture and Interior Decoration* (with an improved edition in 1808); *Collection of Ornamental Design after the Manner of the Antique* (1812); and *The Cabinet Makers' and Upholsterers' Guide* (1828).

His designs were much influenced by those of Thomas Hope but were less classical, and tended to be over-adorned with Egyptian motifs such as sphinxes, palm leaves, leopards, lions, griffins, etc. Although he probably did not originate them, he is notable for having popularised circular dining tables, ottomans, convex circular mirrors, and chiffoniers.

TALBERT, Bruce James (1838 to 1881)

He began working with a wood carver in Dundee, later becoming an architect in Glasgow, and moving to London in 1865. He attempted to create a coherent and identifiable Gothic Revival style, and he published *Gothic Forms applied to Furniture and Decorations for Domestic Purposes* in 1867, and *Examples of Ancient and Modern Furniture* in 1876.

VILE and COBB

A partnership between William Vile and John Cobb, trading during the 1750s and 60s in St Martin's Lane, London. They produced several pieces for the Royal Family, and their designs were always in the grand manner with beautifully executed Rococo carving. Vile retired in 1765, and Cobb carried on the business; after his death in 1778 it was taken over by

Library elbow chair c1740 in the 'French' taste of the first half of the 18th century. The cabriole legs, which are carved with shells and acanthus leaves, terminate in scrolled feet. The upholstery is gros-point needlework

Strickland and Jenkins (Strickland was Vile's nephew). Cobb popularised the design of an artist's table which had an adjustable, rising top (see fig 87).

VOYSEY, Charles Francis Annesley (1857 to 1941)

An architect and furniture designer who fully appreciated that industrial design could play a significant part in developing furniture styles. At one time he used motifs from Art Nouveau but later abandoned the fashion in favour of simple construction, natural finishes for wood, and a minimum of decoration, consisting mainly of pierced ornament and metal inlays, which were often enamelled. Most of his pieces were made in oak.

WEBB, Philip Speakman (1831 to 1915)

An architect and furniture designer who joined the firm of Morris, Marshall, Faulkner & Co as chief furniture designer. He was responsible for adapting an original Sussex country design into the successful Morris chair (fig 268); his furniture was frequently stained the green colour that had been introduced by Holman Hunt.

Glossary

'(not already explained in the text)'

acanthus ornament – Carved decoration based on the leaves of the *Acanthus mollis*: a plant known in England as 'Bear's breeches'. The story goes that architects in ancient Greece noticed the plant growing in a pot which had a tile lying on the top; the manner in which the leaves curled round the tile attracted them and the motif was included in the Greek Corinthian order of architecture.

adzing – An adze is a kind of axe with the blade and cutting edge set at right angles to the handle or haft. There are several sizes according to the work being done; Windsor chair seats are adzed out (a process called bottoming), and lengths of rough, riven timber can be smoothed off (*see also* riven).

alkanet root – Alkanet is another name for the Anchusa plant (also called borage); when suitably processed and mixed, the root forms a dye to produce a red oil.

amorini – An Italian word for winged cupids or cherubs. Boys and putti are similar but do not have wings.

antique nail – A brass nail with a domed head.

apron – A shaped piece which is fixed between the legs of a chair or settee, or below the frieze rail of a table, cabinet, or chest; usually it is decorated with carving, or is pierced or shaped.

arabesque – A decorative design with flowing, interwoven lines that are often floral in character; originally from the Near East.

arcading – A series of arches, usually with semicircular heads, used as decoration on panels in the late sixteenth and throughout the seventeenth centuries. A single arch was also sometimes employed in the same manner.

arris – Term for the meeting of two plane surfaces – in other words, an edge.

bail handle – The shaped bar of a looped drop handle; it is fixed at each end.

bead and groove joint – As illustrated; used between the flap and the bed of a flap or gate-leg table (*see also* rule and square joints).

beading – A thin narrow moulding, usually with a rounded edge.

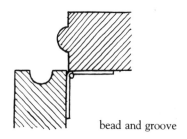

bead and groove

bellflower – A carved, painted or incised ornament consisting of a formalised flower shaped like a bell and with three petals.

bevel – The general description applied to any sloped or slanted inclination of an edge or surface.

boss – An architectural term borrowed by cabinet makers to describe a raised and carved ornament used to cover the intersections of angles in mouldings.

boys – A term used during the Restoration period to describe cherubs or putti (*see also* amorini).

breakfront – Also called broken front. Term applied to a piece of furniture in which the central portion of the front projects beyond the plane of the flanking parts.

brushing slide – A shelf that slides between the uppermost drawer and the underside of the top of a chest of drawers or tallboy; when the slide is pulled out clothes can be laid on it and brushed.

burr – Abnormal growth (resembling a wart) of a tree, caused by buds or eyes that have been unable to develop fully because of lack of nourishment. Such burrs often yield exceptionally beautiful veneers, especially in the case of oak, walnut, and yew.

canted corner – Refers to a corner post that has either been built in deliberately, or has had its front face chamfered, so that it is presented at an angle to the front of the piece.

caryatids – A term for sculptured female figures used as supports, eg on tables.

chamfer – Similar to a bevel (*see also*); in the case of a chamfer, however, it is stopped at a short distance from the end of the piece to which it is applied.

channel; channelling – A continuous depression or wide groove cut in or routed out of a surface.

cherubs – *See* amorini, boys, and putti.

chevron – A decorative motif resembling an inverted V, similar to the stripes worn by non-commissioned officers.

chip carving – A simple form of carved ornament, the pattern being usually geometric. Its advantage was that the carving could be done with basic cuts of chisels or gouges and was well within the ability of a skilled joiner. Used during the thirteenth, fourteenth, and fifteenth centuries.

claw legs – The name given to the curved legs used on tripod tables; the latter were often called claw tables.

cockbeading – A small beading or astragal usually applied around the edges of drawer fronts from the early eighteenth to the early nineteenth centuries.

contre-partie – The lower sheet (usually tortoise-shell) of Boulle work (*see also première-partie*).

cornice – The projecting member, usually moulded and/or shaped, at the top of a bookcase, cabinet or tallboy, or above the tester of a bed.

coved top – A top of curved shape.

crossgrain – Applied to any wooden part that has the grain of the wood running across its width instead of along its length.

C-scroll – As illustrated, a scroll in the form of a letter C.

C-scroll

curl veneer – Also called feather. A veneer resulting from wood taken from the junction of a branch with a larger one, or with the main trunk of a tree.

cushion front – A term usually applied to a drawer front which is pulvenated, that is, bevelled around its edges to give a cushion-like effect.

cusps – An architectural term for the points formed by the intersection of the foils (that is, the circles) in Gothic tracery.

dentils – Small rectangular blocks that form a feature of the Roman Corinthian style cornice.

dog tooth ornament – Resembles four leaves united at one end to form lobes: see illustration.

dog-tooth moulding

dowels – These are short lengths cut from long cylindrical rods from 6mm (¼in) up to 12mm (½in) dia. They were not used in cabinet work but only in chair making instead of mortise and tenon joints. Machine-made dowels date back to about 1850; before then, however, dowels were sometimes employed and were made by hammering roughly shaped strips of wood through holes in an iron plate, known as a dowel plate.

dug-out chest – Also called a monoxylon. The most primitive form of chest, used up to and during medieval times. It was hollowed out of a tree-trunk with an adze, or by burning out a cavity. They were usually bound with iron bands to prevent the splits (which were inevitable) from opening too far.

dustboard – Refers to the thin board interposed between the drawers in some chests of drawers. A misnomer, because such a board was not needed to keep out dust – its main function was to prevent the contents of one drawer from rising to jam the one above; it also acted as a deterrent against theft.

egg and anchor – *See* egg and tongue.

egg and dart – *See* egg and tongue.

egg and tongue – A motif carved on to mouldings, usually ovolos, and based on the Greek *echinus* pattern. Also known as egg and anchor and egg and dart.

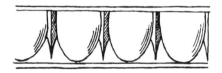

egg and tongue (echinus)

end grain – The grain that shows on the end of a piece of wood which has been sawn across.

end standard – Refers to the upright panel that takes the place of a leg on some designs of table.

entasis – A slight convex swelling about halfway up a pillar or column; without it a perfectly cylindrical pillar appears to be slightly concave.

escutcheon – In furniture the protective plate, usually ornamented, that surrounds a keyhole.

faceted – A term applied to a pillar or leg when its

Mahogany dining chair c1755, with vase-shaped splats and loose drop-in seat. A graceful example of the type – note the finely sculptured arms and back

faces are planed so that it becomes hexagonal or octagonal in section.

fall front – Also called a drop front. The front of a bureau which is hinged so that when opened it forms a horizontal surface for writing.

fan (marquetry) – A decorative motif very widely used from the late eighteenth century onwards.

feather figure – *See* curl figure.

fiddleback figure – This is caused by the layers of grain in a piece of wood undulating so that when sawn it exhibits the kind of figure seen on the backs of violins. Mainly found in mahogany, but can also occur in sycamore.

fielded panel – A panel with a flat centre and the edges bevelled; the latter are inserted into grooves in the framing rails, without glue, so that the wood is free to swell or shrink without disturbing the main frame. The bevelling is normally confined to the front edges, but can also be applied to the rear edges, when it is known as counter-fielding.

finial – A terminal ornament, usually upright and turned, which can be fixed to almost any article of furniture to improve its appearance. A finial that points downwards is called a pendant finial (*see also*).

fluting – Term applied to shallow, hollowed-out grooves which are always vertical. They can either run from the top to the bottom of a post, or side by side as on a frieze rail. In some patterns, the lower part of the flute is filled with reeding (*see also*), when the design is known as return-reeded.

frieze rail – The horizontal rail immediately beneath the top of a table or cabinet stand.

gadrooning – Also called nulling. A form of carved decoration achieved by carving convex lobes or concave flutes side by side as illustrated. A common feature on Elizabethan cup and cover legs.

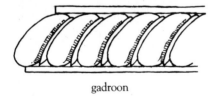

gadroon

gallery – A miniature railing, kerb, or rim around the edge of a table, tray, cabinet top, or shelf. Frequently made of brass; wooden ones were usually pierced.

glazing bars – The slender wooden framing that contains the glass in the barred doors of bookcases, etc.

Grecian key – A very ancient decorative motif, as illustrated.

Grecian key

groundwork – Any kind of base or substrate on which veneer is laid.

guilloche – A decorative motif carved in low relief and consisting of two bands intertwined, as illustrated.

guilloche

hayrake stretcher – A stretcher with bifurcated ends resembling a hayrake.

husks – Also called wheatears. A carved drop ornament comprising a series of buds or flowers; it was popular in the second half of the eighteenth century.

in the white – Term applied to any kind of woodwork that has not been polished, stained, varnished, or painted.

lancet – In the form of a pointed arch; a particularly Gothic decorative motif.

linenfold – A form of ornament in which the wood was carved stylistically to resemble the folds of a piece of linen; there were many variations of the basic pattern.

lists – Trade term for the long, thin rods used in some designs of Windsor chair backs.

loper – A narrow strip of wood that can be pulled out to support a flap, as in a bureau.

lunette – A semicircular decorated motif often carved on Tudor furniture, although it was also used in the form of inlay on later furniture.

mason's mitre – A form of mitre joint where the mitre is carved on the wood rather than being formed by the joint between the two pieces meeting (*see also* mitre).

medallion – A circular, oval, or square decoration inlaid, carved, or painted on a surface. Heads carved in low profile (*see* romayne) were often used

Wing armchair c1700, with hocked cabriole legs terminating in stylised hooved feet; upholstered in damask

on sixteenth- and early seventeenth-century furniture.

mitre – A diagonal joint formed where two pieces of wood meet; although the mitre is usually at 45 degrees this is not necessarily always the case, as the mitre must always bisect the angle at which the pieces meet.

monopodium – An ornamental support for a table or stand, usually consisting of three legs which were carved with lions' heads at the top and lions' paws at the bottom.

muntins – Also spelt muntings. The vertical members interposed between the corner posts of a cabinet, or the stiles of a door, to support and enclose panels.

nulling – *See* gadrooning.

ottoman – Originally a long upholstered seat, with or without a back, on which cushions were distributed for the comfort of the occupants. However, in the Victorian period several variations appeared, including circular and octagonal designs.

parchemin panel – Also called parchment panel. A decorative feature used in the early sixteenth century consisting of two ogee-shaped ribs set back to back, with carved flowers or grapes filling in the background. See fig 376A.

patera – An ornamental feature, either circular or oval, which could be wood, ivory, metal, etc. It was normally carved, incised, inlaid or even painted.

pediment – An architectural term adopted by cabinet makers to describe a triangular or shaped (as the swan necked) feature placed above the cornice of a bookcase, cabinet, tallboy, or longcase clock.

pendant – A general term applied to any kind of drop ornament pointing downwards (*see also* finial).

pilaster – Architecturally, a flat column on which the details and proportions of a classical order are reproduced; the pilaster is then attached to the front of, for instance, a leg; or incorporated in the design of a cupboard panel particularly in the designs of the late sixteenth and early seventeenth centuries.

plank seat – Originally American, this type of seat was adopted by some makers of English Windsor chairs. The seat was made of a single piece of wood and, unlike the English Windsor seat, had no bottoming shape adzed out of it, although most designs had a rolled edge at the front.

plinths – The rectangular moulded or shaped box-like structures which form the bases of many pieces of furniture, and which usually project beyond the limits of the carcases.

première-partie – The upper layer, normally of brass, of Boulle work; the pattern to be cut was attached to it (*see also* contre-partie).

pummel – Also spelt pommel. There are three meanings: (1) a type of finial often called a poppyhead found on a pew or a bench end; (2) the rounding off of a piece of turned wood at the junction of the turned part with the square: (3) a type of handle (see page 23).

putti – *See* amorini, cherubs and boys.

rail – A structural member that joins the vertical stiles of a framework or carcase; also the horizontal members enclosing a panel.

random width – Boards are of random width when the widths are different from each other.

reeded edge – An edge with a profile consisting of a series of parallel convex mouldings, each of which is called a reed.

re-entrant corner – A corner that curves back on itself, as illustrated.

re-entrant corner

riven – Refers to timber that has been split along its grain by inserting a riving iron or froe at one end and hitting it with a hammer. As the only alternative was laborious pitsawing this method was employed whenever possible, especially as the timber so produced was as strong as it could be.

romayne – A decorative feature consisting of small heads in profile enclosed in a medallion; popular in the early sixteenth century.

roundel – A term generally applied to any circular decorative feature or motif; thus it includes medallions, paterae, and plaques.

rule joint – A joint used along the meeting edges of the flap and the bed of a flap or gate-leg table (*see also* bead and groove and square joints).

sarcophagus – Originally a form of coffin with sloping sides used in ancient Greece. The general shape was employed in the late eighteenth and nineteenth centuries for such things as wine coolers, jardinieres, etc.

scalloped edge – Also spelt escallop. An edge with depressions shaped like scallops: see illustration. Such patterns were often used around the rims of tripod table tops.

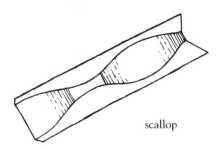

scallop

scratch – More properly, a scratchstock. A sharpened metal blade which was gripped in a wooden handle and shaped to the profile of the required moulding. It was then drawn along the part requiring to be moulded.

scroll-over arm – Also known as a shepherd's crook arm. Made in the form of a double scroll that curved inwards from the seat of the chair, then becoming a convex sweep before re-curving to form an arm rest.

Shaker furniture – Made by an American religious sect, more properly known as the United Society of Believers. Their leader, Mother Ann Lee, said, 'Do all your work as though you had 1,000 years to live, and as you would if you knew you must die tomorrow', and this philosophy produced some of the most functional yet beautiful furniture ever made.

show-wood – A term usually applied to upholstered furniture to define wood that is exposed to view, as opposed to those parts covered by upholstery.

slot dovetail – A form of dovetail joint used to join claw legs to the central pillar or support of a tripod table.

spandrel – Also spelt spandril. A curved, triangular or shaped bracket fitted into an otherwise open corner.

split turning – The wood block to be turned is split centrally lengthwise and the halves are glued together with a piece of paper interposed. The glued-up block is turned when the glue has set, and the two halves afterwards separated to give split turnings.

square joint – Early form of joint used on the flaps of flap and gate-leg tables (*see also* bead and groove and rule joints).

stile – The principal vertical members of a framework in panelled construction (*see also* muntins and rails).

strap hinge – A hinge with a long arm or band as illustrated; used during the sixteenth and early seventeenth centuries.

strap hinge

strapwork – Low-relief carved decoration found on late sixteenth- and early seventeenth-century work. The patterns were varied but normally consisted of interlaced scrolls, arabesques, and lozenge shapes.

swag – A carved, or sometimes painted, representation of a hanging festoon of flowers.

tablet back – Also called tablet top. Any chair in which the top back rail is in the form of a rectangular panel.

toadback moulding – The section of this moulding appears as two shallow ogee mouldings joined by a beading (see illustration); it was sometimes used for chair legs in the late eighteenth century.

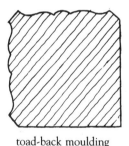

toad-back moulding

trefoil – An architectural term for an arrangement of three interconnecting arcs; at each intersection there is a cusp (*see also*). In furniture the motif was often applied to pierced arches and trefoil feet.

trophy – An arrangement of either weapons or armour, or both; or in some instances groups of musical instruments. They were carved, inlaid or painted as ornamental compositions.

upholstery spring – Properly known as a double cone spring and in use from the late eighteenth century.

volute – The scrolled termination of a spiral: the end of a violin neck is a good example.

webbing – Narrow bands or strips of interwoven jute or hessian, having great strength and interwoven to form the base for upholstery springing.

wheatears – An alternative name for the husk ornament (*see also*).

Chronological chart

This is intended as a quick guide to changes in style, methods of working and finishing, etc. Dates of births and deaths of the principal designers, and the accessions of kings and queens are, of course, precise; but other dates should be regarded as approximate.

1902	Guild of Handicraft formed by C. R. Ashbee
1890	Kenton & Co established; ceased trading 1896
1890 onwards	Bergère chairs and settees in the French style in vogue
1889	French Art Nouveau designs appeared at Paris *Exposition Universelle*
	A. H. Mackmurdo and Herbert Horne set up in business; ceased trading in 1890
1888	Arts and Crafts Movement formed
1884	Art Workers' Guild formed by W. Morris, C. F. A. Voysey, and W. R. Lethaby
1882	Century Guild founded by A. H. Mackmurdo
1880 to 1900	Development of Cosy Corners
1875	Liberty's first shop opened
1869	Charles Rennie Mackintosh born; died 1928
1867	First designs of British Art Nouveau appeared in Bruce Talbert's book *Gothic Forms applied to Furniture*
1865	Captain's low-back Windsor chairs introduced from America
	Sidney Barnsley born; died 1926
1864	Ernest Gimson born; died 1919
1863	Ernest Arthur Barnsley born; died 1926
1860	Morris, Marshall, Faulkner & Co founded. Became Morris & Co in 1865; ceased trading 1939
	First designs of Sutherland tables
1860	Machine-made tacks introduced for use in upholstery
1860 to 1890	Bergère Windsor chairs with heavy bow backs developed
1857	Green stain originated by W. H. Hunt began to be used by Morris, Marshall, Faulkner & Co
	William Richard Lethaby born; died 1931
	Charles Francis Annesley Voysey born; died 1941
1851	Great Exhibition at Crystal Palace
	Arthur H. Mackmurdo born; died 1942
1850	First bentwood chairs introduced
1850 onwards	Roman spindles used in Windsor chair backs
	First machine-made dowels introduced
	African mahogany first imported
	Modern style of screws developed
	Warwick School of Carving produced its own version of Tudor style carving which was over-ornate to the point of vulgarity. The school exhibited at the Great Exhibition of 1851
1845	First copy carving machine invented by T. B. Jordan
1840	First Wycombe Windsor chairs with heavy combs and spindle or lath backs
	First low-back Windsor chairs
	Firehouse Windsor chairs introduced from America

1838	Bruce James Talbert born; died 1881
1837 to 1901	Reign of Victoria
1836	Charles Locke Eastlake born; died 1906
1834	William Morris born; died 1896
1833	J. C. Loudon's *Encyclopaedia* published
1831	Philip Speakman Webb born; died 1915
1830 to 1837	Reign of William IV
1830	First Windsor scroll-back chairs
1830 to 1870	Balloon-back chairs widely used
1828	First coiled and conical upholstery springs patented by Samuel Pratt for mattresses and general upholstery
1825	French polishing introduced from France
1820 to 1830	Reign of George IV
1820 onwards	Bookcase shelves supported on wood or metal lugs inserted into holes drilled in bookcase ends
	Wooden turned knobs become popular as handles
1816	Purchase of Elgin Marbles by public subscription; supervised by Lord Elgin. Their exhibition sustained interest in classical Greek ornament

1815	Louis Gaigneur opened factory for producing Buhl (Boulle) work in Edgware Road, London
1812	Augustus Welby Northmore Pugin born; died 1852
1811	First circular saw for cutting veneers commercially invented by John Barton
1810 to 1880	Rosewood in vogue
1808	Sir Marc Isambard Brunel using machine saws to convert logs to planks; also patented a circular saw for fine sawing
1807	Thomas Hope's *Household Furniture* published
1806	Brunel patented a veneer saw
1805	Battle of Trafalgar and Nelson's death. Commemorated by nautical motifs and black bandings and stringings
1804	Thomas Chippendale (junior) adjudged bankrupt but recovered successfully
	Baron Denon, official archaeologist on Napoleon's Egyptian campaign, published the results of his researches which led to the popularisation of the Egyptian style
1803	Thomas Sheraton's *Cabinet Dictionary* published

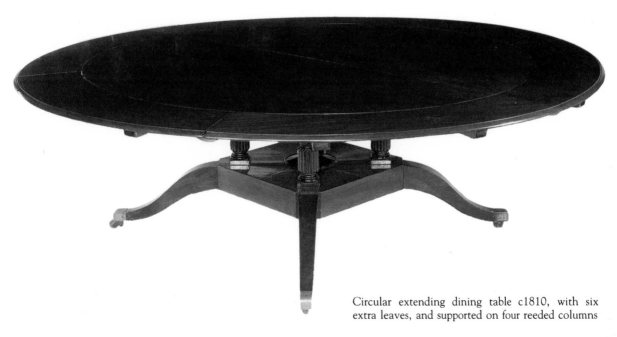

Circular extending dining table c1810, with six extra leaves, and supported on four reeded columns

An early 19th century, French Empire carved salon chair on sabre legs. It has an upholstered panel back with moulded toprail and a stuffover seat

1800	Bail (or loop) handles replaced by small brass knobs, or lion masks holding rings
	The familiar style of bow-fronted chests of drawers introduced
1797	Thomas Maudsley invented a sliding tool holder geared to the main shaft of a lathe, which enabled screw threads to be cut easily
1793	Sir Samuel Bentham patented circular saws, and planing, moulding, and dovetailing machines
1791/4	Thomas Sheraton's *Drawing Book* published
1790	First cylinder and roll top

1790	(tambour) bureaux
	Scagliola factory established in London by Vincent Bellman
	Cheverets (sheverets) introduced from France
	First designs of sofa tables
	Chiffoniers introduced from France; very widely used until early twentieth century
	Whatnots (French *étagères*) began to be popular
	First Mendlesham chairs produced by Dan Day in the village of that name; they were later made by larger manufacturers, particularly during the 1890s
1790 to 1840	Prince of Wales' feathers popular as motif on Windsor and other chairs
1790 to 1820	Tablet-back chairs in vogue
1788	First buttoned upholstery introduced
1788/94	George Hepplewhite's *The Cabinet Makers' and Upholsterers' Guide* published by his widow
1786	Death of George Hepplewhite; date of birth unknown
1784	Bramah factory for making locks established
1783	John Claudius Loudon born; died 1843
1781	Walter Taylor using a circular saw to cut ships' timbers
1780	French horse or English marquetry cutters' donkey introduced
1780	Wheel motif introduced in Windsor chair backsplats
	Chaises-longues introduced from France
	First designs of chiffoniers
	Pedestal tables introduced
	Wine tables introduced
	First designs of ottomans
1779	Thomas Chippendale (junior) took over his father's business
1777	Samuel Miller patented a circular saw driven by a windmill; no record that it was ever built or operated
1776	American Virginian walnut no

longer used because of the War of Independence

1775   The use of solid brass backplates for bail handles was reintroduced; patterns were stamped

1770   Satinwood, amboyna, and other exotic woods began to be used

Lathe-turned screws with slotted heads introduced

Circular nuts, often with slotted heads, used to fasten handles

Ormolu mounts began to be made in Britain; previously imported from France, or made of cast brass

Carlton House table design introduced

1770   First davenport desk designed by Gillow & Co

Thomas Hope born; died 1831

Practice of painting furniture revived; in vogue until 1820s

1763   First work tables, as such; fitted with pouches from about 1770 onward

1762   Matthew Boulton established his factory at Soho, Birmingham. Products were high quality brasswork, and bronze (ormolu) mounts

1761   Royal Society of Arts presented James Stanfield with a prize of £300 for designing a sawmill in Yorkshire. It was a 3-frame saw driven by a water wheel, but it was not generally adopted

Mahogany armchairs c1775, with cartouche-shaped backs, pierced splats with paterae and anthemion pattern carving, scrolled arm stumps, and spade-toe legs

1761 — Gillow & Co opened London shop in Tyburn Road (now Oxford Street)

1760 to 1820 — Reign of George III

1760 onwards — First designs of rent tables (also called drum or capstan tables)

1760 to 1850 — *Bonheurs-du-jours* popular

1759/1803 — Ince and Mayhew in business in London

1758 — Robert Adam returned from Italy and set up in practice

1755 to 1770 — Gothic Windsor chairs fashionable

1754 to 1770 — Chippendale's period of Rococo and Gothic styles

1753/4 — Thomas Chippendale (senior) opened workshop in St Martin's Lane

1751 — Thomas Sheraton born; died 1806

1750 onwards — Many innovations in furniture generally, including:
Astragal mouldings began to be used on glazed bookcase doors instead of solid bars;
breakfronts of bookcases and press cupboards developed;
all-brass castors developed.
Chippendale's period of Chinese styles
The solid backplate on bail handles replaced by two separate roses, one at each end
Serpentine shapes in cabinet and seating furniture became more widely used.
Sideboards with cupboards introduced
First Pembroke tables
Night tables (commodes) replaced old fashioned close stools
Honduras mahogany first imported
Satinwood began to be imported and was most widely used between 1790 and 1830

Window seat c1765, upholstered in floral damask, with carved cabriole legs terminating in scrolled feet

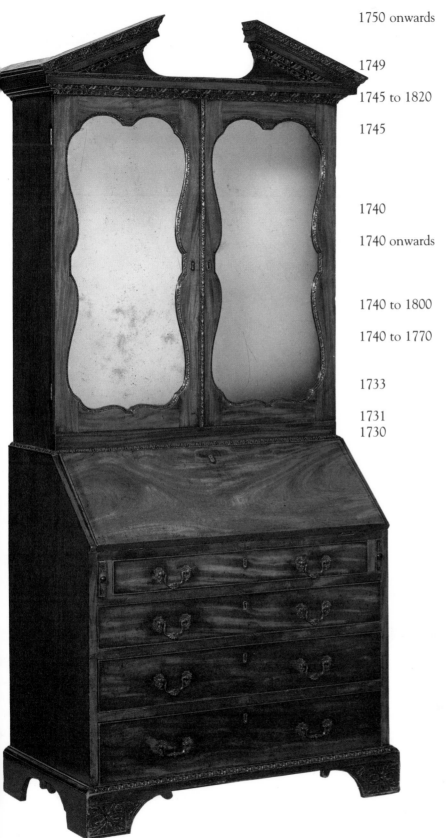

1750 onwards	Rococo style introduced to England; the name was not current until the 19th century
1749	Thomas Chippendale (junior) born; died 1822
1745 to 1820	Free-standing two stage corner cupboards in use
1745	Thomas Chippendale (senior) first recorded working in London at Long Acre
	First designs of piecrust-top tables
1740	Bow backs introduced on Windsor chairs
1740 onwards	Bookshelves supported in rebates worked in bookcase ends; replaced by wood or metal lugs about 1820
1740 to 1800	First designs of architects' and artists' tables
1740 to 1770	French Rococo styles adopted for chairs; style revived in mid Victorian era
1733	All import duties on mahogany abolished
1731	Earliest records of Gillow & Co
1730	Stools began to be made as designs in their own right rather than as adjuncts to chairs
	Card tables with square corners introduced; also with triangular tops and three legs
	First designs of pedestal desks

Mahogany bureau c1745, with mirror-glazed doors which enclose shelves, pigeonholes, and drawers. The sloping flap also conceals further pigeonholes and drawers. The pediment is the broken architectural style and is richly carved; the serpentine shaped edges on the doors are typical of the period

1730 to 1770	Square nuts used to fix handles Corner chairs in fashion
1728	Robert Adam born; died 1792
1727 to 1760	Reign of George II
1726	*Bergère* (birjair, burjair, berjer) chairs introduced from France Cabriole legs began to be decorated with acanthus foliage on knees; and with claw and ball, lion's paw, or eagle's claw feet
1725 to 1810	Cabriole legs in vogue on Windsor chairs
1725 to 1770	Windsor chair legs often shaved instead of being turned
1725 to 1735	Decoration in the form of lions' heads, masks, feet, etc, fashionable
1725	First imports of Cuban and Spanish mahogany
1724	First records of Windsor chairs
1721	Sir Robert Walpole abolished import duties on timbers from the colonies, including mahogany
1720	Exports of French walnut banned due to scarcity First imports of American Virginian black walnut to replaced banned French imports 'Loo' tables introduced Dressers began to be fitted with shelves on back Console table designs introduced from France First designs of nests of tables Ladderback chairs became popular
1720 to 1770	Library, reading, and writing chairs in fashion Regional designs of dressers developed
1718	Thomas Chippendale (senior) born; died 1779
1715	Folding, hinged frames introduced on card tables as an alternative to previous swinging leg hinged at back
1714 to 1727	Reign of George I
1714 to 1730	Heavily built early Georgian fiddleback chairs introduced, with wider seats, lower backs,

Walnut dining chair c1730, with a vase-shaped splat, carved cabriole legs and ball-and-claw feet. The drop-in seat is upholstered with needlework

1714 to 1730	more ornate splats than their predecessors. Hipped cabriole legs 1720 to 1730
1710	Kneehole writing tables introduced Snape fixing on handles replaced by pommel fixing Sofas introduced from France First love seats
1710 to 1730	Chairs by William Kent in Baroque style
1709	Severe winter in France killed many walnut trees; resulted in ban on exports in 1720
1702 to 1714	Reign of Queen Anne
1702 to 1730	Bended back (fiddleback) chairs

1702 to 1730	introduced; at first with plain cabriole legs with club or pad feet; from 1710 with claw and ball feet; hocked cabriole legs from 1710 to 1725; hoof feet 1730
1700 to 1850	Pillar and claw designs of tables in wide use
1700 to 1720	Herringbone bandings fashionable on walnut furniture
1700 onwards	Cabriole leg introduced from Continent. At first plain, then with anthemion or shell motifs on knees, and pad or club feet
	Before 1700 shoe pieces on chair backs were not fixed to back seat rails; from 1700 to 1775 shoe pieces were separate shaped blocks pinned and glued to rails
	Introduction of rebated seat rails to accept drop-in seats on chairs
	Bail (or loop) handles first used; fitted with solid backplate
1695	Gillow & Co established by Robert Gillow
1690 to 1820	Hanging corner cupboards in use
1690 to 1720	Japanning in fashion. It waned from 1720 until the end of the 18th century when it was revived
1690 to 1715	Arabesque designs popularly used in marquetry
1690 onwards	First bureaux and bureau-bookcases
	Boulle work introduced – used intermittently in the 18th century, regained popularity as Buhl in early 19th
	First castors introduced from Europe – hardwood wheels on wooden axles, followed 1700 by boxwood balls on metal axles; these developed into boxwood rollers by 1710. From 1740 castors had leather discs mounted on axles in brass sockets; 1750 saw the first all-brass castors
	Glass first used in bookcases, etc
	Tables for card playing and

1690 onwards	gaming coming into general use
	Division of settee backs to resemble chairs joined together
	Brass began to replace previous iron hinges, handles, etc, which had been made by blacksmiths
	Low backboards added to dresser tables
1689 to 1702	Reign of William and Mary II (Mary died 1694)
1686 to 1700	Braganza feet fashionable
1686 (about)	William Kent born; died 1748
1685	Revocation of the Edict of Nantes by Louis XIV which revoked toleration of the Huguenot religion (originally granted in 1598 by Henri IV). The Revocation led to the flight of many Huguenot craftsmen to Britain, to our great benefit
1685 to 1688	Reign of James II
1680	Earliest Tunbridge Ware produced at Tunbridge Wells. When the town became a spa about 1720 the ware became fashionable and remained so intermittently until about 1880, although some later work was poor quality
	Joined (joyned) chairs no longer made except in remote country districts
	First spoon-back chairs; up to 1700 with turned legs, then cabriole, often with hoof feet
	First designs of tallboys
	First designs of secretaires
1680 to 1730	Restoration upholstered armchairs in walnut in vogue
1680 to 1720	Restoration wing chairs popular; about 1700 the back was extended down to seat level and cabriole legs came into use
1675	First imports of *scagliola* work from Italy; this type of stone work remained popular until the early 19th century
	Drawers with dovetailed fronts replaced those where the fronts were nailed into rebates
	First tea tables, as such, appeared

1670 to 1700	Restoration style chairs in walnut with caned seats and backs introduced from France and Holland	1660	Varnishing introduced as an alternative means of finishing wood
1670 to 1725	Baroque style influenced some furniture designs		First employment of rosewood for inlays; it was used intermittently as a veneer in the 18th century and from about 1760 in the solid, particularly in Victorian era
1670 onwards	First hand-made screws introduced		
	Japanning became fashionable, and was often taken up as a hobby by young ladies; by 1750 it was no longer in vogue. It was revived briefly at the end of the 18th and beginning of the 19th centuries, but tended to be of inferior quality		Introduction of marquetry (as distinct from inlay) by immigrant craftsmen
			Improvements in glues and gluing techniques which resulted in abandonment of pegged mortise and tenon joints
1664	Caning introduced, probably from Holland. By 1720 it had gone out of fashion but was revived at the end of the 18th century. It was used intermittently in the 19th, and was widely employed on bentwood chairs (1850), and *bergère* chairs and settees in the 1900s		Lancashire and Derbyshire chairs appeared
			First dressing tables, as such, in use
			New style day bed introduced from France; it had an adjustable head rest only, instead of rests at both ends
			First wardrobe designs appeared (as distinct from presses)
1663	Duke of Buckingham granted sole right to manufacture mirror glass at Vauxhall		First designs of bureaux
1662	Charles II married Catherine of Braganza; the 'Braganza' foot was introduced	1650	The custom of painting furniture superseded by polishing; however, it was revived in the late 18th century
1660 to 1685	Reign of Charles II		
1660 to 1690	Fashionable period for floral and arabesque marquetry	1650 onwards	Recessed seats for cushions introduced on chairs
1660 to 1790	*Chinoiserie* in vogue		First designs of chests of drawers developed
1660 to 1710	Bun feet widely used	1650 to 1800	*Cwpwrrd tridarns* developed and used in Wales
1660	Restoration of the monarchy after the Commonwealth; many new ideas in furniture and decoration, such as:	1649 to 1660	Rule by Council of State and Parliament (Cromwell)
	Marquetry introduced from France and Holland; it was developed concurrently with veneering	1648	Grinling Gibbons born; died 1721. Recognised as one of the most gifted wood carvers of all time; he was appointed Master Carver to George I in 1714
	First free-standing bookcases appeared; the shelves were supported by bearers nailed to bookcase ends	1642	André Charles Boulle born; died 1732. Master craftsman in Boulle (Buhl) marquetry
	Benches developed into long stools or settles	1632	London Court of Aldermen decided that carpenters should be restricted to making boarded and nailed work; only joiners could use glue, mortise and tenon and dovetail joints, and make panelling. Joiners could also undertake carving
	Oak displaced by walnut as principal cabinet-making timber		

Joined oak side table c1640. It should more correctly be called a 'court cupboard' in the sense that it is a piece for storing and displaying cups and other drinking vessels

1625 to 1649	Reign of Charles I
1620	Pilgrim Fathers embarked on *Mayflower* to America
1617	Sir Robert Mansell took over the glass factory at Vauxhall from Sir Edward Zouche; granted sole rights to manufacture. The factory did not survive the Civil War
1615	First English glass factory founded at Vauxhall by Sir Edward Zouche; in business until 1617
1610	First records of japanning in England
1603 to 1625	Reign of James I
1600 onwards	Locksmithing became a trade in its own right, and hinges, locks, handles, etc, were made by locksmiths rather than blacksmiths, as formerly
1600 to 1710	Wainscot chairs fashionable
1600 to 1630	Splay-fronted cupboards developed and in use
1600	British East India Company founded
1598	John Stow writing his book *Survey of London*
1590 to 1700	Mule chests in use
1590 to 1615	First arabesque patterns in inlay
1590	First back stools appeared
	Pietra dura imported from Italy
	Court cupboards introduced, probably from French designs
1581	Worshipful Company of Painter-Stainers formed
1580 to 1660	Farthingale chairs popular
1577	Rev. William Harrison writing his book *Description of England*
1575 to 1600	Bevelled edges were applied to lock plates, hinges, etc
1573	Inigo Jones born; died 1652
1571	Company of Joiners, Ceilers (panel makers), and Carvers formed
1571	Artificial drying of timber experimented with at Kenilworth but was unsuccessful
1570 to 1700	Glastonbury chairs used, often in churches
1562	First wooden bow fretsaws introduced, using clockspring steel for the blades
1560 (about)	Methods for making brass introduced from Germany
1558 to 1603	Reign of Elizabeth I
1553 to 1558	Reign of Mary I
1550 onwards	Replacement of wooden handles by metal
	Dining tables (refectory type) introduced; with extending tops (pull-out leaves)
1550 to 1750	Side tables (ie dressers without backs) in general use. Press cupboard development
1550 to 1630	Bulbous legs used – eg melon, cup and cover, bulbs
1550 to 1625	*Caquetoire* chairs in use
1547 to 1553	Reign of Edward IV
1544	An Act was passed limiting the number of oak trees to 12 per acre to allow growing space
1540 onwards	X-chairs revived from 12th and 13th centuries
1540 to 1680	Tester bedstead with solid bed-head (tester) and two pillars at the foot in use
1509 to 1547	Reign of Henry VIII
1500	Date generally acknowledged to be when English furniture styles begin
1500	Beginning of oil polishing – eg linseed, nut, or poppy oils; also polishing with beeswax
1500 onwards	Gate-leg tables in general use
1500 to 1800	*Cwpwrrd deuddarns* in use in Wales
1500 to 1700	Turned or thrown chairs in intermittent use, mainly in country districts
	Chair-tables in intermittent use
1500 to 1675	Drawers frequently side-hung by means of runners which slot into recesses cut in sides of drawers
1485 to 1509	Reign of Henry VII
1485	Earliest records of dressers
1400 to 1660	Joined (joyned) chairs used by higher ranks of nobility; designs originally introduced from France

CHRONOLOGICAL CHART OF FURNITURE STYLES

1895 to 1900s	Quaint
1890 to 1950	Cotswold School
1888 to 1920s	Arts & Crafts Movement*
1875 to 1900s	Aesthetic Movement and Liberty style*
1870 to 1900s	Japanese
1867 to 1900s	British style of Art Nouveau*
1840 to 1880	Rococo Revival
1830 to 1900	Victorian Vernacular
1825 to 1860	Abbotsford and Gothic Revival
1820 to 1837	Late Georgian (or pre-Victorian)
1800 to 1820	Regency and Greek Revival
1798 to 1815	Egyptian
1790 to 1805	Sheraton
1775 to 1794	Hepplewhite
1765 to 1790	Adam Neo-Classical
1750 to 1775	Chippendale

1747 to 1760	Strawberry Hill Gothick
1730 to 1800	Georgian
1730 to 1780	Mahogany period
1700 to 1730	Queen Anne and early Georgian
1660 to 1730	Walnut period
1660 to 1700	Restoration (or Carolean and late Jacobean); William & Mary
1645 to 1660	Puritan (or Cromwellian)
1600 to 1645	Early Stuart (or Jacobean)
1558 to 1600	Late Tudor (or Elizabethan)
1500 to 1558	Early Tudor

*These styles appealed only to the intelligentsia and to those who wished to be thought avant-garde; the bulk of the Great British Public bought the popular Victorian Vernacular furniture.

Irish card table c1750, the baize-lined top having guinea pits and recesses for candlestands. The central ornament on the shaped-and-carved frieze rail is a lion mask, and there are satyrs' masks on the knees of the legs

An oak and elm joint stool c1630

Price Guide

This section is exactly what its title says it is – a guide to prices, and the figures quoted indicate a price bracket for each example. It is impossible to give more than an approximation, as there are so many imponderable factors that influence prices; the international exchange rates, the vagaries of fashion, whether the piece is being offered at a specialist collectors' sale, and so on.

The best that can be done is to quote a price bracket into which the price of any particular piece should fall, assuming that it is in good condition – normal wear and tear is accepted; botched-up repairs are not. Good patination (as explained elsewhere) commands a premium, and so does some form of provenance, which may consist of bills, receipts, letters of authentication and the like.

Note A: There are some pieces which, by reason of their individuality or rarity, are difficult to price. These should be submitted to a reputable and expert valuer before being offered for sale.

Note B: Arm and dining chairs are always more valuable when offered in sets – a set should comprise two arm chairs and four single chairs, but a set of four singles is well worth having, as in both instances the prices can be greatly increased.

Fig 25: £400 to £500
Fig 26: £700 to £800
Fig 27: £1,500 to £2,000
Fig 28: £2,000 to £2,500
Fig 29: £2,500 to £3,000
Fig 30: £2,000 to £3,000
Fig 31: £5,000 to £7,500
Fig 32: £5,000 to £6,000
Fig 33: £1,000 to £1,200
Fig 34: £6,000 to £8,000
Fig 35: see Note A
Fig 36: £8,000 to £10,000
Fig 37: £4,000 to £5,000
Fig 38: £100 to £150
Fig 39: £400 to £500
Fig 40: £900 to £1,100
Fig 41: £4,500 to £7,000
Fig 42: £8,000 to £10,000
Fig 43: £4,000 to £6,000
Fig 44: £1,200 to £1,800
Fig 45: £3,500 to £4,500
Fig 46: £1,500 to £2,000
Fig 47: see Note A
Fig 48: £4,000 to £6,000
Fig 49: £700 to £1,100
Fig 50: £1,500 to £1,700
Fig 51: £1,200 to £1,750
Fig 52: £2,000 to £2,500
Fig 53: £700 to £900
Fig 54: £5,000 to £8,000
Fig 55: £4,000 to £5,000
Fig 56: £7,000 to £10,000
Fig 57: £1,500 to £4,000
Fig 58: £750 to £1,000
Fig 59: £3,000 to £5,000
Fig 60: £8,000 to £10,000
Fig 61: £1,500 to £2,500
Fig 62: £250 to £350

Fig 63: £3,500 to £5,000
Fig 64: £2,000 to £3,000
Fig 65: £2,500 to £4,000
Fig 66: £600 to £800
Fig 67: £3,000 to £8,000
Fig 68: £2,500 to £3,500
Fig 69: £5,000 to £7,500
Fig 70: £1,500 to £2,000
Fig 71: £800 to £1,200
Fig 72: £2,000 to £3,000
Fig 73: £4,000 to £6,000
Fig 74: £2,000 to £2,500
Fig 75: £3,000 to £4,000
Fig 76: £4,500 to £6,000
Fig 77: see Note A
Fig 78: £5,000 to £7,000
Fig 79: £25,000 to £30,000+
Fig 80: £12,000 to £15,000
Fig 87: £2,500 to £4,000
Fig 88: £5,000 to £7,000
Fig 89: see Note A
Fig 90: £2,000 to £3,000
Fig 91: £250 to £350
Fig 92: £700 to £900
Fig 93: £350 to £500
Fig 94: £12,000 to £15,000
Fig 95: £10,000 to £12,000
Fig 96: £12,000 to £16,000
Fig 97: £10,000 to £12,000
Fig 98: £4,000 to £5,000 (mirror £800 to £1,000)
Fig 99: £3,000 to £3,500
Fig 100: £6,000 to £8,000
Fig 101: £7,000 to £8,500
Fig 102: £15,000 to £20,000
Fig 103: £14,000 to £19,000
Fig 104: £2,500 to £3,500
Fig 105: £4,000 to £4,500

Fig 106: £5,000 to £5,500
Fig 107: £750 to £900
Fig 108: £1,000 to £1,500
Fig 109: £300 to £400
Fig 110: £900 to £1,200
Fig 111: £2,500 to £3,000
Fig 112: £2,500 to £3,000
Fig 113: £100 to £150
Fig 114: £250 to £300
Fig 115: £3,000 to £5,000
Fig 116: £8,000 to £10,000 (the pair)
Fig 117: £6,000 to £8,000
Fig 118: £750 to £900
Fig 119: £2,500 to £3,000
Fig 120: £2,000 to £2,500
Fig 121: £7,000 to £9,000
Fig 122: £6,000 to £8,000
Fig 123: see Note A
Fig 124: £3,000 to £3,500
Fig 125: £2,500 to £3,000
Fig 126: £100 to £150
Fig 127: £200 to £300
Fig 128: £250 to £350
Fig 129: £800 to £1,000
Fig 130: £750 to £1,000
Fig 131: £1,500 to £2,000
Fig 132: £8,000+
Fig 133: £4,000 to £5,000
Fig 134: £10,000 to £12,000
Fig 135: £1,500 to £2,000
Fig 138: £400 to £500
Fig 139: £2,500 to £3,000
Fig 140: £400 to £500
Fig 141: £1,000 to £1,500
Fig 142: £1,500 to £2,000
Fig 143: £2,000 to £2,500
Fig 144: see Note A

Fig 145: £1,000 to £1,500
Fig 146: £1,500 to £2,000
Fig 147: £2,500 to £3,500
Fig 148: £2,000 to £2,500
Fig 149: £1,750 to £2,500
Fig 150: £5,000 to £6,000
Fig 151: see Note A
Fig 152: £10,000 to £12,000
Fig 153: £8,000 to £10,000
Fig 154: £4,000 to £5,000
Fig 155: £6,000 to £8,000
Fig 156: (set of four) £2,500 to £3,000
Fig 157: (single) £70 to £90
Fig 158: (single) £300 to £400
Fig 159: (single) £6,000+
Fig 160: (single £70 to £90
Fig 161: (single) £300 to £350
Fig 162: see Note A
Fig 163: (single) £100 to £150
Fig 164: (single) £40 to £60
Fig 165: (single) £50 to £70
Fig 166: (single) £50 to £70
Fig 167: (single) £20 to £30
Fig 168A: £15 to £25
Fig 168B: £500 to £600
Fig 169A: (set of four) each £100 to £200
Fig 169B: (set of four) each £100 to £150
Fig 169C: (set of four) each £100 to £150
Fig 170: (set of four) each £100 to £150
Fig 171: (single) £200 to £250
Fig 172: (single) £250 to £300
Fig 173: (single) £250 to £300
Fig 174A: (single) £200 to £250

Fig 174B: (single) £250 to £300
Fig 175: £600 to £700
Fig 176: (single) £350 to £400
Fig 177: (single) £500 to £600
Fig 178: (single) £700 to £800
Fig 179: (single) £700 to £800
Fig 180: (single) £800 to £900
Fig 181: (set of four) £1,700 to £2,000
Fig 182: (single) £700 to £800
Fig 183: (single) £800 to £900
Fig 184: (set of four) £6,000 to £7,000
Fig 185: (single) £900 to £1,000
Fig 186: (single) £250 to £300
Fig 187: (single) £1,000 to £1,200
Fig 188: (single) £900 to £1,000
Fig 189: (single) £600 to £700
Fig 190: £3,000 to £3,500
Fig 191: see Note A
Fig 192: £8,000 to £9,000
Fig 193: £3,000 to £3,500
Fig 194: (single) £500 to £600
Fig 195: (single) £600 to £800
Fig 196: (single) £900 to £1,000
Fig 197: (single) £700 to £800
Fig 198: (single) £900 to £1,000
Fig 199: £1,000 to £1,500
Fig 200: £300 to £400
Fig 201: (single) £700 to £800
Fig 202: £500 to £600
Fig 203: £2,000 to £2,500
Fig 204: (single) £500 to £600
Figs 205–8: see Note A
Fig 216: £400 to £500
Fig 217: £200 to £250
Fig 218: £350 to £450
Fig 219: £250 to £350
Fig 220: £70 to £100
Fig 221: £150 to £200
Fig 222: £250 to £300
Fig 223: £100 to £150
Fig 224: £50 to £100
Fig 225: £150 to £200
Fig 226: £100 to £150
Fig 227: £150 to £200
Fig 228: £150 to £200
Fig 229: £100 to £150
Fig 230: £150 to £250
Fig 231: £800 to £900
Fig 232: £300 to £400
Fig 233: £200 to £250
Fig 234: £600 to £700
Fig 235: £150 to £200
Fig 236: £150 to £200
Fig 237: £100 to £150
Fig 238: see Note A
Fig 239: £100 to £150
Fig 240: £70 to £100
Fig 241: £70 to £100
Fig 242: £100 to £150
Fig 243: £250 to £300
Fig 244: £100 to £150
Fig 245: £100 to £150
Fig 246: £300 to £400
Fig 247: £250 to £300
Fig 248: see Note A
Fig 249: £1,500 to £1,700
Fig 250: £1,500 to £2,000

Fig 251: £1,500 to £1,700
Fig 252: £2,000 to £2,500
Fig 253: £500 to £600
Fig 254: £1,500 to £2,000
Fig 255: £2,200 to £3,000
Fig 256: £2,500 to £3,000
Fig 257: £6,000+
Figs 258–61: see Note A
Fig 263: £150 to £200
Fig 264: £70 to £90
Fig 265: £70 to £100
Fig 266: £150 to £200
Fig 267: £100 to £150
Fig 268: £100 to £150
Fig 269: £100 to £150
Fig 270: £250 to £300
Fig 271: £100 to £150
Fig 272: £150 to £200
Fig 273: £70 to £100
Fig 274: £200 to £250
Fig 275: £50 to £70
Fig 276: £1,000 to £1,200
Fig 277: £60 to £90
Fig 278: £200 to £300
Fig 279: £500 to £600
Fig 280: £500 to £600
Fig 281: £500 to £600
Fig 282: £1,000 to £1,200
Fig 283: £1,000 to £1,200
Fig 284: £800 to £1,000
Fig 285: £1,000 to £1,500
Fig 286: £900 to £1,000
Fig 287: £1,000 to £1,500
Fig 291: £2,000 to £3,000
Fig 292: £2,500 to £3,000
Fig 293: £1,800 to £2,500
Fig 294: £3,000 to £4,000
Fig 295: £2,000 to £2,500
Fig 296: £100 to £150
Fig 297: £300 to £350
Fig 298: see Note A
Fig 299: £500 to £700
Fig 300: £800 to £1,000
Fig 301: £3,000 to £4,000
Fig 302: £250 to £350
Fig 303: £200 to £300
Fig 304: £150 to £250
Fig 305: £300 to £400
Fig 306: £600 to £800
Fig 307: £1,500 to £2,000
Fig 308: £800 to £1,000
Fig 309: £700 to £800
Fig 310: £900 to £1,100
Fig 311: £3,000 to £4,000
Fig 312: £1,000 to £1,200
Figs 313: £700 to £900
Fig 314: £1,000 to £1,300
Fig 315: £900 to £1,100
Fig 316: see Note A
Fig 317: £800 to £1,100
Fig 318: £12,000+
Fig 319: £13,000+
Fig 320: £5,000 to £6,000
Fig 321: £6,000 to £8,000
Fig 322: £7,000 to £9,000
Fig 323: £4,000 to £6,000
Fig 324: £4,000 to £6,000
Fig 325: £12,000 to £15,000
Fig 326: £800 to £1,000
Fig 327: £700 to £900

Fig 328: £800 to £1,000
Fig 329: £2,500 to £3,000
Fig 330: £2,000 to £2,500
Fig 331: £500 to £700
Fig 332: £750 to £1,000
Fig 333: £400 to £500
Fig 334: £450 to £600
Fig 335: £250 to £400
Fig 336: £600 to £700
Fig 337: £1,000 to £1,200
Fig 338: £4,500 to £5,000
Fig 339: £5,000 to £6,000
Fig 340: £7,000 to £8,000
Fig 341: £70 to £110
Fig 342: £900 to £1,100
Fig 343: £2,500 to £3,500
Fig 344: £500 to £600
Fig 345: £300 to £400
Fig 346: £2,000 to £2,500
Fig 347: £200 to £300
Fig 348: £1,000 to £1,500
Fig 349: £1,300 to £1,700
Fig 350: £1,100 to £1,500
Fig 351: £1,500 to £2,000
Fig 352: £800 to £1,000
Fig 353: £1,000 to £1,500
Fig 354: £600 to £800
Fig 355: £600 to £800
Fig 356: £400 to £500
Fig 357: £600 to £800
Fig 358: £500 to £600
Fig 359: £2,000 to £2,500
Fig 360: £300 to £400
Fig 361: £600 to £700
Fig 362: £100 to £200
Fig 363: £2,000 to £3,000
Fig 364: £2,500 to £3,500
Fig 365: £3,000 to £5,000
Fig 366: £2,000 to £3,000
Fig 367: £900 to £1,200
Fig 368: £800 to £1,000
Fig 369: £2,500 to £3,000
Fig 370: £150 to £200
Fig 371: £900 to £1,200
Fig 372: £1,000 to £1,500
Fig 373: £1,000 to £1,500
Fig 374: £700 to £900
Fig 375: £700 to £900
Fig 376: £1,700 to £2,500
Fig 377: £2,000 to £2,500
Fig 378: £900 to £1,200
Fig 379: £400 to £500
Fig 380: £800 to £1,000
Fig 381: £1,700 to £2,200
Fig 382: £1,000 to £1,500
Fig 383: £900 to £1,100
Fig 384: £500 to £700
Fig 385: £500 to £700
Fig 386: £150 to £250
Fig 387: £800 to £1,000
Fig 388: £250 to £300
Fig 389: £2,500 to £3,000
Fig 390: £100 to £150
Fig 391: £150 to £200
Fig 392: £100 to £200
Fig 393: £250 to £300
Fig 394: £700 to £900
Fig 395: £2,000 to £2,500
Fig 396: £500 to £700
Fig 397: £700 to £900

Fig 398: £3,000 to £4,000
Fig 399: £700 to £800
Fig 400: £900 to £1,200
Fig 401: £3,000 to £4,000
Fig 402: £1,500 to £2,000
Fig 403: £5,000 to £6,000
Fig 404: £1,000 to £1,500
Fig 405: £5,000 to £6,000
Fig 406: see Note A
Fig 407: £800 to £1,000
Fig 408: £6,000 to £8,000
Fig 409: £5,000 to £7,000
Fig 410: £1,500 to £2,000
Fig 411: £500 to £700
Fig 412: £1,500 to £2,000
Fig 413: £2,000 to £2,500
Fig 414: £1,500 to £2,000
Fig 415: £2,000 to £3,000
Fig 416: £1,000 to £1,500
Fig 417: £3,000 to £3,500
Fig 418: £3,000 to £4,000
Fig 419: £4,000 to £5,000
Fig 420: £2,500 to £3,000
Fig 421: £3,000 to £4,000
Fig 422: £5,000 to £6,000
Fig 423: £5,500 to £6,500
Fig 424: £5,000 to £6,000
Fig 425: £4,000 to £5,000
Fig 426: £5,000 to £7,000
Fig 427: £4,000 to £5,000
Fig 428: £8,000 to £10,000

Bibiography

Bly, John. *Discovering English Furniture* (Shire Publications Ltd)

Butler, Robin. *The Arthur Negus Guide to English Furniture* (Hamlyn)

Edwards, Ralph. *The Shorter Dictionary of English Furniture* (Country Life)

Fastnedge, Ralph. *English Furniture Styles* (Penguin)

Gloag, John. *A Short Dictionary of Furniture* (Allen and Unwin)*

Hayward, C. H. *Antique or Fake* (Bell and Hyman)

Hayward, C. H. *English Period Furniture* (Bell and Hyman)

Price, Bernard. *The Story of English Furniture* (BBC)

Sparkes, Ivan. *English Domestic Furniture* (Spur Books Ltd)

Sparkes, Ivan. *English Windsor Chairs* (Shire Publications Ltd)

Taylor, Margaret MacDonald. *English Furniture* (Evans Brothers Ltd)*

Tomlin, Maurice. *English Furniture* (Faber)

Wolsey, S. and Luff, R. *Furniture in England* (Arthur Barker)*

Woodforde, John. *The Observer's Book of Furniture* (Frederick Warne)

Those marked * are known to be out of print, and some of the others may be as well. In most cases they are still obtainable from libraries and secondhand book shops

FACSIMILE REPRINTS

Chippendale, Thomas. *The Gentleman and Cabinet-Maker's Director* (Dover Publications)

Eastlake, Charles. *Hints on Household Taste* (Dover Publications)

Hepplewhite, George. *The Cabinet-Maker and Upholsterer's Guide* (Dover Publications)

Sheraton, Thomas. *The Cabinet-Maker and Upholsterer's Drawing Book* (Dover Publications)

Index